HOW INTERNATIONAL LAW WORKS

HOW INTERNATIONAL LAW WORKS

A Rational Choice Theory

Andrew T. Guzman

OXFORD

UNIVERSITY PRESS

2008

OXFORD
UNIVERSITY PRESS

Oxford University Press, Inc., publishes works that further
Oxford University's objective of excellence
in research, scholarship, and education.

Oxford New York
Auckland Cape Town Dar es Salaam Hong Kong Karachi
Kuala Lumpur Madrid Melbourne Mexico City Nairobi
New Delhi Shanghai Taipei Toronto

With offices in
Argentina Austria Brazil Chile Czech Republic France Greece
Guatemala Hungary Italy Japan Poland Portugal Singapore
South Korea Switzerland Thailand Turkey Ukraine Vietnam

Published by Oxford University Press, Inc.
198 Madison Avenue, New York, NY 10016

www.oup.com

Oxford is a registered trademark of Oxford University Press

Library of Congress Cataloging-in-Publication Data
Guzman, Andrew T.
How international law works : a rational choice theory
/ Andrew T. Guzman.
p. cm.
Includes bibliographical references and index.
ISBN 978-0-19-530556-2
1. International law. I. Title.
KZ3410.G89 2008 341—dc22   2007016343

9 8 7 6 5 4 3 2 1

Printed in the United States of America
on acid-free paper

To Mom and Papa,
Who taught me to question
and showed me the world.

CONTENTS

PREFACE

When teaching international law, one is confronted with foundational questions from the very start of the course. Does international law affect state behavior, and if so, how does it do so? Why would states pay any attention to international law in the absence of coercive enforcement mechanisms? What do we mean when we say international law is "binding," given that states can almost always choose to violate it? Every instructor of the subject must find a way to respond to these questions, if only so that the class can get on with the business of learning the rules of international law.

But no matter how these questions are addressed, there is no escaping their importance. Those of us who study international law tend to believe that it affects state conduct and that it can usefully be deployed to address serious problems among nations. But if we venture outside the comfortable community of international legal scholars, that belief is challenged. And rightfully so. Whatever the strengths of international law, it remains almost entirely without coercive enforcement—the primary tool used to generate compliance in domestic systems. Those of us who believe in international law, then, need to offer a persuasive explanation of why and when it works. This book seeks to do just that.

I am certainly not the first to take up this challenge, and many of those who have done so before me have informed my thinking. What this book seeks to contribute is a comprehensive and theoretically sound account of international law from a rational choice perspective. It seeks to explain how international law is able to constrain states, even when those states are selfish and have no intrinsic preference for compliance with the requirements of international law. Building this theory sheds light on a range of international law issues. The theory explains why the arguments advanced by skeptics of international law are insufficient to reach the conclusion that international law is impotent, and why many traditional views of international law need to be adapted to account for what the theory teaches us.

Academic debts last a lifetime and can never be properly repaid, and I certainly have my share. My earliest efforts at legal scholarship took place under the guidance of Lucian Bebchuk, who provided flawless advice and counsel and who invested in my intellectual development despite the fact that my substantive interests diverged from his. Many other mentors also guided me through the early stages of my career, and helped me find my way as an international law scholar. These include Louis Kaplow, Steven Shavell, Anne-Marie Slaughter, Elizabeth Warren, David Wilkins, and Joseph Weiler.

The list of people who have contributed to the book by reading early drafts, discussing ideas, and providing feedback is long, reflecting the enormous amount of intellectual support I have received from colleagues. Among those to whom I have a debt of gratitude are Ken Abbott, Jose Alvarez, Jeff Atik, Dan Bodansky, Margaret Boittin, Richard Buxbaum, David Caron, Howard Chang, Stephen Choi, Allison Danner, Miguel de Figueiredo, Dan Farber, Allen Ferrell, Jesse Fried, Jack Goldsmith, Ryan Goodman, Joanne Gowa, Laurence Helfer, Robert Keohane, Benedict Kingsbury, Christopher Kutz, Gillian Lester, Margo Meyer, Erin Murphy, Jide Nzelibe, Anne Joseph O'Connell, Eric Posner, Kal Raustiala, Giesela Ruhr, Anne Sartori, Paul Schwartz, Beth Simmons, David Sklansky, Anne-Marie Slaughter, Michael Stein, Richard Steinberg, Paul Stephan, Edward Swaine, Alan Sykes, Eric Talley, Anne van Aarken, Erik Voeten, Joseph Weiler, John Yoo, and Frank Zimring.

I have used drafts of the book to teach the theory of international law both at my own Berkeley Law School and at the University of Hamburg. Students at both institutions helped me to refine my ideas and presentation and provided invaluable feedback.

I received outstanding research assistance from Leah Granger, Raechel Groom, and Michelle Mersey. Jennifer Zahgkuni provided unwavering assistance. I owe particular thanks to Timothy Meyer, whose research and critical comments were indispensable throughout and whose tireless work greatly improved the book. I also thank Dedi Feldman and David McBride, my editors at Oxford University Press, for their encouragement and guidance throughout the publication process.

Finally, and above all, nothing I do would be possible without the love and support of my wife, Jeannie Sears, and our children, Nicholas and Daniel Guzman. Whatever else international law achieves, I hope it helps my generation give my children's a more peaceful and prosperous world.

HOW INTERNATIONAL LAW WORKS

1

INTRODUCTION

International Law at Work

In June 1993, Jose Ernesto Medellin participated in the rape and murder of two girls in Houston, Texas. He was subsequently arrested by the Texas police, and informed them that he was a Mexican national. He was convicted of murder in September 1994 and sentenced to death in October of the same year. Medellin appealed to the Texas Court of Criminal Appeals, which affirmed both the conviction and the sentence.

In April 1997, Mexican consular officials learned of Medellin's situation. A few weeks later, Medellin filed a state *habeas corpus* petition in which he raised, for the first time, the claim that he had been denied his rights under the Vienna Convention on Consular Relations (VCCR), an international treaty to which the United States and Mexico are both parties. Under this treaty law enforcement authorities are required to inform foreign nationals, upon their arrest, of their right to contact their consulate and have their consular officials notified of the arrest.[1] At the time of his arrest, Medellin was not informed of these rights.

Medellin's state *habeas* petition was denied, and that was followed by similar failures in his appeal of this state *habeas* petition, his federal *habeas* petition, and his appeal of that federal ruling.[2]

While these domestic legal proceedings were moving forward, Mexico pursued the issue at the international level by filing a case against the United States at the International Court of Justice (ICJ). Mexico alleged violations of the VCCR in the Medellin case and in the cases of 53 other Mexican nationals sentenced to death in the United States. Jurisdiction was based on article 1 of the Optional Protocol of the VCCR, to which both Mexico and the United States were parties, which provides that disputes related to the VCCR are within the jurisdiction of the ICJ.

The ICJ issued its decision, in what is known as the *Avena* case, on March 31, 2004.[3] It ruled that the United States had violated its obligations under the VCCR, and ordered the United States to provide the affected individuals with a review of their convictions and sentences "with a view to ascertaining whether in each case the violation of Article 36 ... caused actual prejudice."

On the basis of the *Avena* decision, Medellin renewed his federal *habeas* petition, but was again denied by the Fifth Circuit. In December 2004, the United States Supreme Court granted certiorari on the question of whether the United States must follow the ICJ ruling.[4]

At this point in the proceedings, President Bush had several options, including the option of simply waiting for the Supreme Court to rule on the relevance of the ICJ decision to federal and state courts in the United States. By doing nothing, Bush could hope that the Supreme Court would deny Medellin and others the relief ordered by the ICJ. Indeed, in 2006 the Supreme Court delivered just such an opinion in a different VCCR case known as the *Sanchez-Llamas* case;[5] the Court ruled that ICJ decisions are "entitled only to ... respectful consideration" and are not themselves binding on U.S. courts.[6] Had such a ruling emerged from the Supreme Court in Medellin's case, there would have been no need under domestic law for the president to insert himself into the issue at all. Even if the Supreme Court had ordered the state courts to take some action in response to *Avena,* the president could have remained comfortably above the fray.

Rather than wait, however, President Bush acted. On February 28, 2005, he issued a memorandum stating: "pursuant to the powers vested in me as President by the Constitution and laws of the United States of America ... the United States will discharge its international obligations under the [*Avena*] decision ... by having State courts give effect to the decision." In other words, the president was ordering the states to follow the instructions of the ICJ. By issuing this order, President Bush generated a conflict between his administration and the governments and court systems of several of the states and exposed himself to the accusation that he was doing violence to the federalist structure of the United States.

As of this writing, the president has lost this battle with the states and has done so in ways he surely would have liked to avoid. Four judges from the Texas Court of Criminal Appeals concluded, for example, that "the president has exceeded his constitutional authority by intruding into the independent powers of the judiciary."[7] A *New York Times* headline stated: "Texas Court Ruling Rebuffs Bush."[8] The *ABA Journal*, a publication of the American Bar Association, featured the headline "Texas Court Tells Bush to Back Off."[9] The United States Supreme Court granted certiorari and will hear the case in late 2007, and so it is conceivable that the president's memorandum will ultimately be viewed as binding on the states.[10] Even this result, however, delivers no real benefit to President Bush, and the alternative of a defeat is surely politically costly, as is the entire conflict between the president and the states.

Looking only to the domestic side of things, then, one wonders why the president injected himself into this case where he had a lot to lose and so little to gain. Looking to the international level for answers fails to reveal any obvious pressure on the United States to follow the *Avena* ruling. The ICJ has no ability to enforce its ruling on the United States, and there were no credible threats of sanctions by any states. One might think that perhaps the president or the United States wanted to support the ICJ as an institution or uphold the integrity of the VCCR, or that it hoped to preserve its ability to use the ICJ in future cases to protect the rights of American nationals arrested abroad. All of these possible explanations are ruled out, however, by the fact that on March 7, 2005—one week after the executive memorandum instructing states to give effect to the *Avena* decision—the United States announced its withdrawal from the VCCR's Optional Protocol, depriving the ICJ of jurisdiction over future disputes.

Why would the United States (through the president) do this? Why would the country respond to a ruling of the ICJ, even as it was denying that institution authority over future disputes? How does international law work?

One answer to these questions is that the ruling in the *Avena* case generated an international legal obligation for the United States. This explanation, however, raises a deeper question: why would a "legal obligation" for which there are no obvious enforcement mechanisms affect the behavior of the world's most powerful country? Why did the president and the United States not choose to simply ignore the ICJ decision? How could the mere fact that the United States has an obligation under international law—without more—make it do anything it does not want to do, including engage in an internal constitutional struggle between the different levels of government?

The Medellin case is not, of course, the only example one can find in which international legal rules affect state behavior. The judicial organs of the World Trade Organization (WTO) have decided many cases, and one could assemble a long list of disputes in which those decisions led to either compliance by a losing defendant or acquiescence by a losing complainant (Wilson 2007). For example, in 2003 the United States removed its safeguard measures on steel following a loss before the WTO's Appellate Body;[11] and in 2005 Mexico reformed its telecommunications regulations so as to come into compliance with the decision of a WTO panel.[12] Similar examples of changed behavior to come into compliance with international law are visible in other areas. A 1996 decision of the ICJ resolved a longstanding border dispute between Namibia and Botswana in favor of Botswana. Namibia accepted the judgment, bringing the dispute to an end.[13] On January 12, 2000, the British government bowed to two 1999 rulings from the European Court of Human Rights (ECHR) requiring that openly gay individuals be permitted to serve in the armed forces.[14] Speaking before the House of Commons, Britain's defense secretary, Geoffrey Hoone explained the British government's decision: "The . . . ruling makes very clear that the existing policy in relation to homosexuality must change."[15] The ECHR also issues monetary judgments under article 41 of the European Convention on Human Rights that are routinely paid by states (Scott and Stephan 2006).

State efforts to come into compliance with international law are not limited to the way they react to judicial decisions. There are many instances in which states have made changes to domestic legislation in response to the demands of international agreements. For example, in response to the 1972 Biological Weapons Convention requiring signatories to ensure that the treaty's fundamental prohibitions are enforceable under domestic law, Britain adopted the Biological Weapons Act in 1974.[16] Following negotiation of the North American Free Trade Agreement (NAFTA), the United States, Canada, and Mexico each made a host of changes to relevant laws. To list just one such change, the United States altered the immigration rules for professionals from Canada and Mexico.[17] The Mine Ban Treaty of 1997 requires states to "take all appropriate legal, administrative and other measures, including the imposition of penal sanctions, to prevent and suppress any activity prohibited" by the treaty.[18] As of 2004, 36 countries had enacted domestic legislation to comply with the treaty, and 23 countries were in the process of adopting legislation.[19] In 1994, the United States passed the Foreign Relations Authorization Act;[20] section 506 of which includes implementing legislation for the Convention against Torture and Other Cruel, Inhuman or Degrading Treatment or Punishment.[21] This legislation amends title 18 of the United States Code to establish criminal penalties for persons committing or attempting to commit torture outside the United States. The Chemical Weapons Convention Implementation Act requires that the U.S. government (through the State Department) seek the issuance of a search warrant in response to a demand from the Organization for the Prohibition of Chemical Weapons to engage in a challenge inspection of a public or private facility.[22] The Basel Accord on International Convergence of Capital Measurement and Capital Standards, a soft law instrument that sets standards governing the capital-asset ratios maintained by central banks, was initially signed by the G-10 countries and Luxembourg, but has subsequently been implemented by more than 100 states.[23]

Of course, even implementation of domestic legislation does not provide an absolute guarantee that a state will comply with its obligations. It can, after all, change the legislation at some future point. Nevertheless, changes to domestic legislation in response to an international agreement are powerful evidence that the agreement is exerting some influence.

Further evidence of how international law affects state behavior can be found by examining individual state decisions and drawing inferences about whether those decisions are motivated by the relevant international rules. It is widely accepted, for example, that the Helsinki Final Act, a soft law agreement including the United States, Canada, a number of European countries, and the Soviet Union, served to reduce Cold War tensions and solidify then-existing national boundaries. Following each of the successfully completed rounds of negotiation at the WTO and its predecessor, the General Agreement on Tariffs and Trade (GATT), states complied with the obligations they had accepted by reducing their tariff levels and making other changes to their domestic systems. Extradition treaties routinely govern the handling of even very controversial cases. In July 2006, for example, Britain concluded that Gary McKinnon, a British citizen accused of hacking into American military computers, should be extradited to the United States. This was done despite concerns about potential human rights violations should he be turned over to the United States and anger over the terms of the treaty itself. Countless more examples of states entering into agreements and changing their behavior as a result could be listed.

It comes as no surprise to most international lawyers that international law can affect states, though social scientists are sometimes more skeptical. But whatever one's perspective on international law, its ability to alter state behavior raises the same critical question—how does it do it? With rare exceptions, no coercive force will be applied to get states to comply with international law. Indeed, in many instances there is no explicit enforcement of any kind.

The puzzle of how international law gets sovereign states to alter their behavior is what motivates this book.

It has long been an article of faith among international legal scholars that international law affects state conduct, and a number of the field's most eminent scholars have written on the question (Chayes and Chayes 1995; Franck 1995; Henkin 1979; Koh 1997). Though these contributions shed considerable light on international law and help us to understand the international legal system, they do not offer a satisfying theory of how and when states comply with international law or when international law is more or less likely to work.

Social scientists—most prominently political scientists—have used a different set of methodological tools to examine international law. This literature has produced a range of important insights into the international legal system (Downs, Rocke, and Barsoom 1996; Keohane 1984; Krasner 1999; Lipson 1991; Mearsheimer 1995; Mercer 1996; Morgenthau 1973; Morrow 1994) but has not generally been focused on international law as such and has not generated a comprehensive account of the field.

Finally, a number of scholars, working at the intersection of law and social science (often falling under the heading "international law and international relations") have studied the workings of the international legal system (Abbott 1989; Brewster 2006; Dunoff and Trachtman 1999; Ginsburg and McAdams 2004; Goldsmith and Posner 2005; Hathaway 2002; Raustiala 2005; Scott and Stephan 2006; Setear 1997; Slaughter 2004; Swaine 2002; Sykes 2004). This book fits most easily into this third category, and like these other works, it borrows from both traditional legal scholars and social scientists.

Despite the important contributions from the authors listed here and many others, the field of international law remains largely without a comprehensive and coherent theory that seeks to explain how the system works across its full spectrum. This book offers just such a theory.

The book explains how international law is able to affect state behavior despite a lack of coercive enforcement mechanisms. In contrast to much of the existing literature, it seeks to explain the various sources of international law within a single framework. Indeed, as the following chapters make clear, agreements and practices that are normally not considered "law"—soft law and norms—must be part of the discussion about international law if we are to make any sense of how the international legal system influences state behavior. More specifically, formal treaties, soft law, customary international law, and international norms all operate through the same basic set of mechanisms. The difference among these sources of legal or quasi-legal rules is a matter of degree rather than of kind. Formal treaties lie at one end of a spectrum of commitment, with mere norms at the other end and customary international law and soft law in between. The matter of legal form—treaty, soft law, custom—however, is only one factor affecting the impact of international law. States have myriad ways to increase or decrease the credibility of their promises (e.g., dispute resolution, escape clauses, reservations, monitoring, etc.) and these tools are also part of what must be understood.

The theory developed in this book explains how what I call the "Three Rs of Compliance"—reputation, reciprocity, and retaliation—allow international legal arrangements to bolster international cooperation. Because reputation, in contrast to reciprocity and retaliation, is poorly understood and undertheorized, I develop a model of reputation to explain how and when reputational concerns can provide states with an incentive to comply with international legal rules.

Establishing a more theoretically satisfying approach to international law yields immediate payoffs. With respect to treaties, the book demonstrates (among other things) that both bilateral and multilateral agreements have the potential to influence state behavior, how states choose between hard and soft law instruments (and why it makes no sense to treat these alternatives as conceptually distinct), how substantive content and form interact within an international agreement, and why agreements vary so widely in their scope and membership. With respect to customary international law, I show that a rational choice model of state behavior is fully consistent with customary legal rules that affect the actions of states, and that such a model of customary international law requires a rethinking of some of the traditional doctrinal approaches to the subject, including the very definition of customary international law and the role of state practice in its creation. Specific doctrinal issues within customary international law, including the doctrines of persistent and subsequent objectors, and the treatment of new states, are recast in light of this model.

It is also worth noting some of the claims this book does not make. It does not assert that international law is always respected or always effective. Such a claim would be extremely difficult to make as a matter of theory, and would fly in the face of what we observe. Nor does the book make any strong empirical claims about international law. The most a theoretical discussion such as this one can do is offer an explanation of how international law can influence states. It cannot compare the power of international law to the many other pressures a state faces and, therefore, cannot come to any strong conclusions about how effective international law is in practice. Critics of international law might charge that I have failed to disprove the claim that international law is irrelevant. That is true, but it seems to me that this charge places the burden of proof on the wrong side of the debate about international law. The empirical evidence that we have—imperfect though it is—offers good evidence that international law does, indeed, affect state behavior.

It takes a very powerful prior belief in the irrelevance of international law to conclude that the burden of proof should be placed on those who believe that international law matters. A number of commentators have carried out case studies that provide examples of international law at work. Mitchell (1994) studies the role of international law in the context of oil pollution and concludes that international treaties are able, under certain conditions, to elicit compliance from states. Haas (1990) examines the causes of compliance with the Mediterranean Action Plan, an environmental protection regime for the Mediterranean Sea, and concludes that the existence of the regime made states more supportive of the underlying substantive standards. Roberts (1994) explores the role of the laws of war in the first Persian Gulf War, concluding that they were effective in constraining the activities of coalition troops. Tomz (2007) looks at sovereign debt obligations and finds that even without a threat of coercive sanctions, states have honored these legal commitments.

Case studies can, of course, be criticized because they do not represent a random sample of behaviors or because their conclusions rely on subjective judgments by the author of the study. An alternative approach that does not suffer from these problems uses large data sets and econometric techniques. Studies of this sort have similarly found evidence that international law matters. Simmons (2000b) shows that legal obligations have an effect on state conduct in international monetary law. Tomz, Goldstein, and Rivers (2005) demonstrate that the GATT led to an increase in trade. Neumayer and Spess (2004) offer evidence that bilateral investment treaties cause an increase in foreign direct investment between developed and developing countries. Morrow (2006) finds evidence that international humanitarian law affects state conduct. Leeds, Long, and Mitchell (2000) find that alliance obligations are honored at a much higher rate than earlier studies had indicated, suggesting that alliance agreements constrain state behavior to a greater degree than previously thought, while Leeds (2003) analyzes the conditions under which compliance and violation occur. Though some of the foregoing evidence is controversial (Rose 2004; Tobin and Rose-Ackerman 2004; Von Stein 2005) there is a growing body of evidence that international law can affect state conduct in some instances and under certain circumstances.

The attitude of states and nonstate actors toward international law also provides evidence that the institution is important. Virtually every individual and state that participates in international dealings appears to take international law seriously, suggesting that the institution of law has some force. The case for international law is further supported by the remarkable resources that are invested in the creation of international rules and in discussion and debate about compliance with them. If international law does not affect the behavior of states, why would they invest so many resources to create international law, to evaluate the legality of their own conduct, to persuade domestic and foreign observers that their actions are consistent with international law, to monitor the legality of foreign conduct, and to dispute the content of international law? Wouldn't they be better off spending time and money on the many other problems they face?

Put simply, given that international law is an expensive proposition, why do states participate? Why, for example, do states work so hard to obtain a Security Council resolution authorizing the use of force? Why has the United States argued so aggressively and for so long that there is a customary international law requiring "prompt, adequate, and effective" compensation when foreign investment is expropriated? Why has the United States government invested resources in multilateral environmental agreements, whether to encourage their formation or to prevent

U.S. participation? Why does the country maintain a large and expensive cadre of lawyers in the State Department and elsewhere who spend much of their time evaluating the legality of American and foreign conduct?

The answer, at least within a rational choice model, must be that international law matters in some fashion. That is, states must experience some gain as a result of their engagement with the international legal system, and that gain must be larger than what they invest. The most obvious interpretation is that states get benefits from international engagement in the form of reliable commitments from other states. If that is correct, international law must be having an effect.

Though this is the most obvious inference, others are possible. It may be, for example, that international engagement helps leaders with their domestic constituencies without affecting the behavior of states. This can only be true if the relevant domestic constituencies are persuaded that international commitments serve their interests even when in fact these commitments have no effect on behavior. For example, if human rights agreements fail to affect state behavior, they may be explained by the desire of the proponents of these agreements to persuade their domestic constituents that they are working to improve human rights internationally. There may be something to this explanation in some instances, but it is difficult to believe that it can explain international rule-making across the many different substantive areas in which law is made or that it could be true for every state in the international system.

Another possibility is that international law serves primarily to shape preferences and express the views of states or other actors. Returning to the human rights example, states may be prepared to invest in human rights agreements as part of an effort to change the preferences and priorities of other states or of other actors within states. Under this view, the agreements do not have a direct impact on state behavior, but instead influence conduct indirectly by encouraging the internalization of certain norms.

The foregoing alternatives involve a relaxation of the rational choice assumptions that are made throughout the book. To be persuasive, these theories would have to be elaborated in a more comprehensive fashion than we have seen to date. Needless to say, that is not the task of this book, and so I put those theories to one side.

As far as I am aware, the only attempt to reconcile a view that international law fails to affect state behavior with the observed enthusiasm of states for creating and fighting over international law argues that state activity in this area is a form of "cheap talk" (Goldsmith and Posner 2005). In essence, the claim is that states' engagement with the international system (or with parts of the system) does almost nothing to affect behavior but takes place anyway because it costs virtually nothing and a failure to engage in the expected rhetorical dance will cause others to think that you are noncooperative. One problem with this notion is that there is little reason for states to avoid being seen as noncooperative with respect to international law if international law does not help states to achieve their goals. Another problem is that participating in the international legal system is, in fact, quite expensive. To illustrate, many poor states have quite limited staffing of their WTO missions when compared to the practice of richer states. This difference in staffing—which reflects one aspect of the cost of participating in the WTO system—affects the ability of these states to participate and influence WTO activities. For these states, it is simply too expensive to devote additional resources to the WTO. Finally, if participation in the international legal system is meaningless chatter, there is no reason for states to infer from the failure to engage in it that a state is noncooperative.[24]

All of the foregoing evidence suggests that international law affects the behavior of states in at least some instances and that international law has an important role to play in facilitating cooperation among states. The theory developed here helps us to understand how international law can fulfill that role.

Beyond simply addressing skeptics of international law, this book speaks to those, including traditional international law scholars, who believe that the system affects states. The study of international law has been (slowly) embracing a social scientific methodology since at least 1989 (Abbott 1989), and this book represents another step in that direction. Starting with a set of rational choice assumptions, the book seeks to develop a theory that can be used to understand how international law works. At times, the conventional wisdom regarding international law cannot be reconciled with the theory that emerges. Rather than attempting to defend that conventional wisdom, I have sought to explore why it might be wrong and what alternative view, consistent with the theory and what we observe in the world, should be adopted in its place. At times, this has led me to disagree with the views of international law scholars, international relations scholars, practitioners of international law, or all of these. It is my hope that the claims made in the book will stimulate discussion with all those interested in international law.

Before turning to a discussion of methodological issues, it is worth saying a brief word about the European Union. Sixty-five years ago, Europe was embroiled in World War II—the single deadliest conflict the world has ever seen. Today, the European Union (EU) represents perhaps the single greatest example of international cooperation on political, social, and economic issues the world has ever witnessed. States that had been bitter rivals for centuries joined in a political union featuring the free movement of goods, persons, services, and capital. The evolution of Europe is a remarkable story of states cooperating in an anarchic world. Ironically, the dramatic success of the EU makes it a problematic model for cooperation among states, at least as discussed in this book. Because European states successfully delegated authority to European institutions such as the European Commission (EC), the Council of the European Union, and the European Parliament, the consent of all EU members is not required to establish rules governing their conduct. This causes the EU to take on some characteristics we normally think of as belonging to states, including its own laws, regulations, and courts. Furthermore, the EU represents such a deep level of integration that matters of compliance and defection take on a different character. State decisions are informed by the fact that they are engaged in the grand project of building Europe. To the extent a new Europe offers all states significant benefits, there is a greater incentive to accept individual arrangements that are costly.

These features of the EU—the presence of a Europe-level government and the increased incentive to be cooperative—make it a problematic case for the analysis that follows. Lessons drawn from the European experience—at least the recent experience—are unlikely to have general applicability because of the unique features of Europe. On the other hand, considering this extreme example of cooperation is likely to raise important questions and offer clues about what makes cooperation work. Ultimately, I have chosen to place less rather than more focus on Europe. There is not enough room in the book for a proper discussion of Europe within the context of the theory presented here, and extensive use of European examples strikes me as having little persuasive value when illustrating a general point about cooperation among states. The decision to focus on cooperation outside Europe does not imply that the theory has no applicability to the European context.

International law has played an important role in Europe, and I believe that the theory advanced herein helps us to explain that role. Because Europe is the most advanced example of cooperation in international law, it offers an interesting and important case study. It might, for example, help us to understand whether (and under what conditions) extensive cooperation makes reputation more valuable and allows for an upward spiral of cooperation; or it might help us to understand the reasons why states are sometimes willing to make important international commitments that compromise national sovereignty. To explore these questions properly, however, would take another book, and that project is left for another day.

Methodology

Even the most casual observation of the international system demonstrates that states do not always comply with their legal obligations. Any sensible theory of international law, then, must account for and seek to explain both instances of compliance and of violation.[25] For example, the simple and oft-repeated claim that states must comply with the law (*pacta sunt servanda*) is at times mistaken for a theory about how law works. But it cannot be such a theory because it tells us nothing about when compliance will come about and when it will not. It also, incidentally, fails to explain why states will or should comply with the law.

Fundamental to understanding international law is a recognition that it is just one of many factors that affect the incentives of states. Because a state's chosen course of action will depend on all relevant factors (rather than only international law) the relevant legal rules can at most put a finger on the scale in favor of compliance. International law obviously cannot render all other issues irrelevant.

One way to explain cooperation among states, consistent with the observation that international law operates at the margin, is to assume that states have a preference for such cooperation or that they have some other closely related preference that generates cooperation. For example, one could assume that states somehow find it costly to violate international law simply because of its status as law.

The most developed version of this approach comes from Chayes and Chayes (1995), the founders of the "managerial school" of international law. They claim that a focus on matters of enforcement and sanctions in international law is misplaced. In their view, the primary source of noncompliance with international law is ambiguity in agreements and limits on state capacity to comply. It follows from this perspective that increasing compliance will come about through improved information flow, greater clarity in rules, increased capacity, and the like, rather than through enforcement efforts.

Critical to the Chayeses' approach is the assumption that there exists "a general propensity of states to comply with international obligations."[26] Under this assumption, the resolution of problems of cooperation becomes easier because the act of entering into an agreement, by itself, alters the costs and benefits of state decisions. Specifically, it imposes a cost on states that violate an agreement. By assuming an underlying preference for compliance, then, the Chayeses' approach can turn at least some difficult problems of cooperation into relatively simple ones.

Translated into the language used in this book, a propensity to comply with international law converts some problems of cooperation into easier to resolve problems of coordination. It seems clear, however, that many of the most challenging problems in international relations (human rights, environmental protection, use of force, and nuclear proliferation, to name a few) cannot be transformed into simple coordination problems by the signing of a legal document. So, although the managerial approach is a sensible frame through which to view a certain class of cooperative problems, and although within that class of problems, that approach complements the discussion in this book, there remain many other challenging cooperation problems with respect to which the managerial approach is of limited use.

An additional problem with the managerial approach is that it does not offer any underlying theory or explanation of why states prefer to comply with international law. Nor does it help us to understand when this preference for compliance will trump other concerns and when it will not prevail. It is conceivable that such a theory could be developed. There may be historical, behavioral, anthropological, or sociological reasons why such a preference exists. I am not aware, however, of any literature discussing the strength of state preferences for compliance, the factors that enhance or diminish the preference, the source of the preference, and so on.

In contrast to the Chayeses, I do not assume that states have a preference for compliance with international law. In the place of this assumption, the book adopts a set of rational choice assumptions. States are assumed to be rational, self-interested, and able to identify and pursue their interests. Those interests are a function of state preferences, which are assumed to be exogenous and fixed. States do not concern themselves with the welfare of other states but instead seek to maximize their own gains or payoffs. States, therefore, have no innate preference for complying with international law, they are unaffected by the "legitimacy" of a rule of law (Franck 1995), past consent to a rule is insufficient to ensure compliance, and there is no assumption that decision-makers have internalized a norm of compliance with international law (Koh 1997).

These assumptions have at least two things to recommend them. First, they are standard assumptions among social scientists and many international law scholars (examples in the latter category include Abbott 1989; Brewster 2006; Dunoff and Trachtman 1999; Ginsburg and McAdams 2004; Goldsmith and Posner 2005; Hathaway 2002; Scott and Stephan 2006; Setear 1997; Swaine 2002), indicating that they are widely viewed as useful, though obviously imperfect, approximations of reality. Second, and more important, the assumptions are basically hostile to cooperation. They imply that states will only cooperate when doing so increases their own payoffs. Under these assumptions, it is relatively easy to construct scenarios in which cooperation fails (as often happens in the world). It is somewhat more difficult, however, to generate cooperation. Because the model is built on assumptions that make cooperation difficult, we can have greater confidence when the results suggest ways that cooperation can come about. If cooperation can be achieved in this model, it can also be achieved in the same way under a wide range of assumptions that are friendlier to cooperation.

Though this rational choice approach is conventional in economics and international relations and gaining in popularity among legal scholars, it is not without its critics. The difficulty with the criticisms is not that they are incorrect or misguided, but rather that there is no workable set of assumptions that can satisfy all relevant concerns. It is, therefore, possible for reasonable people to disagree with respect to their preferred set of assumptions. There should be no disagreement, however, with the fact that progress requires that some set of assumptions be made, and that the rational choice assumptions used here offer a reasonable starting point. That said, it is worthwhile to examine some of the possible objections.

Consider first the realist critique. The basic realist assumption of international relations is that security is the core concern of states and that they evaluate these concerns on a relative rather than absolute basis. Thus, for example, if all countries would benefit in absolute terms from a cooperative venture as a result of an increase in economic wealth, those that stand to benefit the least will perceive themselves as having lost relative to others and will, therefore, attempt to undermine cooperation. The implication is that meaningful cooperation is very difficult to achieve and international law and international institutions are generally unable to influence the behavior of states (Mearsheimer 1995; Morgenthau 1973; Waltz 1979).

The merits and demerits of realism have provoked heated debates within political science departments. Indeed, the disagreement between realists and institutionalists is one of the central themes of international relations scholarship, with institutionalists challenging realist assumptions as well as criticizing it on its own terms (Legro and Moravcsik 1999; Milner 1998). Rehashing these issues and critiques here is not fruitful, and this book makes no attempt to settle these decades-old debates. I instead simply observe that, at the end of the day, I do not find the realist assumption about the significance of relative gains to be appropriate in many of the contexts in which international law exists. Efforts to promote international trade or environmental cooperation, for example, are not closely tied to matters of power and security—the issues that realists tend to focus on the most. Even in the security realm, the bipolar standoff of the Cold War has been replaced with a more multifaceted set of interactions and conflicts that make simple calculations of relative payoffs less relevant. With many relevant players, even a realist approach does not rule out the possibility of bilateral cooperation. If two (or a few) states come together to cooperate in some way, it may be that they both benefit, even under the relative gains approach of realism. This is so because a state must be concerned with its position relative to all other states and not only those with which it interacts in a particular agreement. If states A and B both enjoy absolute gains as a result of their cooperation, and if those gains are not enjoyed by countries C and D, which are outside the agreement, then A and B may well find it in their interest to cooperate, even under realist assumptions.

Other approaches to state behavior are more complementary to the institutionalist approach taken in this book. Liberalism, for example, opens the black box of the state and considers the role of substate actors

(Moravcsik 1997). The most prominent legal scholar working in this tradition is Anne-Marie Slaughter (2004), who has famously argued that the modern state is "disaggregated," in the sense that informal networks of government officials engage in international legal governance. These government networks are, in Slaughter's opinion, critical to understanding international law. More generally, liberal theory and its close cousin public choice theory attempt to offer more realistic models of behavior by relaxing the institutionalist (and realist) assumption that the state is the primary entity and actor. This allows much greater flexibility, as one can consider, for example, the interaction of the legislature with the executive in the formation of public policy or evaluate the relative influence of competing interest groups.

The flexibility of these approaches, however, comes at a cost. To construct a liberal model of international behavior requires, first, the construction of a model of the inner workings of the state and substate actors. The interaction of interest groups is extremely complex, and the result of such interactions may not be stable over time. It is difficult, and perhaps impossible, to construct a general, tractable, and predictive liberal theory of policymaking in a single state, let alone one that also captures the interactions of many states. Moreover, although Slaughter's insight into the important role informal networks play in international governance is useful and important, it would be taking her argument much too far to say that the state does not retain a substantial measure of cohesiveness. After all, governments retain vertical lines of accountability, and at present, with the exception of Europe, supranational institutions remain relatively weak, in terms of their ability to affect legal outcomes, compared to those at the command of the state. Recognizing these issues, and wanting to provide a predictive model of state behavior, this book for the most part retains the assumption of a unitary state.

An alternative critique can be made from a constructivist perspective. Constructivism asserts that state preferences and, therefore, state objectives, are not exogenous to the system. International institutions, including rules of international law, therefore, are not simply inert structures established by rational states but are instead participants in the international legal system that influence the norms and attitudes of states. As a descriptive matter, there is an appealing plausibility to this account. Though international institutions are normally created and controlled by states, they also acquire a sort of life of their own that allows them to be players on the international stage. Among international organizations, one might think of the United Nations, the WTO, the International Monetary Fund (IMF), the African Union, and many others that speak on the world stage in their own voice. Constructivists also argue that international agreements and rules can affect attitudes and beliefs. To take a popular example, international human rights agreements such as the International Covenant on Civil and Political Rights (ICCPR) are not simply tools intended to affect the payoffs of states; they also have an expressive function and have the potential to alter state beliefs and objectives (Lutz and Sikkink 2000). Once again, this perspective is likely to be an accurate description in at least some cases. It is surely true that norms matter in international relations and international law, and constructivism attempts to account for the fact that norms can shift over time.

Constructivist approaches have a relationship to this book that is similar to that of liberal ones. Constructivism, with its emphasis on the role of norms, rejects the rationality assumption made in this book (Finnemore and Sikkink 1998; Mercer 1996; Wendt 1999). As is true with liberalism, constructivism has more flexible assumptions that allow it, at least in principle, to more accurately describe state behavior. And as is true with liberalism, this flexibility makes it difficult for constructivism to produce a general and tractable theory of state behavior. Constructivist writers have to date not advanced a general model of state behavior. Until such a model exists, there is no way to use constructivism to study the full field of international law within a single framework.

Though this book adopts institutionalist assumptions, I recognize the value in both liberal and constructivist approaches. The most sensible approach when studying international law is to recognize that different approaches are suited to different tasks. Constructivism, for example, may be an important part of the explanation for broad changes in state behavior over relatively long periods of time. Since World War II, for instance, states have come to take issues of human rights much more seriously, and concerns for the citizens of other states have come to be much more accepted. This change is difficult to explain without resort to changing norms and preferences. Similarly, constructivist discussions of norms are a productive way to consider how human rights can be improved in the future (Goodman and Jinks 2004).

Liberalism or public choice can sometimes offer an explanation of events that are puzzling from a strictly rational perspective. A rational choice model of international trade, for example, often fails to offer a plausible account of why the international trading rules look the way they do. An approach that recognizes the fact that political leaders may have interests that differ from their citizens can sometimes explain these puzzles (Sykes 1991).

Both liberalism and constructivism can be reconciled, at least partially, with an institutionalist approach. Institutionalism assumes that state preferences are given and fixed. One can think of liberalism and constructivism as theories that help us to understand how these preferences come about. Consider first a liberal approach under which it is assumed that the interplay of domestic interest groups determines state policy preferences. Once the domestic political process plays itself out, however, the state may pursue those policy goals on the international stage in a rational and unitary way. From this perspective, the liberal model serves as an input for the institutionalist model. Constructivism can be complementary to institutionalism in a similar way. If we assume that social norms matter but that they change slowly (or rarely), and if we model them as a form of preference, then it is reasonable to think of preferences as fixed at least over certain time horizons.

Neither liberalism nor constructivism can be reconciled with institutionalism in all instances, however. If one assumes that substate actors are themselves engaged in transnational interactions with other nonstate actors, liberalism is at least partially at odds with the approach used in this book. And if norms are thought to change quickly, then the assumption of fixed preferences that is necessary for a rational choice approach becomes problematic.

And so this book does what virtually all writing on the subject must do—it chooses its assumptions and makes them explicit. Of course, I have selected those assumptions that I believe to be the most promising for the study of international law. In my judgment, rational choice assumptions yield theory that is more parsimonious and predictions that are crisper and more falsifiable than is the case for alternative approaches. It is not the purpose of this book, however, to offer a defense of rational choice or to mount an attack on other methodologies. There is surely room within the study of international law for a multiplicity of methodologies. Our understanding of international law has been and can further be improved by serious inquiries using each of the aforementioned approaches (and no doubt others as well). With rational choice assumptions in hand, however, the task of the book is to explore where they take us.

Because it starts with a set of assumptions, rather than observations, about state behavior, the analysis is primarily a theoretical one. Throughout the book, however, examples of events from the world are also included. These are intended to illustrate the theoretical points being developed and to give some context to the discussion. They are not intended to, and could not possibly, provide proof of the claim being made. Real-world events are often complex and multifaceted and are normally not fully explained by a single theoretical insight. Virtually all of the examples provided in the book, therefore, could be contested. One might argue that in each case some other underlying factors affected the payoffs of the states and that the particular influence at issue in the discussion was not an important factor. This is an inevitable feature of examples and case studies (though the latter have a greater capacity to respond to the critique). So the examples should be taken simply as illustrations. To make stronger causal statements about how and when international law affects outcomes requires more formal investigation, and that is an exercise for another time.

Compliance and Effectiveness in International Law

It is useful at this early stage of the book to clarify a terminological issue that recurs throughout the book. The impact of international law on states is often discussed in terms of "compliance" with international law. In fact, legal scholars have often moved rather quickly from the observed high rate of compliance to a conclusion that international law constrains state behavior. Henkin, who penned possibly the most famous line in international legal scholarship, "almost all nations observe almost all principles of international law and almost all of their obligations almost all of the time" (Henkin 1979), is at times unfairly accused of confusing compliance with effectiveness in this way.

To get an accurate sense of the impact of law requires more than an observation that states comply most of the time. It is necessary to determine if and when international law changes the behavior of states. When law does so, it can be considered effective, and it is this effectiveness that is of interest in this book. In economic terms, law is relevant to the extent it generates a marginal increase in compliance. When evaluating a rule of law, the problem of course is that while we can (at times) observe whether or not there has been compliance, we cannot directly observe whether the law has been effective in the sense of affecting the conduct of states. This poses a challenge for empirical inquiry, whether in the form of qualitative or quantitative investigations. For my purposes, however, the problem is primarily one of terminology. The terms *compliance* and *effectiveness* will both be used in the book. Discussions will often be framed in terms of compliance, but will speak of "improved compliance" or whether compliance is "encouraged." Statements of this sort should be understood to refer to the impact of a rule or behavior on the level of compliance. That is, they are considering how the rate of compliance is affected, which is, of course, the same as asking if the rule in question is effective.

The Scope of the Book

This book is interested in questions relating to compliance with international law and cooperation in international affairs. This area has been the subject of considerable work in political science, economics, and law and cannot possibly be addressed in all its complexity here. It is necessary, therefore, to cabin the inquiry somewhat. To that end, the book focuses on international law and, more specifically, on the conventional sources of international law: treaties and customary international law. It also examines "soft law," which includes international agreements that fall short of formal treaties but nevertheless seek to influence state conduct.[27] Though not among the classical sources of international law, there is little serious doubt that soft law instruments are an important part of the international legal structure that assists states in organizing their relations. Once soft law instruments are considered, however, the distinction between international "law" and other international institutions begins to blur. Soft law clearly includes, for example, resolutions of the UN General Assembly. But to understand those resolutions may require a theory of international organizations, which would take us far afield.

Similarly, the book addresses the role of norms that fall short of any definition of international law. As with soft law, the line between norms that are considered relevant to a discussion of international law and norms that are not (perhaps because they are thought to be "cultural" or "political") is impossible to draw with precision.

The only approach, then, is a pragmatic one. The book will address conventional tools of international law—treaties and customary international law, as well as the related soft law and norms—but will not attempt to offer an expansive theory of all forces that impact state behavior. I recognize that there is no clear distinction between the set of materials included in the book and the set that is outside its scope, but the guidelines provided here are sufficient to move forward in a fruitful way as long as we remain aware that other forces are also at work.

Ultimately, the goal of this book is to advance our understanding of international law and to do so with conventional social science methodology. I believe that the rational choice assumptions made in the book are appropriate for that exercise. The challenge of this book is to advance a coherent and general theory of how international law influences state behavior. It is my hope that the discussion and analysis that follows will be of interest to both lawyers and social scientists interested in international law and, indeed, to anyone interested in the international legal system.

2

A GENERAL THEORY OF
INTERNATIONAL LAW

International law comes in many different guises. It includes treaties, soft law, customary international law, general principles of law, and perhaps more. Though there are plenty of theories of international law that attempt to explain one or more of these categories, there remains a need for a theory that explains state behavior across the full spectrum of international law and legal instruments. It is the task of this chapter to construct just such a theory. The goal is to demonstrate how international legal obligations might influence state behavior, when international obligations are likely—or unlikely—to make a difference, and to begin our exploration—continued in later chapters—of how this theory applies across the various areas and sources of international law.

Games States Play

The subsection that follows describes games in which states find it relatively easy to cooperate, even under our rational choice assumptions. These situations provide only the most modest test for the relevance of international law. The subsequent section turns to the prisoner's dilemma, in which cooperation is much more difficult. It is in the context of this latter game that the theory is applied throughout most of the book.

Simple Forms of Cooperation

Even in a world of selfish states, there will be times when states have common interests that make cooperation valuable and easy to achieve. Consider, for example, the relationship between Canada and the United

States. For a variety of reasons, neither state stands to gain from a military confrontation. Canada would obviously like to avoid such a conflict because it could not hope to emerge victorious, while the United States, despite its military superiority, has no interest in using force against Canada. The ongoing relationship between the two states is worth more to the United States than what would emerge from the use of force. Canada and the United States could choose to sign an agreement explicitly reaffirming the legal obligation not to attack one another, but it is not clear what such a treaty would achieve.[1] They are likely to behave in the same way with or without a treaty because of their shared interest in avoiding a military conflict. Though an international agreement may be put in place in such a situation, it has little role to play beyond perhaps generating some good feeling between the states and their citizens and providing a cheap signal of good intentions that is in line with both parties' prior expectations.

When treaties or other international agreements exist in such situations, one would expect a high rate of compliance, but one would not conclude that international law is achieving anything. An agreement of this kind is akin to a treaty stating that the citizens of treaty signatories will breathe in oxygen and breathe out carbon dioxide. The treaty is in some sense complied with, but it does not do any work.[2] These games lead to cooperation as a result of the underlying payoffs (e.g., both Canada and the United States enjoy higher payoffs if they refrain from military action against one another) rather than anything the international agreement does. An international agreement that imposes an obligation on each party to behave as it would do anyway does not advance international cooperation in any meaningful way, and can hardly be described as effective international law.

International law does only slightly more work in pure coordination games. These are games in which all players have an incentive to cooperate, but cooperation requires that they coordinate their actions. One classic example of such cooperation is the system of rules and regulations governing international air travel and air safety. A series of international agreements, beginning with the Convention for the Unification of Certain Rules Relating to International Carriage by Air (the "Warsaw Convention"), operate to harmonize a range of standards.[3] This represents a successful resolution of the coordination game that air travel presents to regulators. In this and other coordination games, the players in the game (i.e., states) have an interest in coordination that trumps their interest in a particular outcome. The benefits of coordination in the regulation of air travel are obvious. If airplanes in France were subject to one set of safety regulations but those in the United States another, the cost of travel (especially because a single flight might cross over many countries) would rise dramatically. Even for mundane matters such as the tagging of baggage, coordination makes the operation of air travel a great deal more efficient and its regulation more effective.

One might wonder why states bother with formal agreements to address coordination problems of this sort when simpler strategies would achieve the same result at lower cost. States could (and do), for example, use very simple forms of international communication such as a joint memorandum or an exchange of letters to elicit compliance. Research in economics has suggested that such cooperative methods of coordination can be superior to noncooperative, "market leadership" methods of generating coordination (Farrell and Saloner 1988). Though these cooperative measures could be described as forms of agreement, we will not tarry over that semantic question.

In most situations, states do not use formal agreements to resolve coordination problems. Thus, an agreement for two heads of state to meet will involve reliance and the expenditure of resources by both sides but will not typically be the product of a formal treaty or significant international agreement. The date will be agreed to, and officials from both states will exchange information of all sorts, but no international agreement of note will be produced.

In other cases, however, states do use more formal agreements. One explanation for why they choose to do so is that interactions that appear to be coordination games may in fact be some other type of game. States have an interest in certainty and predictability over time and may, therefore, want an agreement that will offer some assurance about how others will behave if the payoffs change at some future date. In other words, once we consider the potential for future developments, the game may not be a pure coordination game, and states seeking some assurance of future cooperation may want a more formal agreement to encourage such cooperation. I discuss this possibility in greater detail later in the chapter. An alternative and consistent explanation is that the creation of a formal instrument to facilitate coordination costs very little. For example, NAFTA is primarily an agreement about trade and investment, but includes a provision stating that the Free Trade Commission, which consists of cabinet-level representatives from each party to the agreement, will meet at least once a year and that each party successively will chair the sessions of the Commission. This particular provision is just a way to ensure that meetings take place regularly. The same result could almost certainly be achieved through an informal agreement, but since the states were already negotiating NAFTA, it was convenient and inexpensive to address the coordination problem of when and where to meet in the same document. Finally, states may use a formal agreement to address a coordination game if there is uncertainty with respect to payoffs. If a state is unsure about the payoffs facing another state, it may be concerned that what appears to be a coordination game may in fact be a more difficult-to-solve cooperation problem. Entering into a formal agreement may help to guard against that possibility.

Coordination games can be distinguished from each other by the degree of tension that exists between the interests of the parties (Ginsburg and McAdams 2004). In the so-called battle of the sexes game, for example, the parties face a distributional conflict. They both strictly prefer coordinating their actions to not coordinating, but the players prefer to coordinate on different equilibria. After a focal point (meaning a solution that seems natural or relevant for the parties) is chosen, the parties have no incentive to defect, but the process of choosing a specific outcome may be sensitive to differences in bargaining power among the parties (Krasner 1991). The allocation of radio frequencies and policies addressing satellite communication is arguably an example of such a situation (Krasner 1991). Other examples of coordination games are easy to find. For example, trains running from Spain to the rest of Europe must pass through France, yet historically Spanish rail gauges were wider than the international standard rail gauges used by France. The result is that trains traveling on the broad-gauge Spanish railways must pass through gauge-change installations when crossing the border. To address this inefficiency, new high-speed trains and rails connecting Spain to France and the rest of Europe have been built using the international standard-gauge width.

Consider one further example, the hosting of the Olympic Games. States that would like to host the games in a particular year have conflicting interests. If Paris hosts the games, New York will not be able to do so. Cooperation is more difficult than in a pure coordination game, because the United States would like the games to be in New York while France would like them to be in Paris. Until a location is chosen, then, the parties' interests are, to some extent, divergent. Once a host city is chosen, however, neither state has an incentive to defect. If New York is chosen for the Olympics, France is better off sending its athletes to New York than boycotting the games or attempting to stage some competing set of games in Paris.[4]

Once again, although states sometimes use international law to resolve such games, there are many other ways to achieve the same goal. It can be done through unilateral actions, repeated practice, informal or tacit agreements, third-party intervention, and so on. In the case of the Olympics, the International Olympic Committee, which is a nongovernmental organization (NGO) over which states have no direct control, determines the host city and state. Once that decision is announced, no state—including one that wanted but failed to be chosen as host—has an incentive to defect. Cooperation is achieved without any need for enforcement, any international legal commitment, or even any action by states.

This set of three games (common interest, pure coordination, and battle of the sexes) does not exhaust the list of games in which cooperation is straightforward and enforcement is not required.[5] It is, nevertheless, sufficient to illustrate the point that in some circumstances cooperation is easy. In such situations, international law does no heavy lifting and might even be said to be superfluous. It may be used to facilitate cooperation, but even then its role is modest. International law is only worthy of study if it does more.

Notice that one would expect a high level of compliance with international law if a large share of international law commitments existed to solve coordination games. This illustrates why, in addition to the possibility that international law often calls on states to do what they would have done anyway (Downs, Rocke, and Barsoom 1996), the observed high rate of compliance (Henkin 1979) may not indicate that international law has a significant effect on state behavior.

Difficult Cooperation: Prisoner's Dilemma

Many international problems are more difficult to solve than those represented by the aforementioned games. It is these more challenging problems that are of primary interest in this book. The greatest value of international law, after all, is its ability to facilitate cooperation in an anarchic world, and this is especially true when cooperation is difficult to achieve in any other way. Focusing on situations where cooperation is difficult is also helpful as an analytic matter. If international law is able to generate cooperation in these situations, it is because it is having a real impact on behavior.

The bilateral prisoner's dilemma is used to get a sense of how international law can deal with these more difficult problems of cooperation. Similar issues and similar problems of cooperation arise in multilateral contexts. Multilateral cooperation also generates some additional challenges that I will address later in this chapter.

As will be familiar to many readers, a prisoner's dilemma is a game in which the parties can maximize their total joint payoff through mutual cooperation but each player does better by defecting. The familiar result is that in a one-shot game the only equilibrium is for both parties to defect, leading to a low payoff for both players.

Bilateral arms control negotiations provide a clear example of a prisoner's dilemma at work in an international law context. Though any number of arms agreements could be considered, the focus here is on the negotiations between the United States and the Soviet Union leading up to the 1972 Anti-Ballistic Missile (ABM) Treaty. Though the United States and the Soviet Union had many conflicting interests, they had a shared interest in curtailing the nuclear arms race. A series of arms control agreements, both multilateral and bilateral, (the Strategic Arms Limitation Treaties, known as SALT I and SALT II; the Non-Proliferation Treaty (NPT); the Limited Test Ban Treaty) were negotiated over the course of the 1960s and 1970s. The ABM Treaty was aimed at solving a special problem within the broad area of arms control. The acquisition of weapons and technology by both sides represented a significant drain on the resources of these two states. As long as both states were doing the same thing, it did not deliver an increase in security to either one. Furthermore, if one side developed an ABM system capable of protecting against ballistic missiles, the other side would have to invest heavily in developing its own ABM system or missiles that could penetrate the opposition's ABM system. A defensive ABM system, therefore, had the potential to greatly accelerate the arms race. While both sides stood to gain from arms control, each also had much to gain from unilateral defection from an agreement. If one side could continue with its arms program while the other side did not, the former faced the potentially enormous payoff that would come to whichever side developed the ability to wipe out the other's second strike capability. The problem, then, was a classic prisoner's dilemma. The best collective outcome was mutual cooperation (arms control), but the dominant strategy for each side was to cheat (arms race). The ABM Treaty represented an attempt to overcome this prisoner's dilemma and allow the states to achieve the first best outcome of mutual arms control.

To illustrate how cooperation can come about in the ABM context as well as in other prisoner's dilemmas, imagine a simplified version of the payoffs facing the United States and the Soviet Union. If both sides lived up to their commitments, they would each enjoy a relatively high payoff of, say, 100, representing a world in which the economic strain from the arms race was reduced. If both sides violated the agreement, neither would gain a strategic advantage over the other, but both would bear the heavy economic burden of a continued arms race. This behavior would lead to a lower payoff of, say, 80. If the United States complied with the agreement while the Soviet Union violated it, the United States would suffer a strategic loss of power relative to the Soviet Union— precisely the outcome the United States sought to avoid by participating in the arms race. The Soviet Union, on the other hand, would benefit from the strategic advantage it could gain by violating the agreement while the United States complied. The payoffs from this outcome, relative to the case of mutual compliance, would be very high for the Soviet Union and very low for the United States. We can represent this outcome with payoffs of 200 and −50 for the United States and Soviet Union, respectively. Finally, if the United States violated while the Soviet Union complied with the agreement, the payoffs would be 200 and −50, respectively.[6] These payoffs are represented in table 1.

This is a classic prisoner's dilemma. Though mutual cooperation yields the highest total payoff, each party has an incentive to violate the agreement, regardless of what the other party does.

Table 1. The ABM Treaty Prisoner's Dilemma

| | | Soviet Union | |
		Comply	Violate
United States	Comply	(100, 100)	(−50, 200)
	Violate	(200, −50)	(80, 80)

The well-known result for a single play of this game is that both sides will choose to violate and cooperation will fail. Nor can an international law agreement hope to affect this outcome in a one-shot game. An agreement is simply an exchange of promises. Without a system of courts or police capable of enforcing the rights of the parties to the ABM agreement, this exchange of promises has no impact on the payoffs and, therefore, no impact on behavior.

Under these assumptions, if an agreement were put into place, we would expect to see routine violations. Any compliance that might emerge must be attributed to something other than the agreement. Indeed, because the agreement serves no purpose, one would not expect rational states to enter into it at all.

The actual course of events, however, was quite different from the foregoing prediction. The ABM treaty was not only entered into, it was honored by both sides for some time. In fact, the degree of cooperation that it fostered between bitter enemies is impossible to reconcile with the simple one-shot prisoner's dilemma. Something else must have been going on.

That something else was the repeated nature of the game being played. Both states had an interest in future negotiations, and both had an interest in continued compliance by the other side. Violating the agreement would have compromised the agreement reached under the ABM treaty as well as the ability of the violator to make promises about future behavior. It would, therefore, undermine cooperation with respect to both this agreement and future negotiations.

The repeated nature of the interactions between the United States and the Soviet Union allowed cooperation to take place. Each country valued cooperation not only today but also in the future. This gave the parties at least three reasons to comply with the treaty. First, and perhaps most important, is reciprocity. A violation by one side would likely provoke a violation by the other side. The one to violate initially would enjoy a one-period gain, but thereafter the treaty might collapse, in which case both parties would return to the noncooperative outcome. Second, both parties wanted to be able to make credible commitments in the future. By complying with its promises, each country enhanced its reputation as a state that honors its commitments and, therefore, its ability to make future promises. Third, a violation had the potential to trigger some form of retaliatory action, which might further increase the cost of breach.

These three costs—reputation, reciprocity, and retaliation, which I refer to as the Three Rs of Compliance—are the keys to understanding why states comply with international obligations.

The Three Rs of Compliance

Reputation can be defined as judgments about an actor's past behavior used to predict future behavior (Miller 2003). In this book I am interested primarily in a state's reputation for compliance with international law rather than the other types of reputation one can imagine (political scientists, for example, often focus on a reputation for resolve or toughness; Huth 1997; Mercer 1996; Nalebuff 1991). A state's reputation for compliance with legal obligations consists of judgments about the state's past behavior and predictions made about future compliance based on that behavior. Unless some other meaning is specified, I will use the term "reputation" throughout the book to refer to this particular type of reputation. I discuss the relationship between a reputation for compliance with international law and other types of reputation in the next chapter.

The term "reputational sanction" refers to the cost imposed on a state when its reputation is damaged. Reputational sanctions, then, are not punishments at all, or at least they are not intended as such. When a state makes a compliance decision (i.e., when it chooses to comply or violate) it sends a signal about its willingness to honor its international legal obligations. Other states use the information in this decision to adjust their own behavior. A state that tends to comply with its obligations will develop a good reputation for compliance, while a state that often violates obligations will have a bad reputation. A good reputation is valuable because it makes promises more credible and, therefore, makes future cooperation both easier and less costly.

"Reciprocity" refers to actions that, like reputation, will often be taken without the intent to sanction a violator. In response to a violation, states may withdraw their own compliance with an international agreement because once the violation takes place the agreement ceases to serve their interests. A reciprocal action is not costly to the reciprocating state. It is instead an adjustment in a state's behavior motivated by a desire to maximize the state's payoffs in light of new circumstances or information.[7]

"Retaliation," in contrast, describes actions that are costly to the retaliating state and intended to punish the violating party. Retaliatory actions might include, for example, economic, diplomatic, or even military sanctions. Though retaliation and reciprocity often play an important role in encouraging compliance, reputational arguments are required to understand these behaviors. For this reason, I discuss them first.

Reputation

The use of reputational arguments to explain state behavior is familiar in both political science (Axelrod 1984; Keohane 1984) and economics (Abreu and Gul 2000) but remains underdeveloped in the legal literature and has not yet been applied in a systematic way to the central questions of international law. Some parts of the discussion that follows, therefore, will revisit notions of reputation that are familiar to some readers. Other parts, however, are new insights into how reputation can increase the rate of compliance with international law.

The simplest intuition about reputation is that a state that complies with international law will develop a good reputation and be viewed as a good partner, while a state that fails to comply with international law will have a poor reputation and be viewed as an unreliable partner. More concretely, a violation of a commitment today will affect the way a state is perceived tomorrow. A state that is known to honor its commitments will find more partners when it seeks to enter into future cooperative arrangements, will be able to extract more generous concessions in exchange for its promises, and will be able to solve more problems of cooperation than will a state that has a less favorable reputation.

If an observing state knew everything about the acting state, including the extent to which it preferred gains today over gains tomorrow (i.e., its discount rate) and the value for it of all possible interactions, the observing state would be able to calculate the acting state's payoffs and accurately predict its actions. Because these things are not observable, however, observing states form a judgment about an acting state's "reputation," which represents a measure of its willingness to comply with its international legal obligations.

To understand how concerns about reputation may affect behavior requires some understanding of why states care about reputation. One could simply assume that states prefer to have a reputation for compliance with international law, in which case they would be prepared to forgo present gains in exchange for an improved reputation. The problem with this approach is that it is ad hoc and does not give us a way to consider how and when a state will value reputation more or less; or when reputation may matter more or less.

So the theory developed here assumes that states have no particular taste or preference for a good reputation, but rather are concerned with maintaining good standing within the international community only to the extent that changing one's standing or reputation affects payoffs.

To illustrate how a good reputation can be valuable to a state, think of a state's reputation as an estimate of its discount rate. That estimate is made by observing states, and so it may not align perfectly with the state's actual discount rate; furthermore, the acting state may behave strategically in an effort to influence that reputation. When a state violates a rule of international law, it may suffer a reputational loss as other states adjust their beliefs. A state with a better reputation is believed to be more patient and, therefore, more willing to comply with international law and sacrifice current gains in exchange for the ability to credibly enter into cooperative arrangements in the future. Because states cannot rely on external enforcement, reputation represents one of the few ways to make promises credible. As Schelling said, "a potent means of commitment, and sometimes the only means, is the pledge of one's reputation" (1960, p. 29).

The greater a state's reputation, the more credibly it can commit to a particular course of action, the easier it is for it to enter into cooperative arrangements, the more it can extract from other states as part of a bargain, and the more likely it is that it can find other states with which to cooperate (Lahno 1995).

The intuition can be seen through the lens of basic bargaining theory. When two or more parties enter into a contract, they do so with an eye toward maximizing their joint payoffs, taking transaction costs into account. The ability to use contract is valuable to the parties, and in the domestic context relies on the enforcement power of courts. The ability to enter into agreements is similarly valuable to states, but international agreements must make do with weaker commitment devices. In the absence of coercive enforcement, they must rely on reputation as a disciplining device to encourage compliance. The stronger a state's reputation, the more easily it can make credible commitments and resolve cooperation problems.

If improving one's reputation can yield value in the form of higher payoffs, then states have an incentive to develop and maintain a good reputation. They can do so by complying with existing obligations even when, absent a concern for reputation, it might be in their interest to violate them. One can think of decisions to comply in these situations as costly signals that serve to enhance a state's reputation for compliance. The signal is effective because it distinguishes states that are likely to comply in the future from those less likely to do so.

To explore the features of reputation further, it is helpful to work with a specific example, and the previously discussed ABM case can be revisited for this purpose. I have intentionally chosen an example involving only two states so as to keep the discussion simple. The theory and conclusions reached, however, generalize to any number of states without difficulty.

The agreement can be modeled as a two-stage game.[8] In the first stage, states negotiate over the content of the law and their level of commitment. The negotiation might involve a dickering over terms, a take-it-or-leave-it offer from one party to the other, a decision to join a preexisting agreement whose terms are already set, or even a coercive negotiation in which one party has little choice but to consent to the proposed agreement. The way the negotiation takes place will have important implications for the agreement, including the terms that are included, the use of dispute resolution, the choice between hard and soft law, and more. These issues are put to one side for the moment. It is enough here to note that the parties come together and attempt to reach agreement. If no agreement is reached, the legal obligations of the parties are unchanged; for the purposes of this example (and for simplicity), I will refer to this outcome as one in which the states are unconstrained by international law. In a more realistic discussion, one could take into account the fact that states remain bound by any other rules of international law that may be in place. This simplifying assumption, however, has no impact on the analysis or the results.

In the second stage of the game, compliance decisions are made. Each party to the agreement decides whether or not it will carry out its obligation under the agreement. In this stage, there are three possible outcomes. First, the interests of the parties may lead them to comply without regard for the agreement. In an arms control context, for example, a state may choose to limit its acquisition of weapons sufficiently to be in compliance, and this decision may have nothing to do with the agreement. There is compliance in this situation, but it cannot be attributed to the agreement. Another possibility is that the parties face payoffs that will cause them to violate the agreement. If the payoffs from defection in the ABM context are large enough relative to the payoffs from compliance, the parties violate the agreement. Finally, it may be that the agreement itself causes the parties to change their behavior and come into compliance. The agreement itself might have caused the United States and the Soviet Union to limit their acquisition of weapons. It is this last possibility that is of greatest interest. If international law matters, it must be able to generate at least some cooperative behavior that would otherwise be absent.

In the ABM example, recall that the (stylized) one period prisoner's dilemma payoffs are represented as shown in table 2.

To understand the role of reputation, it is necessary to compare present and future gains, and so we must account for the fact that states prefer payoffs today over payoffs tomorrow. Let r represent the discount rate of states, meaning that they are indifferent between a payoff of 1 today and $1+r$ tomorrow. We assume that each state knows only its own discount rate and so must estimate the discount rate of other states on the basis of their observed behavior. For simplicity the variable r will be used to refer to the discount rate of both states, which implies an assumption that both have the same discount rate. Strictly speaking, each state should have its own discount rate which could be achieved by adding an appropriate subscript. I omit this bit of notation in the interests of simplicity. It has no impact on any of the results or the analysis.

The estimate of another state's discount rate can be thought of as its reputation. As I discuss later, reputation refers to more than just the discount rate, but that is a useful place to start.

The total value of the payoffs to states if they both defect in every period, then, is $80 + 80/(1+r) + 80/(1+r)^2 + \ldots = 80(1+r)/r$.[9] This is what each state receives in the absence of cooperation.

Table 2. The ABM Prisoner's Dilemma

		Soviet Union	
		Comply	Violate
United States	Comply	(100, 100)	(−50, 200)
	Violate	(200, −50)	(80, 80)

For an international agreement to influence outcomes, it must be that the violation of that agreement generates some form of cost. If reputational sanctions can increase the costs of noncompliance, cooperation is possible.

At the time of the ABM talks, the United States and the Soviet Union both stood to benefit from an agreement that would reduce the burden of their arms race. If both sides respected the agreement, they would each receive a payoff of 100 in every period. Using the same calculus as above, the discounted value of this outcome is $100(1 + r)/r$. This is clearly a better outcome for the parties than mutual defection. The problem is that in any given period, each party is better off if it defects. Before choosing to violate the agreement, however, a state must consider the impact of defection on future payoffs. If violation generates future costs, these costs may be enough to bring about compliance.

How can a violation generate costs? In the next chapter I present a more detailed discussion of how and when reputations change, but for the moment it will simply be assumed that when a state violates a commitment, other states take note and the violating state's reputation suffers. When the state enters into a treaty, it represents to the other party that it prefers mutual cooperation to noncooperation. Its hope is that this claim will be credible to the other state. Framed in terms of the discount rate, the state asserts that its discount rate is such that it will cooperate. If that claim is credible, the other state will enter into the agreement. If the state then violates the agreement, its ability to make credible promises in the future will be reduced. This is what is meant by a loss of reputation—the state is less able to make credible claims about its willingness to comply (illustrated here through claims about the discount rate).

The loss of reputation matters because it makes future promises less credible. Potential partners will have less confidence that the state will resist opportunities to violate the agreement and capture some immediate gain. In this example, the reputational harm will undermine future arms negotiations and may make it more difficult to enter into other kinds of agreements as well. To the extent it does so, the gains the state can capture through such future agreements are reduced.

So as a state considers a violation of the ABM agreement, the costs of breach must be taken into account. By violating today, the state gets a payoff of 200 rather than the 100 it would get if it complies (assuming the other state complies). As a consequence of the violation, however, the state's reputation is harmed, and future negotiations on arms control issues (and perhaps other things) are undermined. Assume that this leads to payoffs of 80 in each future period. So the payoff from a violation today is: $200 + 80/(1+r) + 80/(1+r)^2 + \ldots = 120 + 80 (1+r)/r$.[10]

All of the foregoing payoffs can be represented in a single figure. Because the parties know the consequences of their decisions and the associated payoffs, and because the game does not change over time, each state will either comply in every period (assuming the other side does the same) or defect in every period. To simplify the presentation, let $R = (1+r)/r$. Notice that R is always greater than 1, and as the discount rate increases (i.e., states care less about the future), R gets closer to 1. The resulting payoff matrix is shown in table 3; the headings refer to the state's action in the first period. In subsequent periods, there is mutual compliance if and only if that is what took place in the first period. If either side violates in the first period, there is mutual violation in all future periods. The payoffs reflect the discounted value of all present and future payoffs.

It is clear from this table that for certain values of R, both states have an incentive to comply with the agreement. In particular, as long as $100R > 120 + 80R$, there is a stable equilibrium in which both states comply. Put another way, as long as the states care enough about the future, mutual compliance can be achieved in this game. In this particular example, the discount rate, r, required to generate cooperation is 0.2.[11] In other words, as long as the parties prefer a payoff of 1.2 tomorrow over a payoff of 1 today, cooperation can be sustained.

This illustration shows that rational states can use international agreements to resolve a prisoner's dilemma. Cooperation is possible because a failure to honor the agreement affects the expectations and behavior of other states. When a state fails to comply in one period, other states observe this and draw negative inferences about the likelihood of

Table 3. The Multi-period ABM Prisoner's Dilemma

		Soviet Union	
		Comply	*Violate*
United States	Comply	(100R, 100R)	(80R−130, 120 + 80R)
	Violate	(120 + 80R, 80R−130)	(80R, 80R)

future compliance. That is, the reputation of the violating state is diminished. This model of compliance has the appealing feature that violations are "punished" through these sanctions but the sanctions themselves are not costly to the sanctioning states.

So when states enter into international agreements, they are in effect pledging their reputation as a form of bond. If they violate the agreement, they give up some of this reputational collateral, and this fact both increases the likelihood that they will comply and makes their promises more credible. The greater a state's reputational collateral, the more credible are its promises, and the easier it will be to achieve cooperation. A state with a great deal of reputational collateral will find partners easily and will be able to extract larger concessions from them. The result of this logic is that states will at times be prepared to forgo short-term opportunities to violate the law and extract higher payoffs in the hope of building or preserving their reputations and thereby enjoying higher payoffs later.

If states do not value their reputations, of course, no incentive for compliance is generated. Though this fact suggests that there are some limits on reputation's ability to generate cooperation (as I discuss in the next chapter), there seems to be nearly universal agreement that states are, indeed, concerned with their reputations. Even critics of reputational theories in political science (Mercer 1996, pp. 19–25) and international law skeptics (Goldsmith and Posner 2005, p. 103) concede as much.

Notice that the potential for cooperation is sensitive to the underlying payoffs in the game. In the foregoing example, some payoffs require unrealistically low discount rates in order to sustain cooperation (indeed, for some payoffs no positive discount rate will sustain cooperation) while for others cooperation will emerge with a discount rate that plausibly captures the trade-off states make between the present and the future.

So reputational sanctions can generate an incentive to comply with international legal obligations and can lead to changes in behavior, even in the absence of formal enforcement mechanisms. Like any other incentive, this one operates at the margin, and will at times be too small to affect state behavior. When a state is deciding whether to comply, it will take into account a variety of cost and benefits unrelated to law—domestic interests, political relations with other states, and so on—but it will also consider the legal implications of a violation. The likelihood and magnitude of reputational sanctions will vary depending on the context, so states must assess them on a case-by-case basis. Because international law increases the costs of a violation, it puts a thumb on the scale in favor of compliance or, as is sometimes said, generates "compliance pull."

Even when breach generates a reputational sanction, it may be in the interest of the country to violate its obligations. In the earlier illustration, for example, if the discount rate of American or Soviet leaders is too high, cooperation will fail. Social scientists have referred to expectations of future cooperation as the "shadow of the future."[12] Sanctions that take the form of reciprocity or retaliation can lengthen the "shadow of the future," in the sense that they increase the future cost of today's violation. Reputational sanctions have the same effect; however, in contrast to direct sanctions, which are contingent on explicit reactions by other states, reputational sanctions (or reputational benefits) are the byproduct of the information produced by a state's compliance decision.

Before proceeding, a note about the theory of repeated games is in order. Once we acknowledge that states interact repeatedly over time and with no known final period, it is possible to demonstrate that this repetition can, by itself, sometimes be enough to allow states to overcome a prisoner's dilemma. This form of cooperation can take place without any international law or any exchange of promises, and can take place even if both states have complete information. The model of reputation developed here is something different. It seeks to address the question of whether international law can affect behavior. Can, for example, the signing of a treaty affect behavior and outcomes even when the treaty itself is just a piece of paper? For international law to matter in this way, it must affect the payoffs of the states. The reputational theory explains how this can be. International law implicates a state's reputation and, therefore, its ability to make credible commitments in the future. This theory only applies if there is some informational asymmetry among states. By entering into an international law agreement, states are signaling something about their discount rate, the nonreputational costs they face, or the relevant reputational costs.

So although some cooperation can be achieved simply because a game is repeated indefinitely, this book is focused on how cooperation can be further enhanced through pledges of reputation.

Reciprocity

Though there is a close relationship between reputation and reciprocity (discussed later) this book often talks of the two concepts separately. This is done for three reasons. First, reciprocity plays an important role in international law that is distinct from reputation and sometimes operates more reliably than reputational sanctions. Second, reciprocity is treated as different from reputation in many discussions. By separating it from the general discussion of reputation, I hope to engage that literature more directly. Third, reciprocity is often considered a separate issue in traditional international law discussions. The Vienna Convention on the Law of Treaties, for example, provides that "[a] material breach of a bilateral treaty by one of the parties entitles the other to invoke the breach as a ground for terminating the treaty or suspending its operation in whole or in part."[13]

Reciprocity can serve as a powerful compliance-enhancing tool in the right circumstances. In the bilateral context, where reciprocity is most effective, it is often sufficient to generate cooperation in a prisoner's dilemma. The conditions for success are the same as in any prisoner's dilemma. If the parties make compliance decisions repeatedly over time, if the gains from a single defection are small relative to the gains from cooperation, and if acts of violation are visible, then the threat to terminate one's own compliance can be enough to induce compliance by the other party. The intuition is fairly straightforward. If the parties both prefer mutual cooperation to mutual defection, and if defection today will undermine future cooperation, then a state is really choosing between ongoing cooperation and a one-time opportunistic gain followed by noncooperation.

To illustrate, consider the Boundary Waters Treaty entered into by the United States and Canada in 1909. The treaty established that the boundary waters of Canada and the United States would remain open to commercial ships of both states, regulated the diversion of these waters, and established the International Joint Commission, which was granted jurisdiction over certain matters pertaining to the obstruction and diversion of water and charged with the preparation of reports on matters of concern to the governments.[14] The underlying problem the treaty sought to address had all the features of a prisoner's dilemma. Each country had an incentive to divert water on its own side without regard for the other's interests, but if they did so, both would be worse off.

The Boundary Waters Treaty succeeded in generating cooperative behavior by both parties, and continues to do so today. In fact, compliance has come about despite the absence of mandatory and binding dispute resolution.[15] What explains the success of the treaty is the fact that each side can credibly threaten its own withdrawal if the other side fails to comply. So Canada chooses to comply with the terms of the treaty because its failure to comply would in all likelihood cause the United States to halt its own compliance. The United States has analogous incentives. Mutual compliance is enforced by a credible threat of nonperformance.

This sort of cooperation is familiar and intuitively pleasing, but one might nevertheless ask why mutual compliance is a stable outcome. Why can't Canada violate the treaty opportunistically and then reaffirm its commitment to the treaty and once again promise to comply? It is true that the United States would like to threaten withdrawal as a mechanism to ensure Canadian compliance, but there is no way for the United States to commit itself to such a course of action. Even though violation by one party absolves the other of any legal obligations, the parties are free to renegotiate the treaty after the Canadian breach. So after violating the treaty, Canada could simply state that it plans to comply in the future. Our intuition is that such a promise will often fail to persuade, but why? Canada's problem is that the credibility of its promise to comply with the treaty is reduced by the earlier violation. If Canada violates the treaty once, it will be more difficult to persuade the United States that promises of future compliance should be taken seriously. And even if the United States does accept Canada's assurances, future Canadian violations are more likely to lead to termination by the United States. The point here is that the violation undermines a state's reputation with respect to the particular agreement and treaty partner at issue. Though the United States was willing to rely on Canadian promises at the time of the treaty's signing and ratification, it would be less willing to do so after Canadian violations have taken place.

It is especially easy to appreciate the way reputation affects behavior in this context. The parties entered into the treaty because each believed it to be in its interest. In the face of a violation by Canada, that calculus may change. There are two reasons why the United States might exit the agreement. The first is at issue in the prior discussion—expectations with regard to Canadian compliance are changed as a result of the violation. The United States can infer from the violation that Canada's incentive to breach is sufficiently strong to compel it to ignore its commitment and, therefore, Canada will likely ignore the commitment again in the future. The breach prompts the United States to update its beliefs about Canada's reputation and its (reputational and nonreputational) payoffs. With this updated information, the United States may calculate that the expected payoff from termination is greater than the expected payoff from compliance.

The second possibility is that the United States may terminate the treaty even if it expects Canada to comply in the future. It may do so to establish its own reputation for being intolerant of violations. This decision would be costly to the United States, because it would be turning its back on a cooperative agreement that made it better off (as evidenced by its original agreement to commit) but might nevertheless be worthwhile if it led to more Canadian compliance in other areas. That is, by exiting the treaty, the United States signals to Canada that it will not put up with violations of this sort and, having received this signal, Canada is deterred from acting opportunistically in other situations. I discuss retaliatory actions such as this one in detail in the next section.

In either case, the threat of termination will be sufficient to discourage Canada from violating the agreement as long as the long-term gains from cooperation outweigh the gains from a one-time violation. This appears to be the case with respect to the Boundary Waters Treaty, which remains in force almost 100 years after its signing, with both sides continuing to operate within its confines.

Though a withdrawal of reciprocal compliance may be sufficient to generate compliance with the Boundary Waters Treaty, this will not always be the case. One could imagine that at some point one side—say Canada—will decide that it could achieve higher payoffs by violating the treaty. In other words, although the treaty may have been beneficial for Canada at the time it was entered into, that may change at some later date, and at that point the threat of a reciprocal withdrawal of compliance will be insufficient to prevent a breach by Canada.

Assuming that this breach by Canada is undesirable, in the sense that the cost of breach to the United States exceeds the gains to Canada, additional sanctions would reduce the likelihood of an inefficient breach. The presence of reputational sanctions can serve this function. Even if, as seems likely with respect to most international law agreements, reputational sanctions are insufficient to generate an optimal incentive structure for states, they will often move the system in that direction.

Reciprocity will also fail to induce compliance when a threat to withdraw one's own compliance either lacks credibility or is of no consequence to a potential violator. Virtually every important human rights agreement, for example, must rely on an enforcement mechanism other than reciprocity. For concreteness, think of the ICCPR, one of the most important multilateral human rights treaties. Among its requirements is a ban on the ex post facto application of criminal laws (art. 15). Suppose one member of the treaty, say Russia, is tempted to violate this commitment. Whatever other forces might be at work to encourage compliance, reciprocity is almost certainly irrelevant. For many member states, it is inconceivable that they would respond to a violation by terminating their own compliance with the obligation not to apply criminal laws ex post facto. New Zealand, for instance, complies with that obligation for reasons having nothing to do with Russia's compliance. There is no circumstance in which a violation by Russia would constitute a reason for New Zealand to change its domestic policies on the question. Furthermore, even if reciprocity were imaginable, it is unlikely that Russia would care about the loss of this human right in other states. So even if New Zealand could credibly threaten to terminate its own compliance, this would have no impact on Russia's payoffs.

Efforts to ban nuclear tests represent an example in which reciprocity works in some instances and not others. As between the United States and the Soviet Union a commitment not to conduct nuclear tests benefited from the threat of reciprocal noncompliance. Compliance with the Limited Test Ban Treaty, for example, was supported by the credible threat that if either the United States or the Soviet Union violated the treaty, the other would do so as well.[16] Notice the contrast between that situation and the role of deterrence with respect to Iran's nuclear ambitions. Iran is a member of the NPT and under that treaty has a legal obligation as a non-nuclear-weapon state (NNWS) (as defined in the treaty) to refrain from acquiring or manufacturing nuclear devices.[17] Whatever other forces might cause Iran to comply with this provision, reciprocity does not play an important role. A violation by Iran is unlikely to trigger reciprocal noncompliance by other parties, and even if it did, it is not clear that this would represent a significant cost to Iran.

Retaliation

Returning to the example of the Boundary Waters Treaty, imagine that despite Canada's breach, the United States still believes that Canadian promises of future compliance are credible. That is, the American view of Canada and of the expected payoffs from the treaty is the same as it was when the treaty was first signed. Canada's violation gives the United States the choice of terminating the treaty or allowing it to continue in force—essentially the same position the United States was in when it decided to sign and ratify the treaty. Despite these similarities, the United States may choose to retaliate by terminating the treaty. Why would it do so?

More generally, why would any state use "retaliatory" sanctions, defined as explicit and costly punishments imposed by an aggrieved party against a violator? These sanctions, because they impose a cost on the retaliating state (as well as the violating state), differ from reputational sanctions or reciprocity, and raise the question of why a rational state would bear the cost of the sanction.

Explaining this behavior requires us to consider once again the reputational consequences of state actions. In this case, however, we must consider a slightly different reputational concern. By hypothesis, the United States is not reacting to a change in the reputation of the breaching party (Canada). Rather, the United States is acting to build or preserve a different sort of reputation—one for dealing harshly with those that violate their legal obligations to the United States.

To see how retaliatory sanctions might work, remember that a rational state would not take action simply out of spite or anger, so there must be some other reason for it to bear the cost of punishing a violator. This implies that retaliation will only take place if it generates some payoff to the retaliating state. A retaliating state is communicating to the violating state and, potentially, to other states, that it will react when its legal rights are compromised.[18] If successful, the act of retaliating will enhance the retaliating state's reputation as one that punishes a violator. The impact of such a reputation, of course, is to increase the expected cost of violating an agreement with that state. By retaliating, then, the state hopes to generate its own reputational capital that will induce its partners to be more compliant with their legal obligations. In effect, a reputation as a state that retaliates against violators creates an additional enforcement tool. For example, in 1993 President Clinton, speaking about possible actions to prevent further Serb attacks in Bosnia, explained the American interest as "an interest in standing up against the principle of ethnic cleansing.... If you look at the turmoil all through the Balkans, if you look at the other places where this could play itself out in other parts of the world, this is not just about Bosnia."[19] In other words, the United States could discourage future atrocities by taking action now because it would demonstrate a willingness to punish certain violations of humanitarian law.

Retaliation may also be used in response to an ongoing violation, in which case the retaliation is intended to persuade the violating state to come into compliance. Notice first that the focus here is on costly actions by the retaliating state. Actions that are not costly and that are taken in response to an ongoing violation are forms of reciprocal non-compliance rather than retaliation. Because the retaliatory action is costly, the retaliating state takes it only to convince the violating state to change its behavior or to establish a reputation for punishing violators, as discussed in the previous paragraph. But the act of actually retaliating is, itself, effective only if it convinces the violating party that further sanctions will be applied if the violation continues. The only reason to come into compliance is to avoid *future* retaliatory sanctions. So when a sanction is imposed, it succeeds only if it evidences a willingness to impose future costly sanctions.

While the reputation I focus on throughout this book is one of compliance with one's own international legal obligations, the reputation that is at work when retaliatory sanctions are applied is one for punishing those who violate their international legal obligations. The former is useful because it serves to make a state's own promises credible, while the latter is useful because it makes the threat of sanctions credible and therefore encourages other states to honor their commitments.

Retaliatory sanctions may take any number of forms. These include taking some economic action, such as refusing to permit imports from the offending state or curtailing one's own exports to that state; reducing cooperation in some other area; terminating a treaty (as in the hypothetical Boundary Waters Treaty example); and in the most extreme cases, using military force.

If retaliation can encourage compliance, one might ask why states can't simply threaten retaliation up to the point at which there is an optimal incentive to comply. This question gets to the most important drawback of retaliatory sanctions: they are not renegotiation proof (Abreu, Pearce, and Stacchetti 1986; Downs and Rocke 1995). To be effective, the threat of a retaliatory sanction must be credible, and that credibility depends in part on the threatening state's reputation for punishing violators. Because retaliation is costly to the retaliating state, the incentive to impose sanctions at an optimal level (or to develop a reputation for doing so) is weak, often making the threat of sanctions noncredible. The close relationship between retaliation and my discussion of reputation in this book should now be clear. A state that imposes a sanction does so to build or protect a reputation for sanctioning those that fail to honor their obligations or possibly to end an ongoing violation. The state accepts a cost today in the hope of getting a larger benefit in the future. The forces at play are analogous to those affecting a reputation for compliance. For a state to impose a retaliatory sanction, for example, it must have a sufficiently low discount rate and the cost of retaliation must be sufficiently small relative to the benefits of encouraging more compliance from other states.

Another point worth noting is that sanctions can at times serve both a signaling and a deterrence function. When a violation has taken place and is ongoing, sanctions can signal to the violating state (and other states) that the sanctioning state will punish violations, but it can also encourage the violating state to bring its actions into compliance. Once compliance is reestablished, the sanction is normally removed. Knowing this, the violating state has some incentive to come back into compliance. This is the way the dispute resolution system at the WTO is intended to work. When a state refuses to comply with a ruling of the dispute resolution organs of the WTO, the complaining state is given the authority to impose sanctions. The stated purpose of these sanctions is to bring the violating state into compliance. For example, in the *Brazil–Aircraft* case, Brazil was found to be violating the subsidies rules of the WTO, and Canada was given the authority to impose sanctions equal to the full amount of the subsidy rather than the amount that affected Canada or the dollar impact of the subsidy on Canada.[20] In their ruling, the arbitrators said "a countermeasure is 'appropriate' inter alia if it effectively induces compliance."[21] This sanction provides Brazil with an incentive to come into compliance and signals that future violations will be met with further sanctions.

International Tribunals and State Responsibility

International Tribunals

The Three Rs of Compliance help us to understand how the repeated nature of international legal interactions can generate compliance and cooperation without a formal enforcement mechanism. The international legal system, however, does have institutions that, at least at first glance, seek to enforce international commitments. In particular, tribunals exist that look something like domestic courts and so might be thought to have some enforcement power. There are also international rules that purport to impose penalties on those that violate international law.[22] Is it possible that these institutions play a role similar to that of domestic courts? Is it possible that, at least in some contexts, international tribunals or other international rules can provide an enforcement mechanism for international law that operates separately from the Three Rs of Compliance?

The short answer to these questions is almost certainly no. International courts and international rules calling for compliance or enforcement, though they likely play a role, cannot by themselves be said to offer an explanation of how international law promotes cooperation.

The critical difference between domestic and international courts is that the former are backed by the state and a system of coercive enforcement. A contract between two parties, for example, represents a credible exchange of promises because the state stands ready to enforce the agreement. A party who refuses to comply with her obligations can be forced to do so or to pay damages. The ability to call on coercive enforcement changes the game from a one-shot prisoner's dilemma into a two-period game in which the promises made in the first period are enforced in the second. This enforcement leads to a sanction being imposed on the violating party that alters the payoffs of the parties (relative to the simple one-shot game) and, if the sanction is large enough, generates compliance. International tribunals lack this ability to summon coercive enforcement, and so they ultimately must rely on the same Three Rs of Compliance I have already discussed. This alters the institutions as well as the way we should analyze them.

International adjudication or arbitration can take place before standing international arbitral bodies or in an ad hoc fashion. In terms of international institutions there are several international bodies that have jurisdiction to adjudicate disputes among states or between states and private parties. The best known of these are the ICJ, the WTO and its mandatory dispute resolution system, the European Court of Human Rights, a number of human rights tribunals, the Law of the Sea Tribunal, and the arbitration bodies authorized to adjudicate disputes under bilateral investment treaties.[23]

It is worth noting that most international agreements exist without any form of dispute resolution. Agreements might be entirely silent on the question of dispute resolution or might include the singularly unhelpful command that the parties work together to resolve the dispute. For example, the Chemical Weapons Convention includes the following dispute resolution provision: "When a dispute arises between two or more State Parties... relating to the interpretation or application of this Convention, the parties concerned shall consult together with a view to the expeditious settlement of the dispute by negotiation or by other peaceful means of the parties' choice."[24]

Furthermore, when tribunals exist, they typically do not have busy dockets. The ICJ has handled 110 contentious cases over its more than 60-year history, the WTO and its predecessor, the GATT has received a total of approximately 650 cases over 60 years, and the International Tribunal for the Law of the Seas (ITLOS) has handled 13 cases in its 12-year history. The precise number of disputes brought under bilateral investment treaties is unknown (because such disputes are not always public), but as of 2004, 160 claims were known to have been filed (UNCTAD 2004). The most notable exception is the European Court of Human Rights, which has seen over 8,000 admissible complaints in its almost 50-year history. The large number of cases before this court is attributable to the fact that private parties are able to bring complaints. Indeed, Scott and Stephan (2006) consider the ability of private parties to initiate proceedings to be one of the hallmarks of an emerging system of "formal enforcement" of international law. Where access to a tribunal is limited to states, the number of cases is consistently modest. Nevertheless, dispute resolution is important to the international system. It is an option available whenever states draft an agreement, and it serves a prominent role in certain issue areas, most notably trade and human rights.

Where they exist, international tribunals often have the look and feel of domestic courts. They often call themselves courts, the adjudicators are often referred to as judges, they feature an adversarial system, they rely on legal arguments, many of them publish reasoned opinions that resemble domestic court rulings, and they are charged with issuing legally binding rulings intended to resolve disputes. These similarities are motivated by a desire to have international courts serve a function similar to that of domestic courts. And perhaps because of the superficial similarities, analyses of international tribunals make frequent analogy to domestic court systems. The domestic system works well, it is said, because courts stand ready to enforce the laws. Enforcement is a central problem for international law, and the establishment of international courts, the argument goes, will make international law more effective. Indeed, the establishment of international courts and tribunals is often said to move the international system from anarchy to order and from politics to law. For example, when the WTO was established and its dispute resolution system put in place, prominent commentators claimed that under the new system, "right perseveres over might" (Lacarte-Muro and Gappah 2000, p. 401).

Such claims cannot be evaluated until we have some understanding of what international courts do and how they are relevant to the international legal system. To understand what courts add to the international system, begin with the fact that when a state loses before a tribunal there is no formal legal structure in place to enforce the ruling.[25] The assets of the noncompliant state will not be seized, nobody will be arrested, and under existing rules the state will not even lose the ability to file its own complaints on other issues before the same tribunal. If these tribunals are effective, then, it must be for some reason other than the system of coercive enforcement that goes with a domestic court's decision.

But if international courts are unable to enforce their decisions, why do they exist at all? What role do they serve? How do they make international law more effective, if in fact they do so at all? Whatever impact international courts have must be the product of changes to the payoffs generated by the ruling itself rather than by associated enforcement mechanisms. The ruling itself, however, is just that—a ruling. Its only possible role, then, is as an information mechanism. Recognizing that international courts serve almost exclusively to provide information changes the way one views and evaluates them.

There are two kinds of informational dissemination that might make an international court effective. First, it may assist the states to come to a common understanding regarding relevant facts or law, and thereby assist in settlement. It may achieve this through a conventional adversarial process, or it may do so through something more akin to mediation. In either case, once the parties have a shared understanding of relevant facts and law, they may be able to reach a settlement that was previously unavailable. Standing courts such as the ICJ are particularly well positioned to clarify the law for future cases both because the judges remain in place over time and because in each case the tribunal is recognized as the ultimate authority on the interpretation of the relevant laws. Though the decisions of these tribunals lack formal precedential authority, judges routinely look to prior cases for guidance and treat them as settled law. The decisions of these international courts, then, reduce uncertainty surrounding the relevant legal rules.

The second form of informational dissemination an effective court might engage in is closer to what domestic courts are normally thought to do. Here the desired impact is not so much to provide information that helps the parties negotiate a resolution as to sanction a party that has violated the law. To do so, the court must be effective in distinguishing states that have violated the law from those that have not. Doing so allows the parties and other states to form a more accurate assessment of challenged behavior and, therefore, to update beliefs about a state and its willingness to comply with international legal commitments, to retaliate, or to reciprocally suspend compliance with an agreement. This is the function, for example, of dispute resolution at the WTO. To be sure, the actions of WTO panels and the WTO's Appellate Body often promote settlement, but they also rule on the question of whether the defendant has violated WTO law. If a state does not bring itself into compliance (or satisfy the complainant in some other way) sanctions are authorized. Wrongdoers, then, face both reputational and retaliatory consequences when they lose a case. To the extent that the panels accurately identify violations, they are able to provide a more effective deterrent to wrongdoing. To do this, it is critical that the panels be perceived as disinterested and beyond the control of the parties. To that end, the WTO appoints panelists through a process that does not allow the parties to control the decisions and actions of the panels or the Appellate Body.

The two aforementioned functions are not, of course, mutually exclusive. Providing accurate information about the facts and the law can serve both to promote settlement and to increase the cost of violation. In some instances, however, one function will dominate the other. If the information provided is confidential, for example, this will tend to serve the interests of settlement rather than sanction. The same will be true if the parties control the adjudicators to a greater extent. In this case, the tribunal is not disinterested and is, therefore, less likely to arrive at reliable conclusions regarding the facts or the law. In the course of the proceedings, however, the parties may overcome critical informational asymmetries.

Needless to say, these different functions will lead to different observed outcomes. If, for example, the parties exercise considerable control over the tribunal, a ruling will emerge only if both parties accept it—or, in less extreme cases of party control, a ruling is more likely to have been accepted by the parties if the tribunal is less independent. When the parties have a greater ability to frustrate the issuance of a ruling they dislike, it follows that a ruling is more likely to be complied with. The ruling, in effect, resembles a settlement agreement, in the sense that the parties have significant control over the terms. Rational parties will resist a ruling unless they expect it to be complied with. It is to be expected, then, that the rate of compliance with the rulings of dependent tribunals will be high. This simply reflects the fact that both parties have signaled that they prefer the settlement to the alternative of a continued dispute.

When a tribunal is more independent, on the other hand, the final decision does not require the consent of the parties. Given that there is no coercive enforcement scheme in the background, one would expect a lower level of compliance. The losing party retains the option of ignoring a decision and living with whatever consequences come with that decision. This is, for example, what the EC has done in the *EC–Hormones* case at the WTO. Rather than abide by the decision of the WTO's Appellate Body, the EC has continued its illegal activity and lives with the WTO-approved sanctions imposed by the United States and Canada as a result.

Because international courts can serve one or both of the aforementioned functions, there is no coherent sense in which compliance rates can be used to evaluate the effectiveness of the dispute resolution process. When courts are dependent, they serve primarily to promote settlement, and effectiveness should be measured by the court's ability to encourage the parties to end their dispute. Where a court serves to impose a sanction, its effectiveness depends on the extent to which it punishes violations or, perhaps more important, deters wrongdoing and causes states to terminate violative practices. Each of these roles has value, and each is to be preferred in some contexts and not others. It is not possible, therefore, to make sweeping claims about whether courts that tend to perform one of these functions rather than the other are in some sense "better" than those performing the other (Helfer and Slaughter 2005; Posner and Yoo 2005).

Because their primary role is informational, international tribunals can be effective even if (as is almost always the case) they are not accompanied by any sanction or enforcement authority. Dispute resolution at the ICJ, for example, provides a mechanism through which information is provided on the state of the law and the actions taken by the defendant. Though there is no enforcement, the ICJ adds value by clarifying whether a state has violated the rules of international law. This action provides information to the parties to the dispute, but it also provides information to third parties, allowing them to remain informed about the relevant behavior even when they are not directly involved (Maggi 1999; Milgrom, North, and Weingast 1990). This increases the reputational consequences of violating the underlying international legal rule, even though the tribunal does nothing more than state the actions taken by the defendant and declare whether such actions violate international law. By reducing uncertainty about legal rules and state conduct, the tribunal encourages compliance. The use of dispute resolution, then, can improve the working of an agreement, even if there is no enforcement of the judgment.[26]

It should be added that international tribunals may play an additional role in the international legal system. Rather than simply existing for the sake of resolving disputes, they may serve to establish or clarify the substantive rules of international law (Danner 2006). If so, this may be a reason, quite apart from the compliance effect of the tribunals, for their existence. Having these institutions operate in a sort of quasi–common law role may be problematic from a legitimacy and democracy perspective, but it also has the advantage that it allows gap-filling and even (to some extent) changes in legal rules. This feature of tribunals may also represent a reason (in addition to those I discuss in chapter 4) that states are at times reluctant to provide for formal dispute resolution in their agreements.

State Responsibility

International law also includes some rules that at least arguably require states to provide compensation to a state that has been wronged.[27] For example, article 31 of the Draft Articles of State Responsibility states that "[t]he responsible State is under an obligation to make full reparation for the injury caused by the internationally wrongful act."[28] This is said to be a codification of a customary international law regarding reparations and can be traced to the *Chorzow Factory* case, decided by the Permanent Court of International Justice in 1927.[29] Even if one assumes that the rules of state responsibility have an effect on states, it remains to be explained why this is so. In trying to understand why a state might comply with an international obligation, it makes no sense to turn to a rule of international law that says a failure to comply generates an obligation to make reparation. If there is nothing else to encourage compliance with the initial obligation, then the rule requiring reparations will be similarly impotent.

In game theoretic terms, any mechanism that induces cooperation must ultimately do what the court system does in the domestic context—it must alter the payoffs received by the states in such a way as to encourage compliance. In other words, there must be some way the decision to violate international law imposes costs on the state. A desire to avoid these costs is what provides the incentive to comply with international law.

Payoffs and Strategies over Time

Up to this point, the discussion has assumed that the payoffs facing the parties remain stable over time. By this I do not mean that they are the same in every period (which is not needed for the analysis) but rather that there are no external shocks that change the payoffs in future periods. This assumption of stable payoffs is convenient, but it is more realistic to assume that payoffs change over time, and often do so in ways that are difficult to anticipate. Returning once again to the ABM Treaty example, the decline of the Soviet Union in the 1980s, and its dissolution and the subsequent weakness of Russia during the 1990s, increased the incentive for the United States to violate the treaty, and ultimately led to its withdrawal from the treaty. Much of the incentive for the United States to comply with the ABM Treaty was driven by the desire to avoid an arms race. Once it became impossible for the Soviet Union/Russia to pay for an arms race, the United States stood to gain from the building of an antiballistic missile system. Russia would simply be unable to counter U.S. technological advances. Meanwhile, U.S. officials felt that U.S. technology had improved sufficiently to make viable an ABM system designed to deter threats from rogue states that had acquired or were seeking to acquire nuclear weapons. This combination of changed circumstances was not something the parties could have anticipated with any confidence, and so their efforts at cooperation were not specifically tailored to account for this confluence of events.

If states know that shocks may occur, they can at most calculate the expected future payoffs. These, however, may differ substantially from the actual payoffs facing the states in a future period when they make their compliance decisions. With only estimates of future payoffs, states may not know whether they will be playing a coordination game, a prisoner's dilemma, or some other game.

Relaxing the assumption of stable, known payoffs yields at least two insights. The first is that a country's decision to comply with a rule at one moment in time does not necessarily imply that it will continue to do so at some other time. For example, a state that is enjoying good economic times may decide to comply with an environmental agreement because it is willing to give up some economic benefits in exchange for improved environmental practices. If that same state finds itself in a recession, however, it may weigh the economic costs of the agreement more heavily, and may decide to violate its commitment. In both the good and the bad times, that state has behaved rationally to maximize its payoffs. The outcome has changed because the nonreputational payoffs have changed.

This illustration suggests a definition for reputational and non-reputational payoffs that I will use throughout the book. Reputational payoffs are generated by changes to a state's reputation. The reputational changes help other states to predict what the state will do in the future. Nonreputational payoffs are those payoffs that are the direct result of a state's decision to act in one way or another. They are independent of how the behavior affects the state's reputation.

The second insight is that states engaged in what appears to be one sort of game may enter into agreements designed to address problems of cooperation in some other game. States concerned about a future shock may structure their cooperation to deal with both the game as it appears on the basis of today's payoffs and the game they may find themselves playing after a shock. This offers a possible (though only partial) explanation for why states sometimes use international law to resolve games that do not appear to require any form of enforcement mechanism (e.g., games of common interest, coordination games, battle-of-the-sexes games). If future payoffs are known at the time an agreement is reached, cooperative games of this sort can normally be resolved at lower cost by using less formal ways to select a focal point. For example, a unilateral declaration by one of the states will often be sufficient to generate a focal point and establish a stable equilibrium.

But if the game in question, though it looks like a coordination game, has some probability of becoming a prisoner's dilemma or some other game in which cooperation is more difficult, the states have an incentive to protect against that outcome. By way of example, the Antarctic Treaty bans the establishment of military bases and the testing of weapons on Antarctica, suspends territorial claims, sets up an inspection system, and provides for periodic meetings of the parties. When it was signed in 1959 (and entered into force in 1961), the prohibitions included in the treaty had little practical effect, because states were generally already in compliance. There were, at the time, no military operations in Antarctica, territorial claims were not immediately threatening to escalate into military conflict, and the territory had little more than speculative strategic value. In this sense, the treaty could be described as an effort to resolve a coordination game. The states involved wanted to preserve the territory for scientific purposes and keep it free of military activity and weapons testing, but it seems likely that this was precisely the equilibrium that had already been reached.

Looking forward from the time of the signing, however, it is plausible that the parties had concerns about how the importance of Antarctica and therefore the payoffs to the parties might change. If the interests of the parties changed, whether for economic (e.g., the discovery of oil or mineral reserves), strategic, or other reasons, the game might become a prisoner's dilemma. By establishing a treaty rather than a more informal set of norms, the parties solidified the cooperative regime. As it turned out, environmental issues have become important in Antarctica, and these have the character of a prisoner's dilemma. Although the original text of the treaty contains no specific references to environmental protection, it quickly became clear that environmental issues were among the most important.[30] The first of a series of additional agreements and protocols on the environmental protection of Antarctica was signed in 1964, only three years after the treaty went into effect. Furthermore, in 1988 the Convention for the Regulation of Antarctic Mineral Resource Activities (CRAMRA) was adopted. Though this agreement contained stringent environmental protections, it nevertheless permitted mining in Antarctica, indicating that states' interest in mining had increased to the point where cooperation under the auspices of the original treaty was necessary to solve the nascent prisoner's dilemma. In fact, the reaction to permitting any mining in Antarctica, however limited, was so negative that CRAMRA was superseded in 1991 by the Protocol on Environmental Protection to the Antarctic Treaty (the Madrid Protocol). The evolution of these environmental agreements illustrates the wisdom of using a formal treaty to establish rules governing Antarctica: as the need for more explicit environmental regulation of Antarctica grew, the consultative bodies established by the original Antarctic Treaty provided a forum in which states could bargain to solve the emerging prisoner's dilemma.

That states may enter into international agreements to generate cooperation in games with payoffs that change over time suggests that in some situations international law is doing more work than it seems. So even if many international agreements, at the time of their formation, function primarily to resolve coordination games, international law may nevertheless be generating cooperation in games that, because of changing payoffs over time, represent more difficult cooperative problems.

Modulating the Level of Commitment

The following discussion of the level of commitment is closely related to the theory developed in Guzman (2002b) and Sartori (2002). In Sartori's model, states issue costless signals about the importance of particular issues. Despite being costless, these signals matter because when a state signals that an issue is of great importance, rivals understand that attacking the state on that issue is more likely to lead to resistance and so are less likely to attack. Though a state could claim that every issue is important to it, doing so would be a poor strategy because this would cause its statements to lose credibility. Instead, rational states admit (at least much of the time) when an issue is of only modest importance because doing so lends credibility to its statements about issues it does consider critical. The result is that states use costless signals to send different messages reflecting their commitment.

In the international law context, states can send different signals about their intention to comply with international legal obligations by using different legal forms. They can refrain from any international agreement, enter into a "soft law" agreement (defined as an agreement that is neither a formal treaty nor customary international law), or enter into a formal treaty.[31] Within the category of soft law, further distinctions are possible. For example, the United States has entered into a number of soft law agreements addressing matters of cooperation in antitrust. These agreements demand very little of the participating states, whereas the Basel Accord, also a soft law agreement, includes quite detailed provisions about what states must do to comply and requires real changes in the practices of the states involved. By choosing one form of commitment over another, states signal their seriousness and the amount of reputational collateral they wish to pledge. A formal treaty represents the most serious form of commitment not because it is more costly to enter into than other commitments but because it is understood to be a maximal pledge of reputation (Guzman 2002b). There is more to be said about the role of soft law and treaties, and that discussion is in chapter 4.

In game theoretic parlance, the choice among different forms of agreement is cheap talk. Even if it is no more expensive to use the treaty form rather than soft law, states may do so to signal a more serious commitment. Choosing between the treaty and soft law forms is not so different from choosing to write an agreement on red paper when states wish to signal a strong commitment and green paper when they wish to signal a weaker commitment. By making a more serious commitment (e.g., a treaty) a state is able to extract more from its counterpart because the promises it makes are more credible. The temptation to make every agreement as formal and serious as possible is offset by the costs that come with such a commitment. Specifically, if the agreement is violated, the violating state suffers a reputational sanction. Where the commitment is less serious, then, the state has an incentive to make this clear by, for example, using a soft law form rather than a treaty.

Coercion and International Agreements

Throughout most of this book, the discussion assumes that international agreements are consensual. Under current international law rules, a treaty is considered void as a result of coercion only if the agreement was the result of the unlawful use or threat of force or if a country's representative was threatened (Vienna Convention on the Law of Treaties, arts. 51, 52).[32] Analytically, these rules seem to leave plenty of room for agreements that could be described as coercive, but it turns out to be difficult to craft a better rule to distinguish agreements that increase the well-being of both states from those that do not.

One way we can be sure that an agreement is Pareto improving (meaning that it makes some parties better off without making any worse off) is to demand that all parties have the option of rejecting the agreement and retaining the status quo. Strictly speaking, because individuals make these decisions on behalf of states, consent only ensures that these individuals prefer the agreement to the alternative of no agreement. If these decision-makers pursue private objectives that are inconsistent with the general welfare of their citizens, even consensual agreements need not improve welfare. Nevertheless, we expect consensual agreements to improve the lot of the parties involved with greater frequency than nonconsensual, coercive agreements. After all, citizens (at least within democracies) have at least some check, through the ballot box, on the international activities of their politicians.

There is no doubt that at least some international agreements are, indeed, coercive. An obvious example is the 1919 Treaty of Versailles, by which Germany surrendered to the Allied Powers following World War I. As is true of many other peace agreements, there is no sense in which that agreement can be described as being entered into voluntarily by the German government, nor could Germany choose the status quo rather than the proffered agreement. Agreement was achieved at gunpoint.

Plenty of other, less obvious examples of coercive agreements exist. In September 2004, for example, the United States signed the Trade and Investment Framework Agreement with Afghanistan. At the time, and indeed still today, the government of Afghanistan relied so heavily on U.S. support that the decision to sign an agreement presented by the United States can hardly be construed as a free choice. Another example from the early twentieth century is the Hay-Bunua-Varilla Treaty of

1903, which gave the United States the Panama Canal Zone and the right to build the Panama Canal. Having successfully declared independence from Colombia (at the urging of U.S. president Theodore Roosevelt), the new nation of Panama was in need of allies in the region. The powerful allure of the aid and protection of the United States against a potentially hostile neighbor, Colombia, surely exerted a coercive influence on the negotiation of the treaty that granted to the United States one of the most valuable property rights in the world.

Other agreements, however, are more difficult to classify as coercive or consensual. A conspicuous and important modern example is the agreement on Trade-Related Aspects of Intellectual Property Rights (TRIPs), which was entered into by all WTO member states at the conclusion of the Uruguay Round of trade talks in 1994. The agreement requires that the signatories establish a domestic regime with certain intellectual property protections. Critics of the agreement point out that most developing countries had almost nothing to gain from the TRIPs agreement, and a great deal to lose. They argue that these states signed the agreement because they were threatened with a withdrawal of access to the markets of developed countries, most notably the United States.[33] Defenders of the agreement respond that it was part of a larger bargain struck by states during the Uruguay Round of trade negotiations in the late 1980s and early 1990s. The TRIPs agreement was just one part of the WTO agreement that emerged from negotiations that included concessions by developed states on agriculture, textiles, and the use of unilateral trade measures. Though it was the result of hard bargaining, it was not coercive, the argument goes, because all parties got something they valued.[34] Who is correct in this exchange? Almost certainly both sides. On the one hand, there is no question that the negotiation of the Uruguay Round was a bare-knuckles affair in which power played an important role. Then again, this is true of virtually all important international negotiations. If the presence of large differences in bargaining power is enough to make an agreement coercive, then virtually any north–south agreement (among many others) qualifies. On the other hand, at some point hard bargaining turns into an exchange of threats. The final WTO agreement was described as a "single undertaking" that required states to accept all the negotiated rules or remain entirely outside the system. Furthermore, the previous GATT regime was effectively dissolved by the new WTO, so states declining the new WTO did not have the option of retaining the old status quo.

Developing states were thus forced to choose between accepting the entire WTO package, including the TRIPs agreement, or remaining outside the newly formed WTO and therefore outside the trading system's most important institution. Because states did not have the option of retaining the pre-WTO status quo, the agreement satisfies my definition of coercion. The problem is that there may not have been any other way to reach agreement, and it is possible that every state was made better off by the WTO agreement. The complex package of concessions that emerged from the Uruguay Round negotiations was fragile. If states were permitted to commit to some provisions but not others, the entire structure threatened to break down as each state withdrew the concessions it had made. And if states could opt out of the new WTO while retaining all their rights under the GATT, there would be a temptation to free ride on the additional liberalization provided for under the WTO. By giving up (or being denied) the option of retaining the status quo, states may have improved their payoffs. The single undertaking, then, can be viewed as a necessary mechanism to preserve the integrity of the agreed-upon terms.

One is tempted, then, to rethink the definition of coercion offered at the start of this section. Perhaps agreements should sometimes be considered consensual even if the parties are unable to reject the terms and opt instead for the status quo.

This example demonstrates the key problem: to the extent that we would like to identify a set of agreements that can be labeled as coercive and that are, for that reason, normatively problematic, there is no straightforward way to distinguish coercive agreements from consensual ones (Keohane 1984). One might seek a definition under which consensual agreements are those that (at least in expectation) lead to a Pareto improvement (i.e., make all parties better off), but there is no reliable way to determine when an agreement satisfies this definition. There is nothing unique about the international arena in this context, of course. The same problem exists in the domestic sphere where we cannot clearly identify the difference between a coercive contract and a noncoercive one. We know that "your money or your life" is a coercive agreement, but beyond that it quickly becomes difficult to establish clear distinctions.

What is the relevance of all of this to the working of international law? As mentioned, coercive agreements (defined as those that do not offer the option of retaining the status quo) are more problematic from a welfare perspective than are consensual ones. Indeed, a coercive agreement need not even lead to an improvement in total welfare, however measured. It is entirely possible that the gains to one side will be out-weighed by the losses to the other, meaning that the agreement destroys value, rather than creating it.

Despite this important difference between the welfare effects of co-ercive and consensual agreements, the two types of agreement can be treated similarly for compliance purposes. A coercive agreement is pre-sumably valuable to the party doing the coercing for the same reason that a consensual agreement would be valuable. That is, the agreement must generate some compliance pull beyond what can be achieved without it. After all, why coerce a state into signing an agreement if that agreement does not affect its behavior? When a state makes a promise to take some costly action and in exchange receives some benefit or avoids some cost imposed by the other side, it has an incentive to refuse performance when the time comes. Whether the agreement is a coercive one or a consensual one, a refusal to comply may provoke reputational sanctions. It is true that the coercing state may threaten to impose some additional sanction if there is a violation (presumably this threat would resemble the one that led to the agreement in the first place), but this threat of sanction works like any other such threat—it is only effective if it is credible, and a costly sanction will only be imposed if it contributes to a state's reputation for penalizing those that violate international agreements.

There may, however, be a natural upper bound on the extent to which coercive agreements can bind a state. At least when it is clear that co-ercion was used, the reputational sanction for violation may be limited. A violating state able to show that it was coerced may be able to limit the reputational impact to its reputation for compliance *with coerced agreements*. The state may be able to preserve a good reputation for agreements that are truly consensual. A state's ability to cabin the rep-utational impact of its breach depends on the extent to which reputa-tion is compartmentalized, a question I discuss in Chapter 3.

Multilateral Cooperation

As mentioned, both reciprocity and retaliation are more effective enforcement mechanisms for bilateral agreements than for mul-tilateral agreements. In fact, some observers have suggested that these sanctions are so ineffective in the multilateral context that multilateral cooperation achieved through international law is virtually nonexistent.[35] This negative conclusion about multilateral cooperation, however, both understates the potential role of reciprocity and retaliation and ignores the fact that reputational sanctions represent an alternative compliance-promoting mechanism in multilateral agreements. In this section I discuss the problem that multilateral cooperation presents for reciprocity and retaliation, explain why it is often (but not always) likely to undermine these enforcement strategies, and discuss why reputational sanctions can be effective even when many parties are involved in an agreement. The conclusion of the section is that multilateral cooperation presents some unique challenges for cooperation, but no theoretical reason exists to think that international law cannot facilitate it in a wide range of contexts.

Reciprocity and Multilateral Agreements

There are several reasons that states might choose to enter into a multilateral agreement rather than a series of bilateral ones. For example, multilateral agreements can achieve uniformity more easily than can bilateral agreements, there may be economies of scale in verification and monitoring that promote a more effective multilateral reputation mechanism, and multilateral negotiations may allow for a richer set of possible exchanges and trade-offs than do bilateral talks—potentially creating more room for agreement.

For my present purposes, however, it is sufficient to focus on just one reason: multilateral agreements allow states to overcome collective action problems that bilateral agreements cannot adequately address.

When state decisions affect all (or many) other states, as is the case with many environmental, human rights, and nuclear arms policies, among others, there are powerful reasons to address these issues multilaterally. The reasons are familiar and are illustrated by the environmental problems that gave rise to the Kyoto Protocol. Greenhouse gas emissions are harmful to the atmosphere and therefore represent a cost imposed on the entire world. The cost of reducing those emissions, however, is borne by individual states (and their private industries) that enact regulatory measures. Because the government of a state takes into account all the costs of tougher pollution standards but only a fraction of the global benefit from reduced environmental harm, states will systematically underregulate. Multilateral cooperation allows states to act collectively and internalize more fully the costs and benefits of their policy choices.

The Kyoto Protocol provides this kind of solution. It is a multilateral agreement that calls on industrialized states to reduce their collective emissions of six greenhouse gases blamed for climate change. The treaty, which entered into force on February 16, 2005, commits ratifying states to reducing emissions or, in the event that they maintain or increase their greenhouse gas emissions, purchasing emissions credits from states that have met their targets. The problem posed by climate change, and addressed by the Kyoto Protocol, has the structure of a multilateral prisoner's dilemma. All states have an interest in the reduction of harm to the environment in general and reducing global warming in particular. Because there are many states involved, however, each state has an incentive to shirk and free ride on the efforts of other states. Absent some effective form of multilateral cooperation, there will be too little investment in environmental protection. Collective or multilateral decision-making, in the form of an international agreement, ensures that the member states more fully internalize both the costs and benefits of regulation.

The very reason that public goods problems (i.e., problems involving nonrivalrous goods, such as the global environment, for which consumption by one individual does not reduce the amount of the good available for consumption by others) are often best addressed through collective action also makes reciprocity less effective as an enforcement device. Imagine that a state fails to honor its commitments under the Kyoto Protocol. It would make little sense for all states to simply cease their own compliance in response. Doing so would undermine the purposes of the treaty and impose a cost on all states. Recognizing this, a potential violator knows that the agreement is likely to continue to exist whether or not it violates its commitment. Since every state recognizes this fact, everyone's incentive to comply is reduced. In short, reciprocity is unlikely to prove an effective tool to sustain compliance in a multilateral treaty aimed at a public goods problem.

Though this problem of reciprocity is real for many multilateral agreements, it will not always present a challenge. In agreements that address pure public goods, states are unlikely to be able to condition their own performance on reciprocity by all other states. For many other multilateral agreements, however, it is possible for a state to respond to a violation by withdrawing its own compliance only with respect to the violating state, making reciprocity a useful and sometimes very powerful tool to encourage compliance.

An obvious example is the WTO system, in which a multilateral treaty is enforced by granting states the authority to selectively suspend their own compliance with portions of the agreement. So, for example, when the WTO's adjudicatory bodies concluded that the European Communities had violated their obligations with respect to the importation of beef containing artificial growth hormones, they granted the United States and Canada the right to suspend certain trade obligations they had toward Europe. Though not perfect, this system of reciprocal withdrawal of benefits represents a meaningful incentive to comply with the multilateral trading rules.

In general it is the case that when the good in question is excludable, reciprocity should work in the multilateral context in much the same way as it does in the bilateral context. When the good is nonexcludable, the use of reciprocity to enforce multilateral regimes becomes significantly more problematic.

Retaliation and Multilateral Agreements

The threat of retaliation can often serve as an enforcement device, but like reciprocity it works less well when public goods are involved. Consider, by way of example, the ICCPR. This multilateral human rights treaty imposes obligations on all member states. Suppose Russia is tempted to violate its commitment. A credible threat to impose a retaliatory sanction—perhaps a ban on exports from other states to Russia—might affect that compliance decision, but such a threat is likely to lack credibility for two reasons. First, it suffers from the same credibility problems that exist in the bilateral context. Specifically, imposing the sanction is costly for the sanctioning party, and a rational state will only take this action if there is some benefit. As discussed in the context of bilateral agreements, one reason to impose the sanction is to acquire or protect a reputation as a state that punishes violators, but this may not be enough.

The second problem that is particular to the multilateral context is the free-rider problem. Even if the threat to sanction a violation would be an effective deterrent, when it comes time to impose the sanction, each individual state has an incentive to free ride on the actions of others. Every party to the treaty (and arguably every state in the world) benefits from compliance by Russia and therefore from the compliance inducing effect of the threatened retaliation.[36] But only those states that impose the sanction (or threaten to do so) bear the cost of the sanction. So every state has an incentive to try to capture the benefits of compliance without bearing the costs of the retaliation, and it is likely to be difficult, as a result, to credibly threaten to sanction a violator. To be sure, multilateral sanctions are imposed from time to time. Prominent examples include the economic sanctions on the South African apartheid regime and sanctions on Iraq following the first Gulf War.

In many other cases, however, it proves impossible to overcome the collective action problem. The six-party talks associated with North Korea's development of a nuclear weapon and its withdrawal from the NPT illustrate this point. The United States, China, South Korea, Japan, and Russia were, at least for a time, unable to impose a sufficiently high cost (or opportunity cost, in terms of benefits forgone under the parties' 1994 agreement) to prevent North Korea from taking these actions.[37] Part of this problem was a failure to overcome the collective action problem and impose a unified sanctions regime. More recently the agreement reached among the relevant states promises to end North Korea's nuclear program.

The collective action problem with respect to retaliation is a real and serious one in many contexts, but in some situations states are able to overcome it. If a violation imposes costs on one (or a few) states, a threat of retaliation may be credible even if the underlying obligation is multilateral. The Vienna Convention on Diplomatic Relations, for example, imposes obligations on every state toward all other states that are party to the agreement, but when a violation occurs it normally injures only one party, and that party can retaliate. The collective action problem is overcome in this context because the retaliating state only threatens retaliation when its own interests are harmed and it is, therefore, able to capture the full benefits of a reputation for punishing such violators. The threat of retaliation in this context is as credible as it would be in a bilateral agreement. Several prominent multilateral treaties in which retaliation of this sort is possible are trade treaties (e.g., WTO; NAFTA; the Dominican Republic-Central America Free Trade Agreement, DR-CAFTA), but the same sort of sanction could exist under a variety of treaties in other areas (e.g., the Basel Accord, Geneva Convention

Relative to the Treatment of Prisoners of War, Vienna Convention on Diplomatic Relations, VCCR).

It is also worth noting that multilateral agreements in which there are only a few (or perhaps just one) leading parties, as is often the case in today's world, will face a smaller collective action problem. If the leading party captures a large share of the gains from compliance, it will have a greater incentive to impose retaliatory measures, and therefore its threat to do so will be more credible. An example of an agreement of this sort might be the NPT.[38] This treaty has 187 member states, but among these the United States plays a leading role in encouraging compliance by others. As the only global superpower, the United States' interests are affected, and its influence diminished, whenever another country anywhere in the world develops a nuclear option that negates the substantial U.S. advantage in conventional weaponry. As a result of this distribution of benefits, the United States has taken the lead in organizing, coordinating, and contributing to enforcement efforts such as the Proliferation Security Initiative (PSI), a voluntary arrangement of states aimed at halting the spread of illicit weapons technology through active and cooperative interdiction of illegal arms shipments.

The PSI, launched in 2003 following North Korea's withdrawal from the NPT, was widely seen as an attempt to halt the North Korean nuclear program. Similarly, Israel stood to lose considerably more than other states in the 1980s if Iraq developed a nuclear capability in violation of its NPT obligations. It should thus not be a surprise that Israel was willing to bear alone the costs of a preemptive strike that destroyed Iraq's Osiraq nuclear reactor in 1981.

Reputation and Multilateral Agreements

So even if one considers only reciprocity and retaliation, it is clear that compliance can often be sustained by international law. But as discussed, neither of these strategies works especially well when the relevant issues involve public goods. Areas in which this is likely to be a problem include, for example, multilateral environmental agreements (where the harms from noncompliance are truly felt by many states), human rights agreements, and many multilateral arms control agreements. In each of these areas, threats of reciprocal withdrawal of compliance and threats of retaliation will normally lack credibility. Even for this limited subset of agreements, however, there is no reason to conclude that international law is ineffective or cannot generate cooperation.

The discussion of reputation already presented, along with the detailed presentation in the next chapter, gives us a theory capable of explaining the multilateral cooperation that we observe, even in these public goods areas. Reputation can provide an incentive to comply with international obligations even when reciprocity and retaliation do not, because reputational sanctions require neither that states choose to impose costly sanctions in an effort to generate future compliance nor that reciprocal withdrawal of concessions is practical. Reputational sanctions, instead, reflect the updating of beliefs by self-interested states. There is no need for coordination, no need for formal adjudication of a dispute (though this can improve the effectiveness of reputational sanctions), and no need for costly actions by sanctioning states.

3

REPUTATION

The basic way retaliation and reciprocity work can be well understood with the brief discussion devoted to each in the prior chapter. Reputation, however, requires elaboration. This chapter provides a more complete picture of how reputation affects state behavior and how it interacts with other issues.

Just about every sort of cooperation that is interesting to us relies, in some way, on reputation. The primary exceptions are coordination games and other similarly straightforward games, discussed in chapter 2, in which compliance can be achieved without resort to reputation and, indeed, without resort to international law. The large number of interactions and games that remain all involve reputation in some way. It is true that cooperation can often be sustained through reciprocity or credible threats of retaliation, but as discussed in chapter 2, each of these relies on some form of reputation. Reciprocity can sometimes succeed because when a state has breached an obligation, its promises of future compliance lack credibility. The state suffers a reputational loss, at least with respect to the particular agreement at issue, and so the state's partner no longer has reason to believe promises of future cooperation. A threat to retaliate is costly to the sanctioning state, and so rational states will only take retaliatory action if it helps them to establish a reputation for punishing those that breach their commitments.

Reputation is also critical to our understanding of multilateral agreements. Where the benefits from such agreements are nonexcludable, reciprocity works poorly. It normally makes little sense for all states to cease their own compliance in reaction to a violation by only one state, and threats to do so lack credibility for that reason. Retaliation in multilateral agreements often suffers from significant free-rider problems, as no state has optimal incentives to bear the costs of retaliation when all parties stand to enjoy the compliance benefits of those actions.

Reputation, on the other hand, can work effectively in the multilateral context. Indeed, it may work better in multilateral settings than in bilateral ones. Parties to an agreement may learn about violations more quickly and accurately than those outside of the agreement, and they may have a more finely tuned sense of relevant nonreputational payoffs. If so, the reputational consequences of a violation will be more severe in a multilateral context—because the reputational information spreads quickly to more countries.

This book is certainly not the first effort to use reputation to explain state behavior, and this chapter is not the first to address how reputation works (Abreu and Gul 2000; Alt, Calvert, and Humes 1988; Downs and Jones 2002; Keohane 1984; Maggi 1999; Mercer 1996; Sobel 1985). This chapter differs from prior writings in two important respects. First, it focuses on international law. Much of the existing writing on reputation addresses a state's reputation in the security arena.[1] This distinction is important because security-related interactions are only a small fraction of the interactions between states. Furthermore, security issues are aberrational because of the enormously high value states place on issues of national security and national survival. The importance of security issues has attracted scholars, but an excessive focus on high-value interactions fails to capture the logic of the more routine, and considerably more frequent, aspects of international legal relationships. Second, this chapter considers reputation in more detail than most previous studies and develops a more complete theory than has been done in previous work.[2]

The chapter first develops a simple model of reputational gain and loss and considers how state behavior is affected as a result. I then examine how relaxing certain informational assumptions affects the role of reputation. In particular, I point out that uncertainty about payoffs, legal rules, and actions taken all reduce the impact of reputation on behavior. I then discuss the extent to which states are likely to have a single reputation for compliance with international law as compared to multiple reputations. Finally, some of the limits of reputation's ability to affect behavior are discussed.

How Reputation Is Gained and Lost

The Compliance Decision

We begin by considering how reputation is acquired and lost. The theory of reputation is relatively new in the international law literature but is more established in economic and political science writings. Despite its use in several disciplines, however, we lack a comprehensive theory of reputation that can be applied in the international law context. The first task of this chapter, then, is to outline such a theory.

Chapter 2 defined reputation as judgments about an actor's past behavior used to predict future behavior. Consistent with that definition, we can define a state's reputation for compliance with international law as judgments about an actor's past response to international legal obligations used to predict future compliance with such obligations. This reputation is an estimate of the state's true willingness to comply even when nonreputational payoffs favor violation. This willingness to comply depends on the state's discount rate; the domestic politics in the state (e.g., the extent to which domestic political structures make violation of international law difficult or costly); the state's willingness to impose costs on others;[3] the value of future opportunities to cooperate (which a current violation may jeopardize); and so on.

Other states are assumed to be unable to observe this underlying willingness to comply, and so they must estimate it on the basis of the actions of the state. In principle, every observing state has its own perception of a particular state's reputation. Thus, the United States may have different reputations in Canada, Argentina, Russia, and Syria. For the moment, I abstract away from this issue and assume that every observer has the same view of the state's reputation. This assumption is relaxed later in the chapter.

In the prior chapter, I treated the acquisition and loss of reputation in an extremely simple way. As described there, states that honor their commitments acquire reputational capital, and states that violate their commitments lose it. A moment's thought, however, makes it clear that things must be more complicated than this. If it were simply a matter of counting the instances of compliant behavior, states could build their reputations by signing many treaties that impose trivial obligations. A sensible model of reputation building cannot, for example, lead to the conclusion that Bolivia, a landlocked country, can improve its reputation by committing to keep its ports open. Similarly, it cannot be that the tiny island republic of Vanuatu, whose total gross domestic product is less than $350 million, can improve its reputation by agreeing to refrain from placing weapons in space. The acquisition of reputation clearly must be more complex than simply complying with commitments.

The loss of reputation, similarly, must depend on more than simply how often a state violates its commitments. A minor, technical reporting violation that is quickly corrected, for example, must have less of an impact on a state's reputation than a large-scale and public repudiation of a major treaty.

When entering into an agreement, states want their promises to be credible, and they must ultimately rely on reputation for that credibility. As the expected costs of performance increase, states require more credibility and, therefore, a stronger reputation for the associated promises to be believed.

An increase in reputation, Q, has value to the state in the sense that a higher reputation allows it to make more credible promises to other states and to extract more gains from its international engagements. To see how reputation can change, consider the following illustration.

Suppose a state has an existing reputation it has acquired as a result of its past conduct or, if it is a new state, it has some baseline reputation that represents the expectations of others regarding the state's willingness to comply with international legal obligations. Faced with a compliance decision, the state either complies with or violates its obligation, and this decision may impact the state's reputation.

It is assumed that other states are unable to observe the state's true willingness to comply with its obligation. Other states can, however, observe the acting state's nonreputational payoffs. They may know, for example, what it would cost the state to comply with an environmental obligation, but they do not know what the state hopes to achieve in the future through international environmental agreements or the state's discount rate. All states also know the legal rules in place and are able to accurately observe the behavior of the acting state. These issues (nonreputational payoffs, legal rules, and the ability to observe a state's actions) may bear on how state behavior affects reputation, and they are discussed later in this chapter, but the presentation is simpler if they are omitted for the moment.

The state must choose between compliance and violation. If the state chooses to comply, it receives a total payoff that consists of the nonreputational payoff plus the reputational payoff. The reputational payoff measures the value of any increase in reputation generated by the decision to comply. If both parties to an agreement comply in every period, the payoffs corresponds to the comply-comply payoff in table 3 in chapter 2.

If, on the other hand, the state violates the legal rule, it receives the associated nonreputational and reputational payoffs. Now the reputational payoff reflects any loss of value to the state as a result of its violative conduct.

In deciding how to act, the state compares the total payoff in the event of a violation to what it would receive should it comply. Violation is only tempting to the state if the nonreputational payoff from violation is larger than the nonreputational payoff from compliance. The question, then, is whether the reputational payoffs can provide some offsetting incentive to comply.

In my later discussion of the way reputation changes in response to either compliance or violation, I show that a state's reputation will be changed only to the extent that the state's behavior differs from what observing states have expected. It is possible, therefore, for a compliant state to enjoy no reputational gain or for a violating state to suffer no reputational loss. But when choosing between violation and compliance, at least one of those actions will generate a change in reputation, because at least one of those actions will be different from what observing states expect. This means that the reputational payoff from compliance will be larger than the reputational payoff from violation. This difference in the reputational payoffs has the potential to offset the gains a state gets from violating an agreement.

Specifically, the state will comply if the reputational gain from compliance exceeds the increase in nonreputational payoffs available if it violates its commitment.

Returning to the question of how reputation is gained and lost, notice that the value of reputation will not be the same for every state or in every issue area. Some states (or states in some situations) are in a better position to extract value from a good reputation. These states might, for example, have many future opportunities for cooperation that require them to make credible promises, or they may have an ongoing relationship with a partner that makes a good reputation especially valuable. Reputation is more valuable for such states than it is for those with fewer or less valuable potential international engagements. When reputation is more valuable, states are willing to bear more costs in order to enhance or protect it. They will, therefore, be more willing to comply with an international legal commitment.

To illustrate, suppose that the value of reputation is measured by a function, V. For simplicity, assume that there are two different types of states. One type can extract a great deal of value from any given level of reputation and faces a value function labeled V^H. The other type gets less value from a good reputation and faces a value function labeled V^L.

States facing the value function V^H have more to gain from a strong reputation than those facing the function V^L. Faced with a compliance decision, a state will take into account how changes to its reputation will affect its overall payoffs. As figure 3.1 indicates, a given change in reputation, Q, has a greater impact on the state that places a high value on reputation than on the state that places a low value on it. It follows that the latter will invest less in reputation (i.e., will violate obligations more readily) than will the former. In equilibrium, then, we expect to find some states (or some state–subject area combinations) with good reputations and others with weaker reputations.

As the value of reputation increases, a state is better able to resist the temptation to violate a legal obligation, meaning that the difference in nonreputational payoff between violation and compliance must be larger to provoke a breach by a state for which a good reputation is valuable. One implication is that we cannot hope to predict compliance behavior

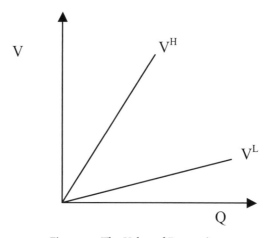

Figure 3.1 The Value of Reputation

without at least some understanding of both the reputational and non-reputational payoffs at issue.

This model of reputation has some similarities to the model developed in Mercer (1996), which focuses on a state's reputation for resolve, defined as its willingness to risk war to achieve its objectives. What he terms "situational" attributes correspond roughly with what I term "nonreputational" payoffs, and what he terms "dispositional" attributes correspond to my "reputational" payoffs. However, unlike Mercer, who takes an approach rooted in social psychology, I assume that states are rational actors. They evaluate the behavior of all other states, whether friend or foe, by using the available evidence and rationally attributing behavior to reputational or nonreputational payoffs on the basis of the information the observer possesses. States in Mercer's model also rely on past behavior, but do so in an asymmetric way. Specifically, he assumes that observers attribute undesirable behavior (from the observer's perspective) by their adversaries to reputation (to use my vocabulary), but attribute good behavior by the same states to nonreputational payoffs. His assumptions about allies are the opposite. With reference to a reputation for resolve, for example, the consequence of his assumptions is that "while adversaries can get reputations for having resolve, they rarely get reputations for lacking resolve; and while allies can get reputations for lacking resolve, they rarely get reputations for having resolve" (Mercer 1999, p. 10). Mercer also understates the relationship between reputational and nonreputational issues. He argues that observers attribute state actions to either reputational issues or nonreputational issues and asserts that a "situational (i.e., nonreputational) attribution cannot sensibly be used to predict behavior in a different situation" (p. 15). When it is recognized that reputational and nonreputational payoffs both influence compliance decisions, however, it is clear that a compliance decision taken in one situation yields information about how a state will behave in other situations. This information, in turn, can be used to predict future behavior.

The next step in developing a theory of reputation is to consider in more detail the circumstances in which reputation is likely to change. There are three key factors likely to determine whether a particular action affects the associated reputation.[4] These are (1) the nonreputational payoffs a state is facing; (2) the state's existing reputation at the time of the action; and (3) the importance of the obligations to other states. These factors help to explain why a decision to violate or comply will have different reputational consequences in different contexts. They also address one of the key arguments advanced by international law skeptics attempting to dismiss reputation.[5] Because reputation acts at the margin and nonreputational factors also influence state decisions, it should come as no surprise that different treaties (or customary international law) generate different levels of compliance at different times. Reputation has an impact on the compliance decision by making compliance somewhat more likely, not by ensuring the same rate of compliance in all circumstances.

Compliance Decisions and Their Effect on Reputation

Because gains and losses of reputation must depend on more than simply whether agreements are complied with, one must also know something about why a state has complied with or violated an agreement. In fact, the reasons for a violation may be as important as the actions itself. In our model, a state acts in an effort to maximize its payoffs, and those payoffs are divided into two categories: reputational payoffs and nonreputational payoffs. Consider first the nonreputational payoffs.

A state that has a powerful national security reason to violate an agreement, for example, faces nonreputational payoffs that provide a strong incentive to ignore the commitment. In contrast, a state whose behavior would be consistent with the agreement even in the absence of a commitment faces nonreputational payoffs that give it an incentive to comply. The reputational consequences of an action (i.e., the reputational payoffs) are closely related to these nonreputational payoffs.

When entering into an agreement, states hope that both sides will comply, but they also recognize that a violation may occur. In fact, they recognize that under certain circumstances, violation is to be expected. Countries that have signed the Kyoto Protocol, for example, have agreed to limit their "carbon dioxide equivalent emissions" of certain greenhouse gases. A failure to do so would represent a breach of the commitment made in that protocol and would normally lead to some level of reputational sanction, but the magnitude of that sanction depends on the context. A violation of the protocol that is plausibly attributable to the fact that the country is at war and devotes its efforts to the pursuit of the war effort rather than compliance with emissions rules will generate a smaller reputational sanction than a violation that cannot be justified in some similar way. Though the protocol does not provide an exception for national emergencies, countries recognize when they sign any agreement that there are circumstances in which compliance will not be forthcoming. Thus, article 18 of the Kyoto Protocol provides that when addressing cases of noncompliance, the governing conference shall develop "an indicative list of consequences, *taking into account the cause, type, degree, and frequency of noncompliance.*" As this section contemplates, there are situations in which compliance is not to be expected. It follows that reputational sanctions will be quite modest in those circumstances. To see why this is so, imagine the position of a state negotiating an environmental agreement. Compliance with the agreement will impose a cost on the signatories, but all parties prefer mutual compliance to mutual noncompliance. The signatories expect compliance in many states of the world, but not in every such state. For instance, assume that every signatory recognizes that a country will abandon its obligation if it goes to war because the environmental obligations are simply too costly to accept during wartime. If military conflict or severe domestic unrest explains why a potential signatory breached a similar obligation in the past, will this fact hamper its ability to participate today? As long as all parties expect breach in the event of a war, there is no reason that past conduct consistent with this expectation would affect the negotiation. In effect, the agreement has an implicit exception in the event of war. If war was the only concern, the parties could, of course, include it explicitly. But if the set of circumstances in which states recognize that compliance is unlikely includes a wide array of reasons for noncompliance, it becomes impractical (or impossible) to specify those reasons in the agreement.

To illustrate more clearly how nonreputational payoffs might affect reputation, consider the NPT.[6] The main provisions of the NPT require that state parties designated as non-nuclear weapons states (NNWS), a category that includes all but five countries (the United States, Great Britain, France, China, and Russia as the successor to the Soviet Union), refrain from seeking nuclear weapons, and that all states refrain from aiding NNWS in acquiring nuclear weapons. Currently, the treaty has 187 member states. For many, if not most, of these states, compliance with the treaty comes as no surprise. The technological expertise and the industrial infrastructure necessary to support a nuclear weapons program would require such a major investment over so many years that a simple cost-benefit analysis dictates compliance for most countries. It is difficult to imagine Trinidad and Tobago starting a nuclear program, even if it were not a treaty member. For other states, domestic politics make a nuclear program quite unlikely. In Germany, for example, there is strong public opposition to any radical expansion of military forces, and there would certainly be strong objection to a proposed nuclear weapons program.

The designated nuclear weapons states (NWS), on the other hand, are not constrained by the treaty's first provision (the prohibition on acquisition of nuclear weapons) and so cannot violate it. For at least some of the NWS, including the United States, violation of the second provision (prohibiting states from aiding NNWS efforts to acquire nuclear weapons) is unlikely, both because the proliferation of nuclear weapons technology would destabilize the community of nations and because it would undermine the NWS' existing nuclear and conventional military superiority over NNWS.

So for many NNWS and NWS, one would expect compliance even in the absence of a treaty. Because the nonreputational payoffs suggest that these states would behave consistently with the treaty obligations even if the treaty were not in existence, observer states have no reason to interpret compliance as any sort of positive signal about reputation. For these states, compliance provides no reputational gain relative to a world in which the treaty did not exist.

Some of the NNWS, however, have an incentive to pursue nuclear weapons. South Africa, for example, had a nuclear weapons program beginning in the mid- to late 1960s.[7] In fact, the program was pursued to completion and produced a weapon in 1982. Within a decade, however, South Africa had dismantled its program and publicly renounced its former nuclear status. Though it is true that South Africa's nuclear deterrent had lost much of its value with the end of the Cold War and the cease-fire leading to the end of the Soviet-backed war in Angola, possession of nuclear weapons would have continued to be of value. Nevertheless, because South Africa in the early 1990s was attempting to reform its image as a global pariah, reputational considerations (along with other factors) dictated that it bring itself into compliance with international norms. It had to choose between its nuclear weapons and participation in the NPT, because the NPT does not provide for an increase in the number of nuclear weapons states beyond the five that qualified by virtue of having tested a device prior to January 1, 1968. In

1991, one year after it began dismantling its nuclear weapons program, South Africa acceded to the treaty. Why would South African want to join the treaty? The obvious answer is that doing so allowed it to more fully rejoin the community of nations and reap the benefits of cooperation with other states. It sought to improve its reputation.

Needless to say, these examples might be contested. These events, like those in any of the examples used in the book, were affected by other forces, and it is possible that these other forces offer a better explanation of events. As I discussed in the introduction, examples such as these are only intended to illustrate the points being made. In this case, the point is that some states that appear to have an incentive to pursue nuclear weapons have chosen to refrain from doing so, and the presence of the NPT may well have encouraged that decision.

Returning to the NPT example, there are states that not only have strong incentives to develop nuclear and other nonconventional technologies (or to traffic in them) but have gone ahead and done so. For some states, this behavior is expected because they have an existing reputation that is sufficiently low that they are not actually expected to comply, and they may have nonreputational payoffs that provide a strong incentive to violate the agreement. This is plausibly the case for Iran and North Korea (especially the latter), both of which were parties to the treaty prior to North Korea's withdrawal in 2003. Already pariah states, these countries have little reputational capital, so other states likely did not expect membership in the treaty to be a meaningful deterrent. Though they could have improved their poor reputations through compliance (or by dismantling existing programs), such a strategy promised no more than modest gains. Rebuilding a reputation can be a slow and costly process that may not suit the needs of these states. Furthermore, it is unlikely that these states would have developed extensive and important cooperative arrangements to which a better reputation would have added value. Whatever reputational gains they might expect are too small to offset the incentive they have to develop nuclear weapons.

Another possibility, illustrated more clearly by the Russian experience, is that the payoffs from noncompliance are too great, even for a state that has a lot to gain from an improved reputation. Russia, a party to the NPT, agreed to complete the construction of first one, and then possibly a second, nuclear reactor for Iran at Bushehr. The deal was financed in large part by loans from Russia to Iran, so failing to complete the project would have had, among other things, an opportunity cost in the form of a loss of exports for the cash-strapped Russian state.

As Russia emerged from communism, however, it continued to have an incentive to engage the rest of the world and to enter into a broad variety of international agreements. With concern about Iran's nuclear ambitions mounting in the West, the United States tried to persuade Russia to cease cooperating with Iran, linking a cessation of cooperation with Iran to future cooperation with the United States. This U.S. strategy brought reputation into play explicitly, as well as introducing a threat of retaliation. Despite this and other potential costs, however, Russia continued to cooperate with Iran for several years. The potential payoff from dealing with Iran was simply too large to be offset by either the harm to Russia's reputation or the threat of sanctions by the United States. Eventually, Russia began to express misgivings about Iran's intentions and capabilities at Bushehr. While the United States and Europe have been the most critical of the Iranian nuclear program, Russia has steered a middle course, offering to enrich uranium for use in the Iranian reactors, thus denying Iran the enrichment technology essential for making a uranium bomb. Russia also stalled before eventually voting on the International Atomic Energy Agency's governing board to report Iran to the UN Security Council for possible penalties stemming from its nuclear program. These compromise actions likely reflect Russia's desire to balance its reputational risk against its nonreputational incentives to cooperate with Iran on nuclear technology. In other words, Russia does not wish to forgo the benefits, economic and otherwise, of cooperating with Iran, but Russian leaders are aware that if other states perceive Russia as aiding Iranian efforts to obtain a nuclear bomb, Russia will suffer greater reputational harm. Russia's hesitation as to whether to continue to assist Iran indicates that the issue is a close call, and thus one in which international law can influence state decisions.

The NPT example demonstrates how a single international legal obligation interacts with the payoffs of states. For some states the obligation will have no effect, because they would have behaved consistently in any case. For other states behavior is not changed, because the treaty is insufficient to prevent a violation. For a third group, however, the obligation can change behavior, because the reputational consequences of a violation can be enough to tip the scales in favor of compliance.

The Role of Nonreputation Payoff and Existing Reputations

Sticking with the NPT example, I now turn to a more thorough examination of how reputation and payoffs interact. For concreteness, I focus on the Russian experience with the NPT. Other nations' expectations of Russian behavior were not the same as their expectations of, for example, Great Britain or the United States. First, Russia's economic circumstances are considerably different from those of the Western nuclear powers. The incentive to export nuclear technology for economic profit would be considerably higher for Russia than for a more financially secure Western nation. These incentives, and the fact that they are known to other states, leads to a reduced expectation of strict compliance with the NPT.

Second, Russia's preexisting reputation for adherence to the NPT was likely not glittering. In other words, other states would think it more likely that Russia, compared, again, to a Western nuclear power such as Great Britain, would undertake an unauthorized transfer of nuclear technology. This preexisting reputation has the same effect as public knowledge of incentives to not comply; it means that if Russia were to transfer technology to a nation with nuclear ambitions, Russia's reputation will not suffer to the same degree that Great Britain's would if it did the same thing. Thus, perhaps counterintuitively, the fact that everyone believes Russia is more likely to violate the letter or spirit of the NPT actually reduces the reputational sanction when such a violation occurs.

Assuming that Russia behaved consistently with the expectations of other states, no change in the beliefs of those states was warranted. This could be so, for example, if Russia faced payoffs that so forcefully called on it to violate the NPT that existing beliefs about Russia and its reputation led observing states to expect violation.

More generally, in order to determine if a state's actions will affect its reputation, it is necessary to know something about both reputational and nonreputational payoffs. When the nonreputational payoffs generate a sufficiently strong incentive to violate an agreement, a decision to breach may not lead to any change in reputation. Similarly, if a state's nonreputational payoffs provide an incentive to comply with an agreement, the decision to comply will not lead to a reputational gain.

In addition to the nonreputational payoffs, the impact of an action on reputation depends on that state's existing reputation. Consider, for example, a state that complies with a treaty, despite nonreputational payoffs that counsel violation. If that state has a very strong reputation prior to its decision, the decision to comply will reaffirm that good reputation, but may not increase it. The decision to comply may still offer a benefit, however, by solidifying the state's reputation and making the observing states' beliefs more stable going forward.

On the other hand, if the state started with a poor reputation, the decision to comply would cause observing states to adjust upward their estimate of the state's willingness to comply. The analysis is the same for states that violate the treaty, but the impact is reversed. Suppose a state's nonreputational payoffs suggest violation, but its reputation is strong enough that observing states anticipate compliance. If the state violates the agreement, other states will revise downward their estimate of the violating state's willingness to comply. In contrast, a violating state with little reputation to start with may not face any change in its reputation because its actions simply confirm existing perceptions.

So we can predict that a state's decision to comply with a legal rule will enhance its reputation when the nonreputational payoffs counsel violation and the state's existing reputation (as other states perceived it) is insufficient to cause observing states to expect compliance. A violation will harm a state's reputation when the nonreputational payoffs, combined with the state's existing reputation, predict compliance.

The foregoing is really just a claim that states engage in Bayesian updating of their estimates of other states' willingness to comply with international law.[8] The reputation of a given state is determined by that estimate, which can change over time. Notice that because states update their beliefs in Bayesian fashion, the strength of their *ex ante* beliefs matters. For a given decision to violate or comply, a state with a long established and consistent reputation will suffer a smaller reputational sanction than one with a less established reputation. Other states will have stronger priors about the former state than about the latter, and so the former's reputation will be less affected by an individual action.

The Importance of the Obligation

One would like, of course, to know not only whether a state's actions have reputational consequences but also the magnitude of those consequences. Because this book takes a theoretical approach, however, there is no way to provide an estimate of the magnitude of reputational sanctions. The theory cannot specify (without additional assumptions) the importance of reputation to states either in absolute terms or relative to nonreputational payoffs. It is possible, however, to consider some of the factors likely to affect the size of the reputational sanctions a state will face if it violates an obligation (or, conversely, the magnitude of the reputational benefit if it complies). I will discuss more of these factors later in this chapter; here I want to point out the role played by the importance of the obligation.

The point here is fairly obvious, but nevertheless bears mentioning. The relative importance of an international legal obligation affects the reputational consequences of violating it. Thus, a refusal to allow inspection of nuclear reactors under the NPT represents a serious breach of a state's commitments and will generate a strong reputational reaction. In contrast, minor violations, such as missing a reporting deadline, are unlikely to be viewed as a serious breach and, therefore, are unlikely to lead to significant reputational sanctions. One can think of this measure of relative importance as a measure of the extent to which the interests of other states have been affected. Refusing to allow inspectors onto the site of a nuclear reactor undermines the very purpose of the NPT and compromises the interests of other parties to the agreement. It is true that these other states have not been directly harmed, but the inability to monitor compliance with a treaty of such importance, combined with the negative signal that a refusal to allow inspectors entry sends, raises significant security concerns in other states.

If violations of more important obligations lead to larger reputational sanctions, one might conclude that such agreements are more likely to be honored. This, however, does not follow, and in fact, the opposite is likely to be true. The most important obligations are those where cooperation yields large gains. They are also the ones where the incentive to defect is largest. To say that an agreement yields large gains from cooperation is equivalent to saying that cooperation would be difficult without the agreement—meaning that one or more parties has strong incentives to defect. In such "high stakes" commitments, we should expect both nonreputational and reputational payoffs to be large.

Though both these payoffs grow with the stakes, it seems likely that at least with respect to agreements that implicate the highest stakes (e.g., security), reputational sanctions will normally play a (perhaps vanishingly) small role. Reputational sanctions, after all, can only do so much.

Even a complete loss of reputation is something a state can recover from, and so there is some upper bound on the magnitude of reputational sanctions. As the nonreputational payoffs of a decision increase, the likelihood that they will swamp the reputational aspect of the decision increases. Thus, for example, one should not expect legal commitments regarding the conduct of war to be especially effective. To the extent that we see compliance in such cases, it is likely to be explained by nonreputational rather than reputational payoffs. Furthermore, as Morrow (2000) notes, major future challenges to a state's security or even its existence may be difficult to foresee at the time the decision to comply with an alliance agreement is made. Because such situations arise infrequently or unpredictably, the reputational costs to violating alliance agreements may be negligible (because a reputation for complying in situations that do not frequently occur is worth less than a reputation for complying in more common situations) when compared with the substantial costs of fighting a war.

Managing Reputation over Time

The reputation of a state is contingent on its past behavior, but it is the knowledge that today's conduct will affect tomorrow's reputation that gives reputational sanctions their force. When making any single decision about compliance, the impact of that decision on a state's reputation and future payoffs is taken into account. Because states recognize the incremental effect of compliance decisions on reputation, they are able to make strategic decisions about how to manage their reputation over time. For example, when recent conduct has damaged a state's reputation, the state may set out to rebuild it by complying with international legal rules it otherwise would have been tempted to ignore.

More generally, the process by which states accumulate and erode their reputations should itself be viewed as the result of a cost-benefit analysis. Because different states (or individual states at different times) will face different costs and benefits, they will differ in their willingness to build and maintain strong reputations. For example, a state whose reputation is sufficiently tarnished may find it so costly to repair that it is better off extracting everything it can in the short term and ignoring much of international law. North Korea might fit this category. For such countries, reputational constraints have little or no force, and international law can only play a role to the extent it generates direct sanctions, is made effective through reciprocity, or assists in the management of simple problems of cooperation such as coordination games.

By way of example, consider Libya's role in the bombing of Pan Am Flight 103 over Lockerbie, Scotland, in 1988. This bombing was carried out by Libyan agents, and as such constitutes an "arbitrary deprivation of life," in violation of the UN Covenant on Civil and Political Rights, to which Libya is a party. Libya, at the time, was arguably a pariah state, at least in the eyes of Western states, and so had little reason to be concerned about its international reputation. (We are talking here about a reputation for compliance with international law. Libya's actions implicated other forms of reputation, of course. Later in this chapter I discuss how these different types of reputations interact.) A decision to violate this treaty was unlikely, for example, to significantly hamper Libya's future ability to benefit from international cooperation, because such cooperation was unlikely to come about in any event. So Libya had little reason to resist whatever short-term benefits it gained from its illegal actions. It was only after years of direct sanctions by the United States and the United Nations that Libya agreed, in 1999, to hand over for trial the agents responsible for the bombing. By delivering the two agents accused of the bombing (one of whom was convicted) to Scottish authorities, Libya signaled that it was prepared to begin complying with international law. This action, along with an agreement to pay damages to the families of the victims, played a role in Libya's ongoing reintegration into the international system.

In other contexts, a state may choose to violate international legal norms in one sphere while attempting to bolster its reputation in another. This is arguably what the South African government did during certain periods of the apartheid regime. While that government was oppressing its nonwhite populations in contravention of the international law of the time, it was otherwise "scrupulous in its observance of international law" (D'Amato 1971, p. 30).

These examples demonstrate that states will not always seek to preserve or build their reputations. Reputation, like any other asset, can not only be acquired but also used or "spent." States will sometimes choose to extract whatever short-term gains they can, despite the fact that doing so will erode their reputation. This incentive to defect from international rules will come about when the gains from violation are especially high or the loss to reputation from breach is especially low. Because a state's reputation may be subject-matter specific (i.e., a state may have different reputations over different issues) a decision to behave opportunistically and extract short-term gains may be profitable to states when the long-term value of cooperation in an area is modest.

Consider an example in the foreign investment area. In the 1960s and 1970s, many newly independent states chose to expropriate the assets of foreign investors. These actions were arguably contrary to customary international law, at least early on.[9] The decision to expropriate can be seen as a decision to extract current value at the expense of future reputation. The states involved had the opportunity to capture rents from existing stocks of foreign investment, especially because much of the investment consisted of fixed capital that could not be removed. These states were also attempting to establish their economic independence and often adopting policies that were hostile to new flows of foreign investment. The knowledge that their policies already made large future inflows of foreign investment unlikely made the decision to expropriate much less costly. Put another way, compliance with what many Western states believed was a rule of customary international law (a prohibition on expropriation without prompt, adequate, and effective compensation) was of modest value, because a reputation for compliance in the investment area was unlikely to generate a large increase in investment at the margin.

A great deal of foreign investment into developing countries is now governed by bilateral investment treaties. These agreements explicitly forbid expropriation except for a public purpose and (typically) with prompt, adequate, and effective compensation. They also provide for mandatory arbitration in the event of a dispute between a foreign investor and a host state. By entering into one of these treaties, a host state makes a reputational commitment and, as a result, has an enhanced incentive to refrain from expropriating or otherwise treating investors in a manner that is contrary to the relevant treaty. Notice that the incentive to comply comes both from the fact that the relevant rules now take the form of formal treaties and from the fact that the value of a reputation in this area is higher than it was 30 or 40 years ago. Developing countries today are more likely to consider foreign investment to be part of their development strategy for the future. A loss of reputation in this area would reduce the future flow of foreign investment, which these states perceive as costly.

Consider one more example. Following the Russian Revolution of 1918, the new Bolshevik government repudiated the debts accumulated by the tsarist government, claiming, among other things, that they were the personal debts of the tsar. This action was a clear violation of Russia's international legal obligations.[10] The Bolsheviks, however, had no reason to invest in their reputation for compliance with international legal rules. In the early days of the regime, they expected a communist revolution to overwhelm Europe in the wake of World War I. Such a revolution would make past reputations irrelevant, as a new era of international relations would be born. This view was so ingrained in the Soviet leadership that Leon Trotsky, the first Soviet foreign minister, defined his role as being merely to "issue a few revolutionary proclamations to the peoples of the world and then shut up shop" (Carr 1985, p. 16). The potential gains from cooperation, then, were perceived to be modest, making repudiation of the debt more attractive. Even if Trotsky's words were mere rhetoric and the Soviet leadership in fact anticipated ongoing relations with the West, the repudiation of the debt is easy to understand. The new Bolshevik government was sufficiently hostile to the West that it had no reason to expect a continuing flow of loans and so no reason to be concerned about whether promises to repay loans would be credible. Whatever reputational harm it incurred by repudiating the debt was of little consequence because, at least with respect to financial matters, the Soviet Union had nothing to lose.

In the late 1980s and early 1990s, the Soviet Union and (after its collapse) Russia were attempting to do just the opposite of what the Bolsheviks had done; they were going to considerable lengths to rebuild a reputation for compliance with international legal obligations. Following the collapse of the Soviet Union in 1991, the new Russian government announced that it would honor existing Soviet debt, despite the change in regime. Had it chosen to repudiate the debt, the new Russia would have compromised its reputation and undermined its efforts to develop financial ties with the West. Abiding by international norms helped Russia to build a new reputation that, in turn, increased its ability to attract financial assistance from the West.

This example illustrates another feature of state reputations. Older, more stable states will have more established reputations. Each instance of compliance or violation will have less impact on the reputation of such states because other states' prior beliefs will be stronger. Once a state is established, improving its reputation, as Mikhail Gorbachev, the

Soviet President, sought to do in the final days of the USSR, can be a difficult and expensive proposition.

Political scientists have used signaling theory to model the cost to a state of demonstrating that it is trustworthy. For example, Kydd (2000a) notes that if state A wishes to engage state B in a cooperative venture, but state B distrusts state A, costly signals will be necessary to reassure state B that state A is a reliable partner. In the case of Gorbachev, Kydd analyzes the Soviet capitulation over the Intermediate Range Nuclear Forces (INF) Treaty in 1987 as just such a costly signal. That treaty called for the United States and Soviet Union to eliminate all ballistic and cruise missiles with ranges of 500–5,500 kilometers and provided for verification procedures, including on-site inspections. This treaty represented a significant concession by the Soviets for a variety of reasons, including the fact that at the time the verification procedures in the treaty were the most stringent in history, including intrusive on-site inspections previously opposed by the Soviets; the category of missiles in question gave the Soviet Union many more targets (e.g., American allies in western Europe) than it gave the United States; and the treaty did not govern the disposition of the nuclear weapons of other Western nations, meaning that American allies remained free to deploy intermediate-range missiles in Europe if they so chose.

For a signal to work, it must be cheap enough for the sender to decide to proceed but expensive enough that the target, in this case the United States, updates its prior beliefs about the reliability of its prospective partner. In reference to reputation more generally, we should expect the cost of the signal necessary to cause such an updating of priors to be higher when the sender is an old state with a well-established reputation, or when states A and B have a long history of interaction with a large number of data points supporting their prior beliefs. Because well-established reputations are less responsive to individual interactions, the magnitude of the interaction, in other words the cost of the signal, must be greater for it to have a significant reputational effect.

New states, or states with new regimes, on the other hand, have reputations that are less well established, so more is at stake when they make compliance decisions. Because observing states have only weak priors about the new state's willingness to comply with international legal obligations, each individual compliance decision has a larger impact on the new state's reputation. It follows that, all else equal, the incentive to comply is increased. This may lead new states to be especially diligent about complying with international legal obligations (Shihata 1965), as is illustrated by the efforts of the Russian Federation (a new regime) to comply with its obligations in the early 1990s. The theory predicts, then, that states with more fragile reputations will make greater efforts to comply with international law than would a similarly situated state with a stronger reputation.[11]

Following the disintegration of the Soviet Union, several of the 15 new republics were "born nuclear," in the sense that they inherited an extensive nuclear arsenal from the Soviet Union. Global leaders hoped that Russia would succeed to the Soviet Union's status under the NPT as a nuclear nation and that the remaining states, Ukraine, Belarus, and Kazakhstan, would return their nuclear arsenals to Russia and accede to the NPT as NNWS. Considering Russia's history of imperialism with respect to its neighbors, it would have come as no surprise if those states had elected to retain their nuclear deterrent. Instead, all three complied, returning their weapons to Russia and acceding to the NPT as NNWS. A study of Ukraine's motivation for this action, taken in the face of realist incentives to the contrary, suggests that Ukraine was motivated by the desire to build its international reputation (Sagan 1996).[12]

Notice that this might be perceived to be inconsistent with the earlier discussion of newly independent states and their decision to expropriate investment. Closer consideration, however, reveals that there is no conflict here. As mentioned, newly independent states in the investment context had reason to think that future investment flows would be modest, so the expropriation of existing investment, even if it had a profound impact on the state's reputation for compliance with customary international law rules governing expropriation, generated modest costs.[13] The former Soviet Republics, on the other hand, generally sought relations with the West and could hope to extract value from a strong reputation.

The Role of Information

Up to this point, it has been assumed that states have complete information about existing nonreputational payoffs, legal obligations, and one another's actions. We now relax those informational assumptions.

Uncertainty about Payoffs

When states interact, they have some information about the goals and objectives of their counterparts but normally do not have complete knowledge of what they seek to achieve. There may, for instance, be domestic pressures that are not evident to a counter-party, or international objectives that are not known to outsiders. To model this fact, assume that states have imperfect information about one another's reputational and nonreputational payoffs. Rather than knowing these payoffs with precision, they have only unbiased estimates of them. Formally, one can think of the nonreputational payoffs in a particular instance as being drawn from a probability distribution where the observing states know the relevant distribution but do not observe the individual draw.

This imperfect information with respect to payoffs makes it more difficult to draw inferences from observations of compliance or violation. Suppose, for example, a state is observed violating a rule of international law despite the fact that other states expected it to comply on the basis of their estimates of its reputational and nonreputational payoffs.

An observing state might conclude that the nonreputational payoffs are just as it estimated, in which case its estimate of the other state's willingness to comply (i.e., its reputation) needs to be adjusted downward. Alternatively, the observing state may conclude that its estimate of the nonreputation payoffs was incorrect. If the short-term payoff from violation was larger, relative to the payoff for compliance, than the observing state expected, the violation can be explained. If so, the acting state may have behaved precisely as its existing reputation predicted, and so there is no reason to adjust beliefs about its willingness to comply.

In one circumstance, an observed violation is consistent with a state's existing reputation, whereas in the other, the violation signals that the state's reputation should be adjusted downward. Because both the willingness to comply with international law and the payoffs are uncertain, however, observing states have no way of knowing which of these two interpretations is correct (or if it is a combination of both). Lacking information, observing states must estimate the probability that the violation is due to unexpectedly high costs of compliance, and the probability that the state's reputation is weaker than was thought.

Uncertainty about the payoffs facing a counter-party, then, makes the process of estimating its reputation less accurate. Actions that should be attributed to nonreputational payoffs will be partially attributed to reputation, and actions that should be attributed to reputation will be partially attributed to other payoffs.

The lesson here is that uncertainty about nonreputational payoffs reduces the reputational consequences of a violation. These consequences are still present, but they are smaller. The same, of course, will be true of decisions to comply. Though they may increase a state's reputation, the magnitude of that increase will be reduced to the extent that observing states are uncertain about the associated nonreputational payoffs.[14]

Uncertainty about Legal Rules

A similar problem arises if there is uncertainty about the legal rules in effect. Uncertainty of this sort may exist for any number of reasons. The rule at issue may be a rule of customary international law, in which case there is a good chance that its very existence is contested. Even when dealing with a treaty, there may be uncertainty because the treaty is ambiguous or incomplete with respect to the action in question. To illustrate, the U.S. government initially interpreted treaties pertaining to the treatment of captured al-Qaeda operatives and Taliban soldiers in ways that greatly enhance the freedom of American military and intelligence agencies to determine the manner in which they hold and interrogate prisoners. The United States contended, for example, that Common Article 3 of the Geneva Conventions, which provides certain rules governing conflicts "not of an international character," did not apply to the conflict with al-Qaeda and the Taliban. To the extent that these claims and the related protests from other governments and human rights organizations evidence some international uncertainty regarding the content of the relevant obligations, they reduce the reputational consequences to the United States for its alleged violation. In June 2006, the United States Supreme Court ruled that Common Article 3 does apply to individuals captured in Afghanistan, eliminating doubt about the meaning of Common Article 3, at least under U.S. law.

Faced with uncertainty as to the law, a state may have difficulty determining if it will face a reputational sanction for its conduct. Because the reputational sanction is the result of an updating of beliefs by observers, what ultimately matters is the attitude of observing states. It is often clear to all that the law is ambiguous in some way, but different states may have different beliefs about what the law means or what it should mean. If the behavior of the acting state prompts observing states to adjust their estimates of the acting state's reputation downward, this represents a cost for the acting state.

This presents a dilemma for a state that is considering actions of uncertain legality. Even if the state determines, in good faith, that a particular action would be legal, it cannot be sure that other states would reach the same conclusion. To the extent that legal rules are uncertain, then, the acting state must tread cautiously.

An observing state has a related problem. If it observes conduct it considers illegal but the acting state argues is permitted, what conclusion should it draw about future compliance by the acting state? On the one hand, the acting state may consider itself to be in violation of the law and be attempting to muddy the waters by claiming that its actions are permitted. On the other hand, the state may have attempted in good faith to comply with the relevant rule and may simply have reached a different conclusion about its content. In either case, the reputation of the acting state may be affected, but the former would surely provoke a more significant reduction in reputation than would the latter. A good faith effort to comply indicates that the acting state sought to comply and its violation indicates a difference of interpretation. Had the contours of the law been clear, it may be that the state would have complied, in which case no reputational adjustment is called for. A state making a bad faith claim of compliance, on the other hand, knowingly violated the law and, in so doing, delivered a stronger signal about its willingness to do so.

The only sensible strategy for an observing state is to adjust its perception of the acting state's reputation on the basis of its estimate of that state's actions. That it violated a legal rule (as interpreted by the observing state) suggests that there will be some reputational loss (putting aside the possibility that the violation was expected on the basis of the nonreputational payoffs), and the magnitude of that loss will reflect some estimate of the likelihood that the acting state acted in good faith.

A closely related question is how states come to believe that a particular interpretation of a text is correct. That is, when there is ambiguity in an agreement, how do the states come to a view as to its meaning and determine what constitutes a violation? It seems clear that norms arise around specific terms and that these norms influence interpretation. Less clear is where these norms come from. Some arise during the course of the negotiations, some from the general context (e.g., if a term is used in many existing agreements, it may be understood to mean the same thing in a new agreement), and some from interactions that take place after the treaty enters into force. Strictly speaking, of course, it is usually only the text itself that has legal force, but in practice, norms of interpretation are relevant.

But if norms serve to clarify the meaning of text, one must also acknowledge that norms can alter that meaning. In other words, norms may generate a de facto legal rule that the text of an agreement does not provide. Consider, for example, Trinidad and Tobago's withdrawal from the Inter-American Convention on Human Rights and the Optional Protocol to the ICCPR in 1999. Both of these withdrawals were facially legal, in that they were made pursuant to withdrawal provisions in both agreements.[15] Nevertheless, Trinidad and Tobago received an enormous amount of criticism for its withdrawal, which had the effect of denying supranational review of alleged domestic human rights abuses.[19] Denying this review was, in the critics' view, tantamount to denying the underlying substantive rights (Trinidad and Tobago did remain a party to the ICCPR itself). The overall effect was to undermine the perception of Trinidad and Tobago's commitment to its human rights obligations. One might interpret this as a signal that Trinidad and Tobago is unwilling to comply with customary international law rules embodied in the relevant instruments, or one might interpret it as a norm-driven de facto ban on withdrawal from the treaties themselves. In either case, despite the textual legality of its actions, Trinidad and Tobago's reputation for compliance with its human rights obligations suffered as a result of these withdrawals.

This same reasoning helps to explain how an agreement can come to be either partially or entirely obsolete. Even without formal termination, the relevant parties may all come to share the view that the treaty is inappropriate and no longer in effect. If that happens, a violation would have no reputational effect. Consider, for example, that the U.S. State Department lists as treaties in force a series of agreements the United States signed with Iran before the Iranian revolution of 1979, including a Mutual Defense Assistance Agreement;[17] economic cooperation agreements;[18] and educational assistance agreements.[19] It is clear that the United States' failure to come to the aid of Iran during the

Iran–Iraq war, and indeed its decision to assist Iraq, did not harm the United States' reputation for compliance with international law. Events had made the treaty obsolete, and all observers understood as much.

This discussion of information sheds light on one of the ways international agreements can affect behavior. By providing greater transparency with respect to the relevant rules, international agreements make it easier to classify behavior as compliant or violative. This, by itself, improves the probability of compliance because it distinguishes violators from nonviolators. Clarity in the rules makes it less likely that a violation will be perceived as compliant or that compliant behavior will be perceived as a violation.

This discussion also offers an explanation for why states go to such lengths to claim that their behavior is in compliance with international law. To the extent that a state is able to persuade others that its actions were actually in compliance with a reasonable interpretation of the law, the reputational sanction will be reduced.

Uncertainty about Actions

An analogous discussion applies to uncertainty about a state's actions. For example, it is not entirely clear how the United States is treating detainees in Guantanamo. There are credible allegations of human rights abuses, but uncertainty remains regarding the scale and scope of behavior that violates international law.

Needless to say, a violation of international law generates a reputational sanction only if some other country knows about the violation. It follows that a violation will lead to a smaller reputational loss if fewer countries know about it. By reducing the visibility of their violations, then, states reduce the reputational consequences.

Things are more complicated if a state's actions can only be observed imperfectly. This is true in the Guantanamo example, as well as a host of other contexts. For example, a state's environmental laws can be examined, but it may be difficult to evaluate the application of those laws or the degree of corruption associated with them. Other examples are easy to find—compliance with arms control agreements is often difficult to verify (e.g., Iran and its nuclear ambitions), the extent to which a state subsidizes an industry may not be clear (making it difficult to tell if it is violating its trading obligations), and so on.

In other instances, some states will observe a particular action but others will not. Those that observe the illegal action obviously do not face uncertainty with respect to the activity. If these observing states publicly announce that there has been a violation, however, those that did not observe the conduct may be uncertain about whether to believe the allegations or the denials of the accused state (assuming that the accused state makes such denials). These situations, and others like them, cause uncertainty about the actions taken by a state.

When there is uncertainty about whether a state has acted illegally, observing states must draw inferences from the information they have. They will estimate the probability that a violation has taken place and update their beliefs accordingly. An accused state, therefore, will face some reputational loss, but the lower the estimated probability that a violation has taken place, the smaller the impact on its reputation will be. Not only will violating states face a reduced sanction as a result but also some nonviolating states that are suspected of having committed a violation will suffer an undeserved reputational loss because they are wrongly suspected of having breached their international legal obligations.

The net result is to reduce the incentive to comply that the reputational sanction provides, because the consequences of violation relative to compliance are reduced by the uncertainty about the actions a state takes.

The Impact of Uncertainty

So each type of uncertainty—whether it relates to the payoffs at issue, the legal rule in place, or the actions taken—reduces the incentive to comply by reducing the cost of a violation. Inferences about reputation become more difficult to draw on the basis of available information. The reputational stakes of a particular action, then, are reduced. The result is that some states that would have complied may breach because the reputational sanctions are reduced.

However, states are not helpless in the face of this reality. To the extent that they are able to promote more complete information, they help to retain the compliance pull of reputation. Among the strategies they use are efforts to clarify legal rules (e.g., codification of customary international law); transparency requirements in international agreements (e.g., the WTO's Sanitary and Phytosanitary Agreement, which governs health and safety, includes a variety of transparency requirements, including that trade measures justified on health and safety grounds must be published prior to their enforcement);[20] measures to ensure ongoing communication (e.g., international antitrust agreements typically provide specific information-sharing provisions, and regulators interact through the International Competition Network);[21] reporting and monitoring requirements in agreements (e.g., the Convention on the Elimination of Discrimination Against Women (CEDAW) requires periodic reports from states); and so on. And of course states are able to discuss conflicts and disagreements and share information directly with one another when problems arise.

This effort to improve the flow of information sounds a great deal like the sort of behavior that the "managerial school" would like to encourage (Chayes and Chayes 1995). The Chayes focus on how communication among parties to an agreement can improve compliance by resolving interpretative ambiguities; generating consensus as to what constitutes compliance; suggesting new methods of fulfilling obligations; and persuading the parties to comply with the agreement. The actual mechanism through which compliance occurs, however, is quite different in the managerial model. To the extent that model provides an account of why states comply, it asserts that states have a "general propensity to comply" with commitments. In the rational choice model developed in this book, of course, no such general propensity is assumed. The informational mechanisms discussed earlier (along with others) are useful because they increase the relevance and force of reputational sanctions. That is, better information leads to payoffs that promote compliance.

When states make informational claims, of course, the goal is not always to simply share truthful information with others. Because informational issues affect payoffs, states have an incentive to attempt to manipulate the information sets of others. This is most obviously done when a state attempts to hide its illegal conduct, but attempts to affect the views of other states are common with respect to each of the three informational categories mentioned in this section (payoffs, legal rules, and actions). For example, on March 31, 1939, Britain's prime minister, Neville Chamberlain, declared in a speech on the floor of the House of Commons that Great Britain and France would guarantee the security of Poland against a possible German invasion. This statement was intended to lend credibility to France's commitments to Poland under the 1921 Franco-Polish Military Alliance, and it foreshadowed the signing of an Anglo-Polish mutual defense treaty in August of 1939. In effect, the speech alleged that Britain's payoffs were such that it would not stand by if Poland were attacked. The strong rhetoric of states on the subject of a customary international law of expropriation is another example in which states have attempted to influence the content of the law. For many years the United States, among others, insisted that the "Hull Rule" of prompt, adequate, and effective compensation applied when foreign investment was expropriated. Many other states resisted this notion and argued that some lower standard applied.[22]

So the role of information helps to explain why states expend so much effort to influence perceptions of other states and nonstate actors. These efforts include official denials (whether true or not) regarding the conduct of the state, participation in debates about existing rules of international law, and claims about the stakes involved in decisions. The more successful such efforts, the smaller the reputational consequence for a violating state.

The same considerations explain how the work of some human rights NGOs, such as Amnesty International, can affect state behavior. Credible reports that shed light on the conduct of states reduce the uncertainty regarding their compliance and, therefore, increase the reputational consequences of a violation.

Interestingly, many human rights NGOs are also engaged in an effort to push the frontier of human rights law and expand the legal rules to include more types of conduct. To this end, they advance arguments about why particular actions should be considered human rights violations, or they may even assert that a particular rule exists even when a disinterested observer might disagree. This effort is intended to generate greater consensus on human rights obligations and persuade at least some people that additional human rights norms should be considered legal obligations. This behavior may not generate any increase in certainty (if successful, it may simply expand the set of actions that is considered illegal without generating any additional clarity at the edges), but it can serve to expand the set of behaviors that international law proscribes.

One result of these actions is that the difference between a violation of a human rights treaty—where the law is relatively clear—and the violation of an alleged rule of customary law, where the rule is often less clear, is not emphasized. This generates a tension for some human rights groups. When reporting on human rights violations, it is important that they retain a high level of credibility. If a group is perceived to be highly partisan or overly eager to condemn the practices of governments, its reports will lose credibility and cease to be useful tools of information dissemination. When attempting to extend the boundaries of the law, however, a human rights group has an incentive to argue for an expansive definition of human rights. Though the groups need some credibility here as well, this work is more in the style of advocacy and less in the style of disinterested reporting. A group that engages in its advocacy function in an evenhanded and neutral fashion will have less success influencing the course of human rights law. But a group that pushes too hard in its advocacy work will be less credible when it attempts to shed light on existing violations.

The Compartmentalizing of Reputation

To say that states want and pursue a reputation for compliance with international law leaves open the question of whether a state has a single reputation for compliance or whether that reputation varies by subject area, by who the counter-party to an agreement is, or by regime. Some commentators argue that states have different reputations with respect to different agreements (Downs and Jones 2002; Mercer 1996, p. 7), while others speak of states having only a single reputation (Chayes and Chayes 1995).[23] Most of the following discussion concentrates on the question of whether states have different reputations in different issue areas. Analogous discussions could investigate the extent to which different regimes within a state have different reputations, and the extent to which reputation depends not only on the acting state but also on the observing state. Because the same basic ideas apply to these other dimensions along which compartmentalization of reputation may take place, I discuss them in a more abbreviated way after considering issue-specific reputations.

Reputation by Issue Area

The extent to which violations affect a state's reputation generally, and the extent to which the impact is limited to one issue area, depends primarily on what it is that observing states learn as a result of a violation. When a state violates a commitment, it reveals that its expected payoff from a violation is larger than its expected payoff from compliance. Observing states must try to infer why this is so. One possibility is that the direct gains from violations relative to compliance are relatively large. If this is so, there is no reason for a violation in this issue area to affect other issue areas. Suppose, for example, Venezuela enters into and subsequently violates an environmental agreement it. If observing states conclude that this violation reflects a Venezuelan view that future environmental harms will be small (and therefore Venezuela is not prepared to bear significant costs to protect the environment), then those observing states will update their beliefs about Venezuela's attitude toward the environment. This updating will have no impact on international commitments in, say, trade or security. Another possibility, however, is that observing states will conclude that the violation reflects a more generalized reluctance to bear costs today in exchange for future benefits. It might, for example, reflect the fact that Venezuelan leaders have a higher discount rate than previously thought. If so, the violation will lead to an updating of beliefs about Venezuela's willingness to comply with international law in general and will, as a result, impact all of Venezuela's efforts to achieve international cooperation.

It is helpful to be clear about what it means to have one or several reputations. If a state has a single reputation across all issue areas, then all actions of that state impact this reputation. At the extreme, actions in the human rights area have no greater reputational impact on future human rights commitments than on, say, future economic or environmental promises. If, on the other hand, a state's reputation is fully compartmentalized by issue area, actions in one area have no bearing on the state's reputation in another area. A state can engage in widespread and flagrant violations of commitments in, for example, the security area without affecting its reputation in the economic area. Even within a particular area, a state may have a number of reputations depending on the particulars of the interaction. Huth (1997), for example, disaggregates a reputation for resolve into four different categories.

The sensible answer to the question of whether states have one reputation or multiple reputations, given current understandings about reputation, is almost certainly "both." For several reasons, it is implausible for violations in one issue area to be strictly limited to that area. First, a violation (or compliance) provides information about a state's attitudes toward a particular area of law. It signals how important that area is to the state, how important it feels future cooperation in the area will be, and so on. This is simple enough, but it requires some sense of what constitutes an "area" of law. Would the Geneva Convention Relative to the Treatment of Prisoners of War, for example, be its own area, meaning that violations would not implicate other areas? Or would violations of those conventions speak to a state's reputation with respect to humanitarian law generally? Would they have implications for other security issues such as a state's reputation for compliance with bans on land mines or other military technology? Or would violations instead, or perhaps also, affect a state's reputation for compliance with human rights treaties? The answer, of course, is that there is no answer. What constitutes an area for this purpose will depend heavily on context, and even with respect to a single compliance decision there will not be a single "area." A violation of a fisheries treaty may signal both that the state is relatively unconcerned about harm to the fishing stocks and that there is little domestic support for environmental measures more generally.

Second, violations of international commitments will at a minimum provide information about a state's underlying discount rate. Even if that rate varies somewhat from subject matter to subject matter, the relevant discount rates in each area will be determined in part by the state's general willingness to accept present costs for future benefits, as determined by, for example, the state's domestic structure.

Finally, observation suggests that reputations are generalized, at least to some extent. This is most clearly visible in the form of rogue states that have sacrificed whatever reputational capital they once had. These states are normally not considered to be violators in only some small number of discrete areas (though there may be a few areas that are most responsible for their loss of reputation) while simultaneously being thought of as reliable partners in other areas. It appears instead that sufficiently egregious violations in a few areas are often enough to compromise a state's reputation across the board. This is consistent with the model of reputation developed here, because egregious violations in several areas might indicate that the state has a high discount rate or simply expects few benefits from a strong reputation. If so, it is appropriate for other states to draw negative inferences about the acting state's general reputation.

If the notion that a state has multiple reputations that are completely isolated from one another seems far-fetched, it is similarly difficult to believe that states have a single reputation across issue areas.

Consider, for example, the Pinochet regime in Chile in the early 1970s. Pinochet came to power in a military coup in 1973 that removed the leftist government of Salvador Allende. The Allende government had nationalized industry, seized land and factories, and implemented price controls, all of which had combined to leave the Chilean economy in tatters and make international investors extremely anxious. Pinochet's military junta thus came to power with two goals: economic stabilization and political reform designed to prevent the recurrence of polarizing and self-destructive policies. The political aspect of the agenda was carried out through repression, much of which constituted a violation of the ICCPR, which Chile ratified in 1972 and which entered into force in March 1976. In contrast, the neoliberal economic reforms were carried out with an eye toward economic stabilization and restoration of Chile's credibility with the global financial and business communities, a program that yielded fruitful results from 1977 to 1981 and then again following Chile's graduation from IMF assistance in the late 1980s. In this example, Pinochet's Chile benefited from a reputation for compliance with economic commitments but surely had a much weaker reputation on human rights issues. The 2003 American-led invasion of Iraq offers another example. Though there was some spillover to other areas, in the main the reputational harm to the United States seems to have been limited to matters of peace and security.

So it is likely that states have different reputations in different issue areas, but that these reputations are related to one another. One can think of the ripples a stone dropped in a lake creates, with the place where the stone enters the lake being analogous to the location of a violation. The reputational consequences are greatest at the point of impact, and at points further from the specific violation, the reputational consequences diminish. Though a state is likely to have multiple reputations, it is unlikely that these reputations are entirely independent of one another. A violation of an environmental agreement, for example, may have its largest impact on a state's reputation for compliance with environmental commitments, but will often also have at least some spillover impact on other areas.

Notice that the acting state cannot control the extent to which its behavior in one area affects its reputation in other areas. The extent to which reputation spills over from one area to another is determined by the extent to which a state's actions provide information about characteristics that are relevant only to a particular context (e.g., whether the state values ongoing cooperation on a narrow issue) as opposed to a broader set of situations (e.g., the state's discount rate). If an observing state believes that another state's breach in the human rights area signals an unwillingness to comply in the trade area, for example, then that breach will carry reputational costs in the trade area.

The question of whether states have one or several reputations has implications for the effectiveness of international agreements. Among other effects, the number of reputations a state has determines the extent to which decisions about compliance in one area are influenced by reputational concerns in other areas. Can decisions on peace and security, for example, be made without affecting present and future economic commitments? The answer to this question has important implications for the decisions governments make. Consider, for example, American efforts in the war on terror. If reputation is highly compartmentalized, the United States can be much more aggressive in some of its actions than would be the case if there were large reputational spillovers into other areas. Suppose the United States violates international rules governing the treatment of prisoners. If it suffers reputational harm only with respect to humanitarian law, the associated costs are modest. Future U.S. efforts in the humanitarian law area are unlikely to be of central importance to the country, so even if reaching agreement in this area is more difficult in the future, the costs to the United States are very small. The important caveat to this point is that the United States may wish to use humanitarian law as a tool to protect its own citizens and soldiers and current U.S. violations may hamper this effort. If, on the other hand, U.S. violations produce reputational spillovers that affect other areas of international cooperation, the costs might be higher. If, for example, U.S. violations hinder negotiations regarding North Korea's nuclear ambitions, the costs are much higher.

One area where the compartmentalizing of reputation is important is human rights. Consider, for example, the potential for international law to constrain the human rights conduct of a state. Venezuela, for example, is party to the ICCPR, which prohibits, among other things, torture, degradation, arbitrary arrest, and detention. It also guarantees rights to certain legal processes. The breakdown in recent years of law and order in Venezuela has compromised these rights on a broad scale, prompting inquiries by the UN Commission on Human Rights as well as the Inter-American Commission on Human Rights. If reputation is fully compartmentalized, these developments impose reputational consequences only on Venezuela's human rights commitments. Unless those commitments are linked to international benefits that the leaders of Venezuela care about (e.g., international trade), it is hard to see why that reputational loss would concern them. If, on the other hand, the state suffered a general loss of reputation, this would be costly to decision-makers, who would find it more difficult to pursue whatever other objectives they may have in the international arena.

Generalizing from these examples, if reputations are compartmentalized, it will be more difficult to generate compliance in areas where states have little interest in building a good reputation. It will, conversely, be easier to do so in areas where states have much to gain from a good reputation. This may imply that cooperation will be difficult in, for example, human rights and easier in, for example, economic interactions.

It has been argued that the existence of a single reputation implies that compliance rates should be comparable across issue areas (Downs and Jones 2002). This, however, need not be true. Compliance rates are determined by the reputational and nonreputational costs and benefits of compliance. A single reputation does not imply that either the costs or the benefits of compliance are constant across issue areas. Consider, for example, the decision to violate an extradition treaty. Even if we assume a single reputation, the compliance decision will reflect, in addition to the state's existing reputation, the nonreputational costs and benefits and the reputational consequences of violation or compliance. There is no reason to think that the nonreputational payoffs in the extradition area bear any particular relation to those relevant to, say, a treaty governing the establishment of national borders. There may be powerful domestic pressure to ignore the extradition treaty, and this may generate nonreputational payoffs that make violation the state's best strategy. With respect to national borders, the state may have no reason to challenge the established borders, and so compliance is a better approach. With respect to reputational payoffs, the violation of an extradition treaty may be a relatively minor issue that has little impact on a state's general reputation, whereas the violation of a treaty establishing a boundary may have a profoundly negative impact on reputation. The point here is that differences in reputational consequences do not require that states have multiple reputations.

If, indeed, states have multiple reputations but they are interrelated, as discussed, what are the implications for international law and compliance? Most obviously, state actions in an area will have their greatest impact within that area. So a decision to violate a trade agreement will, first and foremost, affect a state's reputation in trade and especially with respect to the agreement at issue. But the reputational consequences will not be limited to one narrow area. There will be spillover to other "adjacent" issue areas such as other economic agreements. For more distant issues such as environment or human rights, the reputational impact will presumably be still less. So while a state's reputations may differ from one area to another, they are not entirely independent of one another.

When making a compliance decision, then, a state will take into account the reputational impact of its actions across all issue areas, but will also recognize that the reputational sanctions will be largest in the areas closest to the one at issue.

Reputation by Regime

Once we recognize that states are likely to have different if interdependent reputations across issue areas, it is easy to see that reputations may vary along other dimensions as well. For example, the reputation of a state is likely affected by the regime in place. This is most obvious in the case of extreme regime changes. To illustrate, consider again the example of Chile during the transition from the Allende to the Pinochet government. Under Allende, Chile expropriated the assets of foreign firms and, accordingly, had a reputation among both states and potential investors for disregarding the existing international law on investment.[24] When Pinochet seized power, this reputation changed almost instantly, and foreign investment returned.

When regime changes are as dramatic as in this example, it is easy to see why a state's reputation would change. Though less dramatic, it is likely that more modest regime shifts also affect a state's reputation. For example, the election of a Democrat to the White House might reduce the United States' reputation for compliance with its free trade agreements. Because Democrats rely on organized labor for much of their political support, their commitment to free trade agreements such as the recently signed DR-CAFTA might be in doubt. To be sure, shifts of this sort occur only at the margin, and the new regime retains an interest in honoring the commitments made by its predecessor regimes. The point here is simply that some reputational effects can come about in this way.

Reputation by Dyad

Just as reputation may vary from one issue area to another, it is conceivable that a country's reputation (or its reputation in a particular area) varies from one counter-party to another. There is, after all, no reason to think that a state will behave in the same way toward its friends and allies as it will toward its enemies and rivals. If a state's willingness to comply varies based on these factors, rational states will take this into account when they deal with one another. In negotiations with Canada, for example, the United States benefits from a high level of reputation and trust. In dealings with Iran, the United States almost surely enjoys a less positive reputation. On the basis of a review of case studies on the subject of security and deterrence, Huth (1997) concludes that there is some evidence to support the hypothesis that reputations form within country-pairs. The extent to which this evidence speaks to reputation in international law is, however, an open question.

In the context of my model of reputation, it is possible to understand dyad-specific reputations as a reflection of the fact that states have more frequent and more valuable interactions with some counter-parties than with others. As mentioned, the United States and Canada have frequent interactions, many of which yield high payoffs from cooperation. The United States has fewer interactions with, say, Tanzania. In terms of the earlier discussion of the value of reputation, the value the United States places on a reputation may be different when it deals with Canada than when it deals with Tanzania. The United States, then, would have one value function (which could be labeled V^C) with respect to Canada and another with respect to Tanzania (which could be called V^T). Like compartmentalized reputations by issue area, there is no compelling theoretical reason to believe that a state will have either a single reputation across all counter-parties or an entirely compartmentalized one. Both of these outcomes, and many that lie between these extremes, could generate a stable equilibrium.

That said, it seems unlikely that a state's reputation is entirely compartmentalized by counter-party. At a minimum, by observing the behavior of a country with its other partners, a state can draw lessons about that country's discount rate and its attitude toward its legal obligations. Furthermore, if reputation were entirely dyad specific, we would expect more default in instances where one state places little value on its future ability to make credible commitments with its counter-party. For example, when a developing country accepts a World Bank loan, its promise to repay is backed by the country's reputation (at least its reputation with respect to financial obligations). Though it is certainly within the legal capacity of the state to default on the loan, countries have shown themselves reluctant to take such a step for fear that this might generate a negative signal to other potential lenders, including both private lenders and other states. Notice that this is not simply a concern about signaling that the state is in poor financial health. Where default on World Bank or IMF loans is being considered, it is often well known that the state is in dire financial straights. If anything, from a purely financial perspective, defaulting on existing debts would make a state more able to repay because the default would reduce its total debt load. Nevertheless, states do everything they can to avoid defaulting, because they fear the reaction of international financial markets, including parties other than the World Bank or IMF. Their reputational concern certainly extends beyond the specific contractual parties involved. Third parties observing the default will draw inferences about the likelihood of future defaults from the state's conduct (Tomz 2007).

Trade offers another example. When entering into negotiations regarding DR-CAFTA, the Central American participants would be foolish to ignore the behavior of the United States under the WTO and NAFTA. These other agreements suggest, for example, that the United States generally (with some exceptions) respects the decisions of arbitral bodies established by trade agreements.[25]

A more dramatic example is the birth of a new state. For example, after the collapse of the Soviet Union, Ukraine became an independent state. It would have been foolish for Ukraine to treat all other states as having a clean reputational slate. Ukrainian officials had knowledge of how states had reacted to legal obligations in the past, even if none of those obligations had been with Ukraine itself. By taking into account the past actions of states, Ukraine was able to develop a better estimate of the reliability of its future partners.

The Impact of Multiple Reputations

In its most disaggregated form, then, it is possible that every regime of a country has its own set of reputations and that these reputations are different in each issue area and with each partner. And one could probably identify further dimensions along which to compartmentalize reputation. As argued, however, a rational state forms its expectations about the conduct of another state on the basis of all available information, so there is no reason to think that each of these reputations is fully independent of the others. Thus, even if there is a meaningful difference in, for example, Thailand's reputation on economic commitments and its reputation on human rights commitments, and even if each successive regime in Thailand has a set of reputations that are to a certain extent distinct from that of previous regimes, there will still be spillovers from one reputation to another. The most useful information for an observing state will obviously be the past behavior of the current regime within the relevant issue area. But what would an observing state do if there was no such past conduct? A new regime may have not yet addressed, say, human rights issues. It seems clear that, absent unusual circumstances, an observing state would take into account the reputation of the prior regime on human rights issues. It would then adjust that reputation to reflect what it knew about the current regime. If the current regimes accepted and honored international obligations in other areas, even when breach offered a payoff, then the observing state might adjust its reputational estimate upward. In this simple example, both the prior regime and other issue areas have influenced perceptions.

To the extent that reputations can be isolated, however, it is interesting to ask if the force of reputation is reduced if there are few spillovers to other issue areas (or other partners, or other regimes). Downs and Jones (2002) argue that the presence of multiple regimes implies that reputation has less force.[26] This conclusion, however, requires an assumption that as a state's reputation narrows, its force within the area in which it is relevant does not increase. Consider the following example. Japan and Russia have both trade and environmental dealings with one another. Assume that each state has a single reputation and that Russia has failed to honor an environmental agreement with Japan. Its reputation will be hurt as a result, and this reputational sanction will impose costs on Russia when it deals with Japan on either environmental or trade issues. For clarity, assume that the cost of this lost reputation is E in the environmental context and T in the trade context, leading to a total cost of $E + T$.

Now assume that the states have separate reputations for trade agreements and environmental agreements, and that a violation of an environmental agreement has no impact on a state's reputation in the trade area. Assume again that Russia has violated an environmental agreement. By assumption, there is no reputational consequence in the trade arena (i.e., $T = 0$). There remains, of course, a reputational consequence in the environmental area. If we assume that the cost in the environmental area is the same in this case as it would be if the state has a single reputation, then the total cost of the violation is simply E. It follows that the assumption of multiple reputations implies that reputation has less impact on compliance.

But this analysis is flawed. The reputational cost in the environmental area will be higher if there are multiple reputations than if there is a single reputation. This is so because if there are multiple reputations, there are necessarily fewer "compliance opportunities" for a state to establish a reputation in a given area. If Russia has a single reputation, Russian actions in the trade area yield information that allows Japan to form beliefs about Russian behavior in the environmental area. This means that Japan observes a larger number of compliance decisions by Russia and, therefore, its view of Russia's reputation is more stable. In contrast, if Russia has a reputation for compliance with environmental agreements that is independent from all other areas, Japan will have observed many fewer compliance decisions by Russia. Therefore, when Russia does make such a decision, the priors of observing states (including Japan) will be weaker, and the impact of a particular conduct on reputation will be larger. The Russian violation of the environmental agreement, then, will generate a reputational cost in the environmental area of some amount, $E^* > E$. Without additional assumptions, there is no way to know if E^* is larger or smaller than $E + T$.

So we cannot conclude that having multiple reputations somehow reduces states' incentive to comply with their obligations. We can conclude that reputation will have a larger impact in areas where the value of cooperation is high. In these areas, a loss of reputation imposes relatively large costs, so breach is discouraged. This might describe, for example, trade. Though there are plenty of exceptions, it is clear that states tend to comply with their trade obligations even when these obligations impose short-term costs. It seems likely that consistently breaching trade obligations frustrates a good deal of future cooperation and, therefore, is costly. Human rights may represent a useful example in which the opposite is true. States that are tempted to violate human rights commitments are unlikely to be concerned about the possibility that future human rights agreements will be difficult to negotiate or join. This reduces the costs associated with the violation of these treaties and, therefore, makes such a violation more likely.

Limits and Caveats

Before discussing the sources of international law in the next two chapters, it is useful to address some of the limits and questions raised by the theory advanced up to this point. The following subsections discuss the limits on the ability of reputation to influence state conduct and the relationship between a reputation for compliance with international law and other kinds of reputation.

The Limits on Reputation's Ability to Generate Compliance

It should be clear from the foregoing discussion that reputational sanctions can generate compliance in some but not all circumstances. This is a necessary feature of any model of international law. We observe that states sometimes violate their obligations, and so our theory must have some explanation for when that will happen.

Consider one of the more dramatic failures of international law in the last century—the Munich Accord of 1938. Under the terms of this agreement, France and Britain agreed to the German annexation of the Sudetenland, a German-speaking region of Czechoslovakia. In exchange, Hitler promised that he had no further territorial ambitions in Europe. The Munich Accord failed to deter Germany's subsequent decision to seize the rest of Czechoslovakia, or the later decision to attack Poland, which triggered the outbreak of World War II. Nazi Germany's failure to comply with the Munich Accord was, to be sure, a failure of international law, but it is not one that should surprise us. It is clear (at least in retrospect) that Nazi Germany had no reason to value a good reputation. Hitler's ambitions required that he ignore international legal norms, including the national boundaries of other states. These ambitions were inconsistent with the maintenance of a good reputation for compliance with international law, so there was no point in cultivating such a reputation. In other words, the harm to Germany's reputation as a result of its violation of the Munich Accord imposed only a modest cost on the state.

Probably more important than Nazi Germany's lack of interest in a strong reputation was the fact that the decision to violate the Munich

Accord involved calculations about national security, territorial expansion, and European dominance. Though states have a reason to protect their reputation for compliance with international law, the value of reputation is, nevertheless, limited. Even the threat of a total loss of reputation would not normally cause a state to take actions that threaten its very existence. In the lead-up to World War II, Germany sought expansion and control of much of Europe, a prize whose value surely exceeded the reputational consequences of Hitler's actions. The pre–World War II experience in Europe also illustrates how observing states update their beliefs. As Nazi Germany repeatedly failed to honor commitments, other European states adjusted their estimates of Germany's reputation, eventually concluding that they could neither seek nor rely on further German promises.

Indeed, while the violation of the Munich Accord and the seizure of the remainder of Czechoslovakia may have been the signal to Europe that Germany did not intend to honor its own agreements or the territorial integrity of other European states, there had been earlier warning signs. In 1938, prior to Munich, Germany had violated one of the terms of the Treaty of Versailles when it annexed Austria.[27] Earlier violations of the Treaty of Versailles included Germany's remilitarization of the Rhineland in 1936, and Germany's rearmament throughout the mid-1930s. Nevertheless, many western European nations had come to see the Treaty of Versailles as unnecessarily harsh and punitive, and had higher expectations of Germany's compliance with the Munich Accord. So it was the violation of the latter agreement that caused the collapse of Germany's reputation and prompted the British and French to issue the March 1939 guarantee of Polish security against German aggression.

Generalizing this example yields two important lessons about reputation and international law. First, the force of reputation is affected by a state's interest in developing or maintaining a good reputation. States that anticipate little or no return from investments in reputation are less likely to comply with international law. The effectiveness of reputation hinges on the state's desire to be able to make credible promises in the future.

Second, the force of reputation is limited. Even a state eager to nurture its reputation will violate its legal commitments if the nonreputational payoff from doing so is large enough. This implies that when the stakes are very high, the likelihood that reputation can influence the outcome is smaller. Certainly when states have honest concerns about fundamental security interest, for example, international law is unlikely to have much influence on their decisions. If this is correct, we should expect to see (as we do) international law largely put aside during moments of extreme national crisis. Something similar is true of domestic law, where it is sometimes said that *inter arma silent leges* ("in times of war the laws are silent"). In such moments of crisis, more powerful forces than international law are likely to push it aside. As the stakes at issue grow smaller, however, the likelihood that reputational issues might tip the balance toward compliance grows.

The weakness of international law in the face of high-stakes decisions does not imply that international law cannot be usefully deployed in high-stakes areas, however. It seems improbable, for example, that international law can prevent a war that would otherwise take place, but that does not mean that international law is irrelevant to all issues related to warfare. To take one example, though it is unlikely to prevent a war, international law may be able to improve the treatment of prisoners of war. The Geneva Conventions regulate the treatment of prisoners of war and, though they are certainly not always complied with, impose reputational costs on states that choose to ignore the conventions. Provisions of the Geneva Convention Relative to the Treatment of Prisoners of War stipulate that a detaining power must allow visits to prisoners of war by representatives of "protecting powers," that these visitors must be allowed to interview prisoners, and must be allowed to visit the premises in which they are housed.[28] These requirements make it possible for violations of the Geneva Convention to become public and provide the detaining power with an incentive to comply. Notice that even the act of denying access to visitors is a violation that comes with an attendant reputational cost. For example, following revelations of detainee abuse at the Abu Ghraib prison in Iraq, the U.S. army suggested that the Red Cross should no longer be permitted to make no-notice visits to cellblocks. This suggestion became public, and was a source of much embarrassment to the United States.[29] Where this form of reputational cost is insufficient to generate compliance, reciprocity may succeed. Both sides in a conflict may prefer a regime of mutual access to prisoners to one of no access. The international law relating to prisoners of war, then, has some chance of affecting state behavior, because the gains from a violation may be outweighed by its reputational costs (Morrow 2001).

More generally, law can matter in high-stakes areas by targeting individual decisions that do not themselves implicate high stakes for the parties. Compliance with rules governing the treatment of prisoners of war will often (though not always) represent a modest cost, and legal obligations might influence the cost-benefit calculation. The lesson is that international law cannot easily influence high-stakes *decisions*. When trying to create binding obligations, then, negotiators are well advised to find ways to constrain states by influencing decisions with lower stakes. An example is the use of inspections in arms control regimes such as the NPT. A variety of protocols (the International Atomic Energy Agency Protocols), signed pursuant to the NPT, commit states to certain levels of transparency regarding their use of nuclear technology. The stakes involved in complying with these protocols individually are much lower than the relatively high stakes involved in developing a nuclear capability. Thus, reputational sanctions associated with the protocols may deter violation of a protocol, and thus of the larger arms control agreement, when such reputational costs alone would not have prevented a state from defecting from the arms control regime as a whole.

If high-stakes decisions are difficult to influence, one might hope that low-stakes decisions are easy to affect. That is, one might think that a decision to violate the law imposes some fixed reputational sanction and, therefore, that compliance decisions involving modest costs and benefits are systematically more likely to be affected by international law than are decisions that implicate larger stakes. This is only true, however, if one makes the implausible assumption that reputational sanctions are unrelated to the stakes in the case.

It seems much more realistic to assume that a violation of an obligation that is of fundamental interest to other states will generate a larger reputational sanction than will a violation of a minor obligation. The Kyoto Protocol, for example, requires that state parties submit an annual inventory of greenhouse gas emissions as well as greenhouse gas removal by sinks. A state that fails to meet its reporting requirements on time and instead submits the required reports a day late is unlikely to face reputational sanctions of any consequence. In contrast, the same agreement requires a certain percentage reduction in the emission of greenhouse gases, with different countries having different targets. A decision to ignore this obligation would result in reputational sanctions. To put it more generally, some violations of international law will simply be too trivial to trigger reputational sanctions, even when other states can observe the violation. In these cases, reputation will have little or no effect on a state's decision to comply. It is in cases in which observing states view the obligation as a significant basis for forming future expectations of compliance, and in which the stakes for the state deciding whether to comply are sufficiently low, that reputation will be able to exert the most influence.

Other Kinds of Reputation

The discussion of reputation up to this point has been focused on a state's reputation for compliance with international law, which could be called (somewhat awkwardly) the state's "compliance reputation." The basic argument relies on the notion that states wish to be able to make and elicit credible commitments and are willing to forgo at least some short-term gains in order to develop a reputation that allows them to make such commitments.

This focus on a state's reputation for compliance with international law might leave the impression that a state has no other reputational concerns. Indeed, one criticism that has been made of a reputational theory is that states and their leaders may care about many things other than a reputation for compliance with international law (Goldsmith and Posner 2005). A state may want a reputation for toughness, retributiveness, kindness, generosity, or any number of other things (Keohane 1997). In fact, the bulk of the literature on reputation in international affairs is concerned with a state's reputation for resolve rather than for compliance with international law (Mercer 1996). Furthermore, these other reputational concerns may be in tension with whatever interest states have in respecting international law. The problem with this argument is not its premise (that states care about other things) but its conclusion. The fact that other factors are relevant tells us nothing about whether a state's desire for a reputation for compliance generates an incentive to comply with the law.

By way of example, imagine a conflict between the United States and India with respect to intellectual property. This could take the form of a dispute about India's legal obligations under the TRIPs agreement, as was the case in the *India–Patents* case at the WTO;[30] or it could simply be a case of the United States attempting to persuade or coerce India into a particular course of action, in the absence of a legal rule. The latter type of dispute took place during the Uruguay Round of trade talks in the late 1980s and early 1990s. The United States, among others, wanted the Uruguay Round to be approved. India was objecting in particular to the TRIPs agreement, which would have required India to legislate increased protections for intellectual property. Both sides were concerned about the substantive issues at stake, but both sides also had reputational concerns. The United States had good reason to promote a reputation for dealing harshly with those that do not capitulate to its will, especially in the intellectual property area.[31] India, on the other hand, had an interest in resisting an increase in international intellectual property requirements, not least because the pre-TRIPs rules had generated many jobs for Indian citizens and opportunities for Indian businesses, and the TRIPs regime threatened these gains. Internationally, India also had an interest in building its reputation as a leader among developing states and a country that would resist coercion.

Of course, exactly the same reputational concerns were present when these two countries were involved in the already mentioned India Patents case at the WTO. That dispute was the first WTO case dealing with the TRIPs agreement, so both parties had reputational interests in resisting a compromise. After the ruling, which went in favor of the United States, India had an interest in refusing to comply, in an effort to develop a reputation as a country that is not worth pursuing on TRIPs issues. The United States had an incentive to ensure Indian compliance to demonstrate the U.S. commitment to protecting its interests under TRIPs.

None of the reputational effects discussed in these two examples speak to a state's reputation for compliance with international law. Furthermore, India's interests, as described in the preceding paragraph, are in tension with its reputational interest in compliance. This particular case ended with compliance. After the United States won before the dispute settlement bodies of the WTO, India agreed to bring itself into compliance, and did so in 1999.[32] The broader point is that when the compliance reputation and other reputational concerns pull in opposite directions, either of them may dominate.

This point can be made much more generally. There will frequently be many costs and benefits at play when a state is making a decision about compliance. Sometimes the state will have sufficient incentives to comply without worrying about its compliance reputation. Other times the incentive to violate a commitment will be sufficiently large that the state will do so despite its concerns about its compliance reputation. Finally, there will be times when a state's reputational interests with respect to compliance will cause it to comply despite the fact that the other relevant costs and benefits provide an incentive to violate the commitment.

What all of this really means is that there are many influences on a state's behavior beyond its compliance reputation. This observation does not, however, undermine the basic point that the compliance reputation is relevant to state decisions. Like all influences, compliance reputation operates at the margin—putting a thumb on the scale in favor of compliance. If other incentives to violate a norm are sufficiently strong, reputation will not prevent violation. It matters most when the decision to violate or comply is a relatively close call. In these cases, reputation can generate compliance where there might otherwise have been violation.

4

INTERNATIONAL AGREEMENTS

W hen states come together to make an agreement, they have nearly total control over the content and form of the deal. The result is that agreements range over almost every imaginable topic and virtually every conceivable form of strategic interaction and they vary widely in their design. Some are bilateral while others are multilateral; some take the form of treaties that are said to be "binding" under international law while others are much less formal; some provide for mandatory dispute resolution while others do not even mention the subject; some include comprehensive monitoring schemes while others provide no oversight whatsoever; some demand extensive changes to existing practices while others do little more than reflect what states are already doing; some are highly abstract and focused on general principles while others establish detailed commitments.

This chapter applies the rational choice assumptions that form the foundation of this book to international agreements, including both treaties and agreements that are not formal treaties. The great diversity among agreements and their terms makes it difficult (and perhaps impossible) to develop a rich model that covers all aspects of these agreements. Rather than attempting to do so, the chapter identifies a number of key features of international agreements and explores how one might understand them in light of the rational choice theory developed throughout the book.

To cabin the inquiry somewhat, the chapter focuses on how different problems of cooperation are addressed through treaties. Thus, for example, this chapter discusses how the problem of enforcement is handled in agreements. In doing so, it considers not only if there is a dispute resolution provision—the most obvious enforcement tool—but also whether states use hard or soft law, the escape clauses they provide, and more.

The way states construct agreements and the effect those agreements are likely to have depends in significant part on the nature of the problem being addressed. A coordination problem, for example, is solved more easily than a prisoner's dilemma and, therefore, requires fewer credibility-enhancing devices, monitoring mechanisms, or other tools to encourage compliance. So at least one source of the variety in the design of agreements can be attributed to the fact that these instruments are intended to address different sorts of problems.

This chapter draws on the work of many authors who have considered international agreements, but a word should be said about the issue of the political science journal *International Organization* entitled "The Rational Design of International Institutions" (Koremenos, Lipson, and Snidal 2001). This volume represents an important advance in our understanding of international agreements, and the insights developed there have contributed substantially to this chapter and other parts of this book. This chapter makes reference to the "conjectures" made in the introduction to that volume, written by Koremenos, Lipson, and Snidal (2001). They put these conjectures forward for testing in the volume's empirical articles and intentionally did so in a fairly informal theoretical setting.[1] In an important sense, the focus of the volume is on the empirical testing rather than the theory. This chapter adopts a different approach, in that it concerns itself almost exclusively with theory. It is hoped, of course, that these results will be tested empirically, but that is a task for another day. For the moment, the goal is to explore the relevant theory, which remains underdeveloped.

Why Do States Make Agreements?

International agreements present a challenge to the development of a theory of international law because they feature such remarkable diversity. To speak usefully to all (or at least most) of these agreements requires a fairly general framework, and that is what this section seeks to develop. Generality, however, comes at a cost. The arguments and claims made in this chapter are meant to apply to international agreements broadly. There are surely instances in which, for one reason or another, the claims are inaccurate in a particular context. Furthermore, the approach adopted here inevitably overlooks important details in particular subject areas (for example, Barrett [2003] offers an excellent treatment of agreements in the environmental context). The merit of the approach is its broad applicability. The discussion that follows is not contingent on the particular attributes of agreements in any one subject area or among any particular group of states. It applies to all international agreements, whether they take the form of hard or soft law, whether they are broad or narrow in scope, whether they codify existing behavior or demand wholesale changes in conduct, and so on. The analysis in this chapter, then, should be taken for what it is—a general treatment of international agreements that can form the basis for a more careful examination of particular agreements in individual subject-matter areas and among specific states.

Basic Assumptions

Our basic rational choice assumptions imply that states will only enter into agreements when doing so makes them (or, at least, their policymakers) better off. In other words, states enter into treaties for the same basic reasons that individuals enter into contracts. Treaties allow them to resolve problems of cooperation, to commit to a particular course of conduct, and to gain assurances regarding what other states will do in the future.

Rationality implies that states will seek to maximize the joint surplus of any agreement, taking into account transaction costs. This is, of course, just the familiar Coase Theorem (Coase 1960). The same assumption also implies that an agreement can be sustained only if every state and every subset of states are better off with the agreement than with any available alternate arrangement. Thus, for example, if a subset of the parties to a treaty can do better by entering into an agreement with one another and excluding the others, they will do so.

The paradigmatic problem I examine is one in which states can improve their payoffs through cooperation, but have at least some incentive to defect. The prisoner's dilemma is the most obvious such problem, but the analysis also applies to other, similar games. The game can be modeled as taking place in two periods. In the first period, states negotiate and (possibly) enter into an agreement. In the second stage, they decide whether or not to comply. Between the first and second stage, new information may be revealed regarding the state of the world.

If the agreement remains in place, there are subsequent rounds of compliance or noncompliance based on the same agreement. A similar approach to modeling international agreements is adopted by Fearon (1998). Though this basic framework is simple, it captures much of what we are interested in and has the merit of being applicable to a very wide range of interactions, from simple coordination games to prisoner's dilemmas; from narrow technical standards to matters of war and peace.

States and Risk

To evaluate state conduct, it is necessary to model the preferences of states. Though this can be done with a minimum of assumptions, there is no way to avoid specifying some model of states' attitudes toward risk. Agreements almost always involve some chance of noncompliance, and the future is almost always uncertain.

This book assumes that states behave in a risk-neutral fashion. This is in contrast to much prior work on international cooperation, including the *International Organization* Design Project (Koremenos, Lipson, and Snidal 2001), which assumes that states are risk averse with respect to individual commitments.[2] An assumption of risk aversion leads to a range of results in which uncertainty affects behavior and reduces states' willingness to enter agreements or to delegate in some way. Some authors justify their assumption of risk aversion with reference to existing realist and institutionalist scholarship. For example, Koremenos, Lipson, and Snidal (2001) justify the assumption by saying that it is "the bedrock of modern realism, where states' fears of destruction and keen interest in preserving their sovereignty dominate their strategic calculations" (p. 782). Even if one grants that states are risk averse in many of the areas of interest to political scientists, however, it does not follow that they are risk averse with respect to their international legal commitments.

The case for an assumption of risk neutrality with respect to international legal obligations rests on two primary claims. The first is that states will normally be well diversified in their international agreements. The second is that international agreements are rarely themselves high-stakes matters that implicate the security and survival of a state. I will consider each of these points in turn.

Just as diversification can cause a risk-averse investor to behave in a risk neutral fashion in financial markets, it can cause risk-averse states to behave in a risk-neutral fashion with respect to their international commitments. At any given moment, states are engaged in a broad set of activities in both the domestic and international spheres. Think, for example, of the full set of international commitments the United States is subject to at any one time. If one adds to these the many, many domestic activities of the state, it is clear that there are a large number of state engagements at any one time.

A large number of distinct interests and projects represents a form of diversification. For a state and its leaders, what matters is the degree of risk and uncertainty present in the entire portfolio of activities rather than that present in any single engagement. For example, a commitment to an extradition treaty entails a certain amount of uncertainty. On the one hand, the state may find itself obligated to extradite an individual it would prefer to keep within its jurisdiction; on the other hand, it may benefit from the extradition of a wanted individual from another state. The greater this uncertainty—that is, the greater the variance in expected outcomes—the more reluctant an undiversified, risk-averse state would be to enter the agreement. But in addition to the extradition treaty, the state is engaged in a host of other activities. Many are likely to be entirely independent of the extradition treaty, for example, bilateral agreements addressing cooperation in antitrust issues. Other state efforts may be related to the extradition treaty in some sense, but the success or failure of those efforts will not be correlated to the performance of the treaty. For example, a state may be changing its evidentiary rules for criminal prosecutions. Like the extradition treaty, this project impacts the incentive of would-be criminals, the way the state deals with defendants, and the success rate of criminal investigations. The success or failure of efforts to change the evidentiary rules, however, is essentially unrelated to the success or failure of the treaty. The point here is that whatever it is that the state is trying to maximize (more on this later), it will normally have several projects in place that contribute to that goal. Because the outcomes of those projects will not be perfectly correlated with one another, it is possible to eliminate some risk through diversification.

One can see the potential for diversification if one considers state interests at their broadest level. Consider the way policy-makers seek to optimize the overall performance of the state. This goal may be some measure of public welfare, it may be the private welfare of the decision makers, it may be some combination of these two, or it may be some other set of concerns. All that matters is that there be some sense in which the state's performance can be evaluated by decision-makers. Regardless of how the policy-maker's objectives are generated, the entire set of state activities, whether domestic or international, affects them. At any given moment, the state is confronting uncertainty on many fronts. The policy-maker may be risk averse, but she will consider risk as it affects the overall objective function, not as it affects individual projects the state has undertaken. Because the state has many different projects underway, and because the impacts of those projects on the overall objective function are almost never perfectly correlated with one another, as long as the state is sufficiently well diversified, the best strategy is to seek to maximize the expected return from each project, rather than to minimize the risk of individual projects. In other words, even a risk-averse policy-maker should behave in a risk-neutral fashion with respect to each individual project, including each international legal commitment.[3]

One might wonder if the validity of this claim is sensitive to the objectives of the state. Is it necessary to make strong assumptions about what the state is attempting to maximize in order to make this claim? The simple answer is no. As long as the state has a single objective function, risk can be diversified. This means that it is sufficient to assume that states aggregate the outcomes from all of their activities (domestic and international) to generate a single payoff. This payoff corresponds to some measure of utility for the state. Such a result would be consistent, for example, with a public choice model of state conduct in which government leaders respond to strong interest groups or campaign contributions in an attempt to retain and increase their power. Though these politicians will not be pursuing the public good, they will judge activities on the basis of the private payoffs they receive and will be interested in the total payoff from all the state's activities. Even if these decision-makers are risk averse, they will be diversified over the many engagements of the state. Similarly, if the government pursues the public interest (however measured), it will make decisions on the basis of how they will impact the public good, and it will aggregate over all decisions and activities for that purpose.

If states are able to diversify their risk in this way, it is appropriate to model them as behaving in a risk-neutral fashion. They will, of course, attempt to avoid outcomes that generate negative payoffs through the use of exceptions, reservations, escape clauses, termination provisions, and the like, but they will not sacrifice the expected return of projects in order to reduce the variance of their payoffs.

One might be tempted to argue that certain commitments feature payoffs that cannot be diversified away. Military alliances and nuclear weapons treaties, for example, implicate issues so central to the survival of the state that they are probably not diversifiable, the argument would go. Even in these contexts, however, the most appropriate assumption is that the risks associated with international legal commitments can be diversified.

This is so because, as I discussed in more detail in chapter 3 in relation to reputation, the power of international law is limited, especially when critical issues of national interest are involved. Suppose, for example, that a state is considering whether to join the Convention Against Torture (CAT). This treaty requires that states refrain from the use of torture and provides that "[n]o exceptional circumstances whatsoever, whether a state of war or threat of war, internal political instability or any other public emergency, may be invoked as a justification of torture."[4] The legal commitment taken on, then, would not permit torture under any circumstances.

Now imagine the familiar "ticking time bomb" scenario in which a government has in custody a person who knows the location of a nuclear device set to detonate in the near future. Assume that torturing this person will allow the government to extract the information necessary to defuse the bomb and save hundreds of thousands, or perhaps millions, of lives. The risk at issue—whether the bomb is detonated—is not diversifiable for the state. The legal commitment, however, is something different. Faced with this ticking time bomb scenario, the decision as to whether to torture or not will surely not be made on the basis of the international legal commitment.[5] When joining the CAT, then, the state does not have to worry that it will be prevented from using torture in this scenario. The risk inherent in joining the CAT is the risk of breaching the treaty, not the risk of being prevented from torturing.

More generally, though many international agreements demand commitments or actions that implicate matters of a state's security and survival (or other essential interests), there is no reason to think that the legal obligations will trump the state's fundamental interests. Another example is provided by the Charter of the United Nations. When states enter the UN system, they agree to refrain from the use of force except in self-defense or when authorized by the Security Council. In the actual conduct of their foreign affairs, however, it is clear that states use force in many other contexts, as illustrated by the United States' invasion of Iraq in 2003, the intervention in Kosovo led by the North Atlantic Treaty Organization (NATO) in 1999, and any number of other examples.

Agreements that relate to such high-stakes issues do not undermine states' ability to diversify the risks associated with legal commitments, because the modest enforcement tools of international law limit the cost of breaching those commitments. This cost may include reputational harm, reciprocal violations by others, and retaliation, but will not rise to anything like the potential costs associated with a severe compromise of national interests or security. Because states violate agreements when the costs of compliance outweigh the costs of violation, the most a state risks by entering into an agreement is the cost of violation.

The key point here is that the individual international legal obligations of states (as opposed to the subject matter of those obligations) are (almost) never of critical importance to states. The question of whether to comply or not does not implicate the sort of high-stakes issues that might cause a state to behave in a risk-averse fashion.

Return for a moment to the CAT example. Even if the state joins the treaty, the associated risks are modest. If at some point in the future the state concludes that compliance with the treaty is too costly, it can simply violate it (though doing so would not be costless). Viewed this way, the treaty would be just one among many international commitments that contribute to the state's overall goals. The risk can be diversified with other agreements and other projects.

States and Cooperation

The simplest games of international cooperation, as discussed in chapter 2, are those in which states have common interests. In these games, states will behave in a cooperative fashion whether they have an international agreement or not. There is, therefore, no need to invest major resources pursuing cooperation.

States can use international law to play a role in coordination games, though any approach able to generate a focal point will serve equally well. These include treaties, written agreements that are not formal treaties (i.e., soft law), oral agreements, unilateral statements of intent, actions taken by one of the parties, and so on. Because the objective is simply to establish a focal point, there is no reason to provide for monitoring, dispute resolution, or sanctions. Treaties that are straight-forward coordination games, such as the Convention on International Civil Aviation, otherwise known as the Chicago Convention, are, there-fore, simple to understand. The Chicago Convention established the International Civil Aviation Organization (ICAO), which in turn sets standards for international air travel, such as the requirement that all air traffic controllers and flight crew engaged in international air travel be proficient in English.[6] The one puzzle with respect to such agreements is why they ever take the form of treaties at all rather than more informal forms of agreement or cooperation. After all, treaties are difficult and time consuming to negotiate, they typically trigger more significant domestic law procedures, and they require approval from high gov-ernment officials. In contrast, soft law agreements such as the Paris Memorandum of Understanding on Port State Control—which has 20 member nations and harmonizes inspection procedures that are aimed at ensuring compliance with major maritime conventions governing pollution and safety, address coordination problems without the need for approval by domestic legislatures—can be negotiated by relatively low-level officials, and involve fewer formalities. I provide one possible explanation for such behavior in chapter 2, where I suggest that states may want to use the treaty to protect against the possibility that future events will cause the game to change from one of coordination to some other form in which cooperation is less assured. In that case the states are not really playing a coordination game at all, and so a stronger legal form such as a treaty may make sense. The example I used in chapter 2 was the Antarctic Treaty, which started as a coordination exercise but subse-quently changed into a more challenging cooperative exercise. The bulk of this chapter, however, focuses on games in which the interests of states are more directly in opposition to one another than they are in coordination games.

In a prisoner's dilemma, states enter into agreements as a way to exchange promises. In the Convention on International Trade in Endangered Species, for example, 169 states have agreed to curb the trade in international endangered species through a licensing system gov-erning imports and exports of species covered by the Convention.[7] Each state has made commitments regarding its own conduct in exchange for the promises of other states. When analyzing treaties, I normally will assume that the exchange of promises takes this form: states make commitments of their own in order to extract commitments from other states. Put differently, the concessions they make represent costs to the state, and the concessions made by others represent benefits.

Two caveats are necessary with respect to this "contract" model of international agreements. The first has already been explained: in agreements designed to address coordination games or other games in which states have a common interest (e.g., coincidence of interest, battle of the sexes) the promises of states do not fit neatly into this model of costs and benefits. This is, however, not a serious problem because those agreements are readily understood as coordination devices.

Second, a contract model, like the rational choice assumptions used throughout most of this book, assumes that the commitments a state makes are not designed to constrain or empower some domestic constituency. Thus, for example, such a model rules out the possibility that policy-makers consider it a benefit to constrain the behavior of future leaders (Moravcsik 2000) or the legislature (Abbott and Snidal 2000).

Though treaties may be used to achieve domestic objectives from time to time, the decision to put such motivations to one side is a pragmatic necessity. Once one considers the interaction of domestic constituencies, it is necessary to abandon the assumption that states have a set of fixed preferences that motivate their international behavior. If the assumption of fixed preferences is abandoned, the complexity of the model is greatly increased. Without fixed preferences one must generate some model of how the preferences of states are formed and how they change. And to the extent that state preferences change as a result of changes in domestic politics, it is clear that no good general model of how preferences change exists. As a practical matter, then, models that include strong public choice components can often be useful as a form of positive analysis in a specific context, but are less helpful in general models such as the one developed here, or as tools to generate predictions about state behavior (Croley 1998).[8]

These pragmatic concerns do not change the fact that domestic political concerns are surely relevant to many of the phenomena this chapter examines. And so a dilemma must be addressed. The explicit inclusion of public choice concerns would make the model unworkable and undermine the goal of generating useful predictions, unless one were to make strong assumptions about exactly how public choice issues affect government leaders' decisions. Omitting these concerns ignores a factor in government decisions and so risks misrepresenting state behavior. This tension is present in any analysis of state behavior and so is familiar to anyone who studies international law or international relations. This chapter attempts to navigate between the options of building public choice issues into the model and ignoring them altogether. The basic analysis proceeds with states modeled as unitary actors, but when more specific applications of the model are developed (e.g., to consider why a state might choose soft law rather than a treaty) domestic law issues are incorporated. The downside to this approach is that it may be considered an unduly ad hoc way to incorporate domestic political issues. On the other hand, it allows both a functioning predictive model to exist and allows consideration of domestic issues where these are most relevant.[9]

Finally, note that the assumptions made do not imply that domestic politics are irrelevant to national priorities. The model developed here is silent as to how state preferences are formed. It is perfectly consistent with a view that the objectives of states are the product of a complex domestic political process and that the resulting policies may diverge from whatever would maximize the welfare of citizens. It is similarly consistent with any other model of preference formation in which states generate stable preferences.

Negotiation of an Agreement

Imagine two countries coming together to address a shared problem: for instance, Canada and the United States negotiating about fisheries issues.[10] Each state enters the negotiation with some preferred outcome, meaning some agreement between the two states that would generate the greatest payoff for that state. Over the course of the negotiation (and assuming that there is enough common ground to allow for an agreement), as they seek out the agreement with the greatest joint payoff, the parties identify substantive terms to be included.

In a simple model without transaction costs, the parties negotiate terms that maximize their joint payoff and then commit to those terms. Assume, for example, that Canada prefers a more environmentally protective policy than does the United States. The United States will consent to terms that generate protection beyond its preferred policy, but will demand some form of compensation in exchange for that compromise. Recognizing this, Canada will offer compensation up to the point where the marginal amount the United States requires equals the value Canada places on the marginal increase in environmental protection. This may result in a level of protection below Canada's preferred level, but it will maximize the value of the agreement.

Once the terms are agreed to, a standard contracting model predicts that the parties will enter into a formal legal commitment requiring that they both perform their obligations under the agreement. Performance will be subject to monitoring up to the point at which the marginal cost of additional monitoring exceeds the marginal benefit of increased compliance. Finally, the agreement will provide for efficient damages in the event of breach and a dispute resolution system to assign those damages.

In the domestic context, parties entering into a contract are assumed to behave as the foregoing model predicts, though the state provides some of the features of the agreement (e.g., the court system and default damages regime may address the parties' needs in those areas). Even a casual observer of international agreements, however, will immediately recognize that states' practice seems far removed from this description.

How can we explain this divergence between the foregoing theory and practice? Much of the remainder of this chapter is devoted to answering that question. The next section considers the form of international agreements and why states might prefer one form over another. I then undertake a similar analysis of the substantive terms of agreements. Subsequent sections consider the interaction of form and substance and issues related to the membership of international agreements.

Matters of Form

Substance and Form

The assumption of rationality generates important implications for the form and substance of agreements. This section is concerned primarily with the form of agreements; the next will address primarily matters of substance. One of the implications of the discussion is that form and substance are closely related and that states trade one off against the other as they work to design an agreement. The two categories are nevertheless discussed separately for several reasons. First, lawyers and others who work with international agreements are accustomed to thinking of form and substance as separate issues. Indeed, once an agreement is completed, it makes sense to focus first on substance to determine if there is a violation at all, and then on form to identify the consequences of a violation. Second, this categorization connects the discussion more directly to the existing literature on international agreements (Raustiala 2005). Finally, though this chapter emphasizes how trade-offs between form and substance can be made, it is likely that there are differences between the two categories that are important to states. The substantive terms of an agreement are salient in a way that the form of the agreement normally is not. For these reasons, though it is recognized that the distinction between form and substance is somewhat artificial, I maintain it for expositional purposes.

For the purposes of this book, I define the "substance" of an agreement as the set of formal obligations, commitments, or promises that speak to the actions states say they will take in the future. I define "form" as including parts of the agreement that determine the degree to which states have pledged to comply with the obligation, that determine when obligations can be avoided, and that provide for enforcement. Examples of choices as to the form of the agreement include the decision to adopt a treaty rather than soft law, the provision or omission of dispute resolution and monitoring, and the inclusion or omission of reservations, escape clauses, and exit clauses.

One could define these terms differently, and there is no sense in which the definitions proposed here are better than alternatives except that they are convenient for the discussion that follows. As this chapter demonstrates, there is no natural way to divide matters of form from those of substance. States are able to trade one off against the other and can often achieve a particular goal using either a substantive or a formal provision. For example, an agreement with modest substantive provisions might be identical in its effect to one with much stronger substantive provisions accompanied by many reservations and generous escape clauses. To illustrate this point, consider the ICCPR obligation prohibiting arbitrary arrest or detention (art. 9). As actually written, the prohibition is phrased as an absolute one: "No one shall be subjected to arbitrary arrest or detention."[11] The ICCPR, however, provides an escape clause. In times of "public emergency which threatens the life of the nation," a state may derogate from some of the obligations of the ICCPR, including the prohibition on arbitrary arrest or detention.[12] As written, then, and using the definitions adopted earlier, the absolute prohibition might be termed a substantive term, and the escape clause might be termed a matter of form. Article 9 could have been drafted to say that "no one shall be subjected to arbitrary arrest or detention in normal times." "Normal times" could then be defined as "times in which there is no public emergency that threatens the life of the nation." The content of the legal obligation is obviously identical to that provided in the actual ICCPR, but under this alternate version it is provided entirely through the substantive terms rather than through an escape clause that could be termed a provision relating to form.

What States Want

Before moving on, it is essential to get a sense of just what it is that states are trying to do when they enter into an agreement. How do they judge the relative merits of the many design choices they have to make? For example, by allowing reservations, states permit more detailed tailoring of the agreement to states' interests and concerns, and reduce the likelihood of a violation; but they also water down the content of the agreement. To understand the choices made by states, it is necessary to have a sense of how they evaluate the costs and benefits involved.

Recall that the rationality assumption implies that states seek to maximize the total joint value of the agreement. The distribution of the gains from the agreement will depend on the bargaining power of the parties. These distributional issues are, of course, critical to the ultimate form of the agreement. The assumption of rationality tells us that the agreement will be value maximizing, but there are likely to be many value-maximizing agreements available, each with different distributional implications. It nevertheless remains possible to understand a great deal about international agreements within a general framework such as the one used here.

I refer to the various options states face with respect to form and substance as "design elements." Those relevant only to form are called "formal design elements," and those related to substance "substantive design elements." When making decisions about the form of international agreements, then, states seek to identify the combination of relevant design elements that maximize the value of the agreement. Conceptually, states negotiating an agreement face a problem in which they control variables along many dimensions, each of which affects the one variable they are concerned with—the total joint value of the agreement. States will trade off design elements against each other to further their goal of maximizing this joint value. The challenge is to identify the costs and benefits of each element so that we can understand how these trade-offs are made.

It is, of course, impossible to quantify the value of each element in this sort of general theoretical discussion. The value of various design elements depends too heavily on the particular agreement and the states involved to let us draw broad conclusions about even their relative value. We cannot, for example, hope to determine whether a restrictive escape clause is worth more or less to states than stricter monitoring provisions. In the trade context, the escape clause may have great appeal to governments because it allows them to breach in circumstances when doing so is efficient (Sykes 1991). Monitoring provisions, on the other hand, may have only modest value because violations (in terms of border measures, for example) are fairly transparent to a state's exporters, and the states can use reports and complaints from their exporters to learn about potential violations by trading partners. In the context of a human rights treaty, on the other hand, an escape clause might be less appealing, and monitoring might be quite valuable because gaining access to information about the practices of foreign states can be difficult. My analysis will instead have to use what we observe states doing to help draw inferences about what matters most to them. Where monitoring is avoided but dispute resolution is used, I infer something about the relative gains each of these offers. In examining the design of agreements, we can also test and refine portions of the theory against the observed behavior of states. One example of this sort of inquiry is provided in the next section, where I explain the reluctance to use credibility-enhancing design elements.

Commitment, Credibility, and Reputation

As discussed in chapter 2, international agreements are valuable because the forces of reputation, retaliation, and reciprocity give states an incentive to comply with their international legal obligations or, more accurately, with their promises, whether or not these are termed "legal." In other words, international agreements give states the ability to enter into credible commitments. This ability to commit has important benefits in the international context. Most obviously, it allows states to engage in a variety of cooperative behaviors that would otherwise be impossible. It also allows states to modulate their commitments by choosing more or less "serious" forms of commitment. A treaty, for example, is recognized to be a greater commitment, all else equal, than a soft law agreement. The reputational signal the treaty provides is stronger both because it communicates the state's intent to be bound and because it triggers a legal obligation to comply under both the Vienna Convention on the Law of Treaties and customary international law.

But adopting a formal treaty is not the only way for states to increase the credibility of their commitments. In their search for credibility, states have a range of other options with respect to the form of an agreement. These include whether to enter into a formal treaty or some form of soft law agreement; whether to include some form of dispute resolution or omit it entirely; whether to provide for monitoring procedures; whether to permit or forbid reservations; whether to provide liberal exit and escape clauses; and so on.

Each of these formal design elements can affect the seriousness of the commitment. More thorough monitoring practices, for example, make defection less likely because they increase the risk of exposure. This, in turn, makes the original commitment more credible. Mandatory dispute resolution provisions provide a neutral forum before which alleged violations can be proved (or disproved). This makes the violation more transparent both to the affected parties and to other states. More generous provisions governing the use of reservations, exit, and escape make it more likely that one or both parties will be able to avoid performance and, therefore, reduces the credibility of the promise to perform.[13]

With so many ways to alter the credibility of their commitments, it is something of a puzzle that states are not more aggressive in their use of formal design elements to increase their commitment. Even a casual observer of international law would notice that states often enter into soft law rather than hard law agreements, and that agreements rarely provide for mandatory dispute resolution. Monitoring provisions are often very modest and certainly less than one might expect from states attempting to equate the marginal cost of monitoring with its marginal benefit. States also often create agreements that allow for reservations and provide flexibility in the form of liberal exit and escape clauses.

Why would states behave in this way while at the same time being concerned about their ability to make credible commitments? If the inability to make credible commitments is a fundamental problem for international cooperation, why don't states at least do everything that they can to increase the credibility of their agreements?

An exchange of promises is only valuable to the extent that it binds the parties and gives each state confidence that the other states will perform as promised. An agreement that constrains state behavior more effectively, then, should have greater value. This point can be clarified with an analogy to domestic contracts. The parties to a contract typically want to commit themselves to perform and they rely on the domestic legal system to make their promises credible. States, of course, have no analogous enforcement system to rely on. This makes states much less able to commit in a credible fashion. Indeed, the inability to commit lies at the heart of many critiques of international law and much of international law scholarship. The implied assumption in all of these discussions is that a mechanism through which states could make credible and binding promises would be used by states and would be valuable to the international system. But if this is so, why do states not at least use the formal design elements that they have to maximize their commitments?[14]

This mystery is reinforced if one considers a simple contracting model. Once states agree on the optimal substantive terms in an agreement (i.e., those that maximize their joint payoffs), conventional bargaining theory predicts that they will want to commit to perform consistently with that agreement. Having all sides commit to the substantive terms of the agreement allows the parties to rely on one another's performance and to achieve the anticipated joint gains. The ability to commit oneself is essential for contracting to work.

The analysis that follows presents an explanation of why states sometimes resist using formal design elements to maximize the credibility of their agreements. The basic claim is that although increased credibility leads to higher compliance rates, which is good, it also increases the costs the parties face in the event of a violation. This cost is taken into account by the parties when they enter into the agreement and may discourage them from increasing the credibility of the agreement.

The Problem with Flexibility

To the extent the international law and international relations literature addresses the general question of why states do not embrace existing tools to enhance the credibility of their commitments, it argues that states sometimes prefer less binding or less credible commitments because they value the flexibility these less stringent obligations provide. The clearest presentation of these views is in the context of the choice between hard and soft law (Abbott and Snidal 2000, Lipson 1991). The basic notion is that weaker or less binding commitments give states greater flexibility in performance, which is desirable because it helps states to deal with an uncertain world, reduces the costs of termination or abandonment, and makes renegotiation easier. In discussing exit clauses, Helfer argues that "[d]enunciation clauses reduce uncertainty by giving states a low cost exit option if an agreement turns out badly" (2005, p. 1599). A variation of the flexibility argument is sometimes used to explain why international agreements so rarely provide for mandatory dispute resolution. The argument here is that states prefer to retain control over disputes rather than turn them over to a third-party adjudicator (Rovine 1976).[15]

These arguments, however, look only at the impact of flexibility on a party that wants to avoid what would otherwise be its obligation. What is needed is an assessment of the impact of flexibility on the value of the agreement at the time it is signed. When a state joins an agreement, of course, it normally wants its own obligations to be flexible. But it also wants the obligations of other parties to be inflexible—allowing it to rely on the performance of others to the maximum extent possible. The whole point of an agreement, after all, is to establish a set of promised behaviors. At some point, additional flexibility must increase the risk facing states because there is no discipline on the behavior of others. Even if one assumes risk aversion, then, it is not at all clear that greater flexibility with respect to compliance is better for the parties.

At the time of negotiating the treaty, the parties simply want to identify and implement (to the extent possible) an efficient set of incentives with respect to performance of the treaty's substantive obligations. The theory of breach in the contracts literature teaches us that an efficient agreement compels performance unless the joint costs of performance outweigh the joint benefits. This insight from contracts can be fruitfully applied to international agreements as long as we are careful to keep in mind the differences between the two contexts. In the international context, the lesson is that the parties will select an optimal set of terms in their agreements. This includes both the substantive content of the agreement and the associated matters of form. With respect to the nonsubstantive terms, the parties will seek to prevent breach, unless the joint costs of breach are less than the joint costs of compliance.

Recall the prior example of Canada and the United States negotiating an environmental agreement. The states will negotiate with respect to the substantive terms of the agreement and, subject to transaction costs, will maximize the value of the agreement. The final terms will differ from the preferred level of environmental protection of one and possibly both states, but no other agreement will be able (even with available transfers) to make both parties better off.

In the domestic context (or at least in an idealized version of the domestic context), the story ends at this point. It is assumed that once an agreement is reached, the parties will enter into a binding legal contract that reflects that agreement. This contract would reflect an efficient form of commitment and enforcement. The parties would rely on the court—or, perhaps, some form of arbitration—to resolve disputes, breaches would lead to efficient damages, and monitoring would be provided up to the point where the marginal cost of monitoring is equal to its marginal benefit.

In the international context, however, agreement on the substantive terms of an agreement is only a first step. The parties must then decide on a series of issues related to the form of the agreement. To begin with, it is clear that even commitment to a formal treaty is not analogous to entering into a contract in domestic law. Though both are said to be "binding" on the parties, a treaty provides a good deal less in terms of enforcement and, therefore, credibility. Even if one includes mandatory dispute resolution, there is no authority available to compel compliance with court decisions. This fundamental and well-known problem of enforcement in international law suggests that it is simply not possible for states to secure optimal levels of compliance through the use of existing international law forms of agreement. As far as I am aware, this is a consensus view among international legal scholars and analysts.

Given this problem of enforcement, a standard negotiating model would expect states to do everything they can to increase the credibility of their commitments. Notice how this account of state behavior undermines the argument that states seek flexibility. At the time of entering into an agreement, all states seek an efficient agreement. As such, they want commitments to be binding and enforced in an efficient fashion.

As I will discuss more fully, this suggests that states should want less rather than more flexibility in their agreements.

Fear of Losing

There is also an argument in the literature that states prefer to avoid dispute resolution because they fear losing (Rovine 1976). A similar argument could be made about monitoring (they fear being identified as being in violation). To be coherent, this argument must rely on an assumption that states are risk averse. Otherwise, there is no reason why they would want to avoid the identification of violating (or the absolution of those not in violation). Assuming risk aversion on the part of states with respect to international legal obligations, however, is inappropriate, as discussed earlier. The fear-of-losing argument, then, is not persuasive.

Credibility Can Be Costly

If state behavior cannot be explained with reference to a desire for flexibility or a fear of losing, some alternative is needed to explain the fact that states frequently enter into soft law agreements, rarely include mandatory dispute resolution or sanctions, often provide weak monitoring provisions (or omit them entirely), frequently include liberal escape and exit clauses, and allow significant reservations. All of these formal design elements serve to reduce the credibility of the commitments made by the parties to the agreement.

The effect of such choices is to create agreements in which the consequences of violation are weaker than conventional theories of bargaining and negotiation predict. It is true, of course, that a violation of international law may lead to reputational sanctions, reciprocal withdrawal of compliance, or retaliation, but there is no reason to think that these mechanisms are sufficient to generate an efficient level of compliance. As already discussed, reputational sanctions are limited in magnitude, many agreements cannot be sustained by threats of reciprocal noncompliance, and retaliation is costly to the retaliating states and subject to significant free-rider problems in multilateral contexts.

If flexibility fails to explain the form of international agreements, what else might be at work? The assumption that states are rational implies that the decision to design agreements featuring less, rather than more, credible commitments is value maximizing for the parties. The task, then, is to identify reasons why, contrary to the bargaining theory discussed earlier, a weaker commitment can leave the parties better off than would a stronger commitment.

To account for state behavior in this context, it is necessary to recognize not only that domestic enforcement schemes are more effective than international ones but also that the cost of enforcement, as measured by the parties, is normally higher in the international context than in the domestic context. The standard form of enforcement in domestic disputes is money damages paid from the violating party to the injured party. This transfer has a zero-sum character. What is lost by one is gained by the other. When the parties enter into a contract, and when they consider the impact of damages on the overall value of the agreement, they need only consider the impact of the damages rules on compliance—higher damages generate a greater probability of compliance. Because the damages themselves take the form of a zero-sum transfer, they need not worry about how the payment of such damages affects the expected value of the agreement.

As already mentioned, however, money damages are rarely used in the international arena. The consequences of a violation consist instead of reputational loss, reciprocal withdrawal of compliance, or retaliation. These sanctions do not have a zero-sum character. This is obviously true in the case of retaliation, which is costly to both parties. The reciprocal withdrawal of compliance is also negative sum, as evidenced by the fact that the parties were prepared to enter into the agreement in the first place. That both parties consented to the agreement indicates that each was better off with mutual compliance rather than mutual defection, and this in turn means that the cost of performance by one state is smaller than the benefit thereby conferred on the other state. When the nonviolating state withdraws its own compliance, this imposes a cost on the violating state that exceeds the benefit that nonperformance confers on the nonviolating state. For the parties taken together, then, the effect is a net loss. This leaves reputational sanctions, whose negative-sum character I discussed in chapters 2 and 3. Reputational losses to one party are not offset by gains to the other parties to an agreement.

From the perspective of the parties when they negotiate an agreement, then, each of these possible consequences has two effects. First, it has the beneficial effect of increasing the probability of compliance (because it imposes a cost on violators). Second, it imposes a cost on the violating party that is not captured by the other parties to the agreement (i.e., it is negative sum). The second feature represents a cost to the parties in the sense that it reduces the overall value of the agreement. If this cost is large enough, it may motivate states to select formal design elements that reduce rather than enhance the credibility of their commitments. Such behavior would be consistent with rational states maximizing the value of their agreement.

To illustrate the trade-off between credibility and costly sanctions, consider the development of the Universal Declaration of Human Rights (UDHR). Like other examples used in the book, a complex story could be told here, and the foregoing analysis certainly does not explain it all. The example does, however, help to illustrate the balance between stronger and weaker forms of commitment. The UN General Assembly adopted the UDHR in 1948. While it was being drafted, there was considerable disagreement about whether it was to be a formal treaty or convention (perhaps with some form of implementation attached) or simply a declaration of principles. The states involved invested considerable time and energy on this question of form. Though some visions of what was termed an international bill of rights were initially more ambitious, it eventually became clear that the two options were a binding treaty, without enforcement mechanisms beyond perhaps reporting obligations, and a nonbinding declaration.

Given the weakness of international law, and the dramatic evidence of its failure provided by World War II, one might have expected all states to be strong proponents of the most binding form of declaration. If, after all, international law was to contribute to the avoidance of future wars and the prevention of atrocities such as the Holocaust, it would need to be given the strongest possible footing. Yet some countries, including the United States and the Soviet Union, favored a nonbinding declaration rather than a treaty. Why would the two superpowers take the view that a nonbinding declaration is desirable (as opposed to no agreement at all), but a treaty is less so? It cannot be that they simply wished to avoid any commitment, since they could have instead worked against the entire exercise, and they did not.[16] Certainly the United States was well positioned to undermine the drafting negotiations if it wanted to. But the United States was in fact in strong support of the project, as evidenced by the fact that Eleanor Roosevelt chaired the Commission on Human Rights that drafted the declaration.[17]

Though the United States supported a declaration, it was unwilling to go as far as a formal treaty that would subject it (and all other states) to legal obligations. These obligations would not include enforcement mechanisms, but the United States nevertheless resisted the notion of a binding obligation. What sort of loss concerned the United States if it were to commit to a treaty? Certainly it could not have been concerned about enforcement through some formal process, because no such process was envisioned. One could imagine retaliation or reciprocal noncompliance by others, though these sanctions work poorly in a multilateral context. What remains is a reputational concern.[18]

The negotiating states had to balance the benefit of a formal treaty—greater compliance—against its cost: greater reputational loss in the event of a violation. This trade-off between compliance and a non-zero-sum sanction led to the adoption of a nonbinding declaration. Not all states were in agreement on the form of the agreement, of course. Many states, including most of the smaller states that were UN members, the United Kingdom, and Australia, supported a treaty. These states, apparently, were unable to offer the United States, the Soviet Union, and other states that preferred a declaration sufficient compensation to induce them to accept a treaty.

A similar analysis helps to explain why agreements often avoid other credibility-enhancing design elements. For example, the CEDAW established a "Committee on the Elimination of Discrimination against Women" but that committee is primarily charged with reviewing and commenting on self-reporting (a common if unreliable form of monitoring in human rights agreements) by state parties. Though a much more rigorous and effective monitoring function could be imagined, nothing more was provided. The CEDAW does include a mandatory dispute resolution provision in article 29, but the CEDAW also explicitly provides that members may opt out of it, as many countries have done.

Another way the CEDAW could have been drafted to increase the extent to which states committed themselves to the norms of the agreement would have been to prohibit or limit the use of reservations, but it failed to do so. It allows any reservation that is consistent with the rules of the Vienna Convention on the Law of Treaties, which means any reservation that is not "incompatible with the object and purpose of the present Convention" (art. 28[1]).

On the other hand, the CEDAW does not provide an escape clause or an explicit exit clause. The ability to escape the obligations of the Convention temporarily would further reduce the extent to which states are bound. The same would be true if the Convention provided for easy exit from the treaty. In the case of the CEDAW, it seems that the parties concluded that the compliance consequences of a liberal escape or exit clause outweighed the expected reputational cost of omitting them. That is, including such clauses might have avoided the reputational costs to a violating state, but this savings was not enough to persuade the parties to give up the compliance benefit of omitting those clauses.

Soft Law

The category of "soft law" is the subject of a great deal of writing in international law. On a continuum, soft law lies somewhere between "hard law," that is, treaties and customary international law, and purely political agreements that lack any legal component.

As mentioned earlier, a discussion of soft law requires some clarification of the term. The international law literature defines soft law in at least two different ways. At times the term is used to mean binding agreements that are vague, imprecise, or weak (Abbott and Snidal 2000). Such agreements are clearly "international law" in every sense, but are thought to be less effective than more precise forms of international law.

The more common use of the term refers to international promises, obligations, or commitments that are not "binding" under international law. That is, they do not qualify as treaties, custom, or general principles of law. The term, then, is used to refer to a residual category of norms possessing some legal characteristics but not traditionally defined as international law. Examples abound. The Basel Accord on capital adequacy, the 1975 Helsinki Final Act, and the UDHR are just three well-known examples. This is the sense in which I use the term "soft law" here.

Some authors go so far as to deny the relevance of soft law, arguing, for example, that the "sublegal obligations are neither soft law nor hard law: they are simply not law at all" (Weil 1983, p. 414–415 n. 7).[19] As a formal doctrinal matter, this may be correct in the sense that a state's promise either meets the definition of "international law" or it does not. The most authoritative list of sources of international law, the Statute of the ICJ, does not include international agreements that fall short of treaties. Soft law promises might be relevant as evidence of customary international law, but they do not themselves create a legal obligation.

However, this formalistic approach is of little use for this study. International law and international commitments affect state behavior through several channels, and it is often the case that there is no tribunal with jurisdiction over a dispute. Furthermore, there is no doubt that states find it useful to enter into agreements that fall short of formal treaties. To simply dismiss these on the grounds that they do not fit the traditional definition of law does not advance our understanding of these instruments or of international law. Put another way, this doctrinal approach cannot offer an explanation for why soft law agreements exist at all, and does not provide any guidance on how one should view them.

This chapter has already presented reasons states might wish to enter into soft law agreements rather than formal treaties. Those reasons have implications for the way soft law agreements should be viewed. One such implication is that there is no reason to view soft law agreements as different in kind from treaties. The decision to enter into an agreement is motivated in both cases by a desire to address some sort of cooperative problem. The exchange of commitments allows each party to anticipate and rely on the behavior of other parties. Though soft law agreements will normally represent a weaker form of commitment, they should be analyzed and understood in essentially the same way as treaties. One might argue that the "binding" nature of treaties differentiates them from soft law in one important way—they can be interpreted and enforced before international adjudicatory bodies. While it is generally true that soft law agreements are not subject to dispute resolution procedures, it need not be so in principle. That is, one could imagine a soft law agreement that included procedures for identifying states that have failed to live up to the terms of the agreement. Indeed, the Inter-American Court of Human Rights and the Inter-American Commission on Human Rights interpret the American Declaration on the Rights and Duties of Man to be a binding obligation of members of the Organization of American States, notwithstanding the fact that the Declaration is a soft law instrument.[20] While some may view this as an example of overreaching by international tribunals (the declaration itself does not indicate that it is judiciable), it also demonstrates that there is nothing inherent in soft law agreements that prevents a tribunal from reviewing compliance behavior. Strictly speaking, one could not describe the failure to honor that commitment as a violation of "law," and the ICJ may not be able to hear the case (because its "function is to decide in accordance with international law" (ICJ Statute, article 38) and its statute does not provide for the application of soft law rules), but states could obviously set up some other forum to hear that case.

Because states make decisions about soft and hard law on the basis of the costs and benefits of each, it is more productive to view this as one of the choices states make in the course of negotiating an agreement. In essence, they can choose to downgrade the level of commitment and the credibility of their promises by entering into a soft law agreement rather than a treaty. The analysis of international treaties, therefore, is incomplete if it does not take into account the fact that soft law is always available as an alternative.

Rather than viewing treaties and soft law as distinct legal structures, one should view them as different points on a spectrum of commitment. It is true that only treaties deliver a "legal" commitment, but soft law agreements deliver a commitment nonetheless. Both types of agreement affect states' incentives, because both affect the relevant payoffs. A failure to comply with the provisions of soft law can, just as is the case for treaties, lead to reputational harm, reciprocal noncompliance, and retaliation. The incentive may be weaker (all else equal) for soft law, but the basic mechanism encouraging compliance is the same. This helps to explain why soft law agreements can sometimes be very effective and sometimes largely ineffective. Though the soft law form is weaker than the treaty form, it is only one relevant factor. Other factors, including other matters of form and substance, also affect the impact of the agreement. The other factors might cause the agreement to have a significant compliance pull, despite the fact that it is not a formal treaty.

The spectrum of commitment a rational choice approach suggests offers a more coherent view of international law than the one that most writing on international law provides. This view makes clear that states are not making discrete, all-or-nothing choice about the force of their commitments. Instead, they are selecting a location on this spectrum that balances the various costs and benefits (discussed throughout this chapter) they face when they enter into an agreement.

By way of illustration, consider two agreements made between the United States and the Soviet Union, both of which addressed matters of security and the arms race. There is no doubt that the ABM Treaty was, in every sense, international law. As such it was said to be "binding" on the parties. The Helsinki Final Act (which also included other states) was not "law" in this sense. It was not a treaty and, therefore, was not binding under conventional definitions of international law. Despite these differences, both were important agreements, and it is generally believed that both affected states' behavior. To treat these agreements as entirely different in their impact seems absurd—they addressed broadly the same subject matter, featured the same parties, and were motivated by similar concerns (security and peace). If one is interested in knowing how the United States and the Soviet Union sought to cooperate, it is clear that an understanding of both forms of agreement is essential.

Once the relationship between hard and soft law is understood, it is natural to ask what causes states to choose one form over the other. The prior discussion of the relationship between non-zero-sum sanctions and the choice of formal design elements is relevant to the choice between a treaty and soft law alternatives, but other factors also play an important role in that decision.

Perhaps the most important influences on the decision are the domestic law implications of selecting a treaty. This is certainly the most conventional account of the choice between hard and soft law, and is surely an important influence on the decision. The basic argument proceeds as follows. Soft law is attractive to states because it requires less domestic process than do treaties. It does not require ratification and so can be reached more quickly and is more fully within the control of the executive. When speed is of the essence, then, or when the executive prefers to avoid the legislature (more on this later), soft law may be preferred (Lipson 1991). Similarly, soft law may be attractive when the executive prefers to retain the greatest possible authority to renegotiate the terms of the agreement.

If one accepts this explanation for the use of soft law, however, another puzzle arises. The explanation implicitly assumes that states are unable to enter into treaties without at least some domestic process, such as ratification. This assumption is not correct.

Article 11 of the Vienna Convention on the Law of Treaties makes it clear that as a matter of international law, ratification is not necessary for a state to be bound by a treaty. "The consent of a State to be bound by a treaty may be expressed by signature, exchange of instruments constituting a treaty, ratification, acceptance, approval or accession, or by any other means if so agreed."[21] Under international law, then, treaties do not require ratification. There may, of course, be domestic law requirements that affect a state's ability to enter into treaties. In the United States, for example, the Constitution gives the president the authority to make treaties, but requires that "two thirds of the Senators present concur" (U.S. Constitution, art. II). This constitutional provision, however, is understood to define the word "treaties" differently from how it is defined internationally. The president is permitted, under the laws of the United States, to enter into "congressional-executive agreements" or "sole-executive agreements" that are considered treaties under international law. For at least some agreements, then, it is possible for the president of the United States to enter into an agreement that is a treaty under international law but that falls short of that definition under American law.

The key point here is that international law does not require that treaties be ratified. The signature of a treaty can, by itself, be sufficient to bind a state. The triggering of domestic legal process, then, is done by either domestic laws that limit the ability of the executive to enter certain kinds of international agreements or the desire of the parties to require ratification before the treaty enters into force.

This leads to the question of why leaders would ever choose to condition the entry into force of an agreement on some domestic process. Several possibilities suggest themselves. First, the executive branch may wish to increase the legislature's investment in the agreement, and a treaty may serve that purpose (Abbott and Snidal 2000).[22] Second, enlisting the legislature in the ratification process may serve a valuable signaling function. By requiring ratification, the parties to a treaty signal to one another that there is relatively strong domestic support for the agreement and, therefore, the probability of compliance is presumably greater (Martin 2003). Finally, many international agreements require domestic action. They may, for example, require implementing legislation or repeal of some existing rule. Given that the executive has to seek support from the legislature in any event, the additional cost of ratifying a treaty may be small. If this is true, one would expect soft law to be more common in agreements that do not require legislative participation, as is the case for at least several areas in which the United States has entered into such agreements. Soft law agreements in antirust, securities, and banking, for example, have been entered into by the United States without direct congressional participation.

Finally, soft law agreements may represent a balancing of domestic interests that serves the interests of decision-makers. Domestic groups interested in international engagement and cooperation will typically prefer a treaty to soft law, all else equal, because the former is a stronger commitment than the latter. Other domestic groups, however, may prefer no agreement at all. A soft law agreement may allow political leaders to satisfy the demands of the first group without unduly alienating the second. Certain constellations of domestic interest groups, then, make a soft law arrangement the preferred outcome for domestic leaders.

Reservations, Escape, and Exit

Understanding Reservations, Escape, and Exit

When states design international agreements, they often include one or more mechanisms through which parties, under certain conditions, are able to avoid their obligations either temporarily or permanently. The three most important such tools are reservations, escape clauses, and exit clauses. Each of these tools serves to reduce the overall legal burden imposed by an agreement. Reservations except a state from some portion of what would otherwise be its obligations; escape clauses suspend some or all obligations temporarily; exit clauses allow a permanent extinguishing of the obligation (Helfer 2005; Rosendorff and Milner 2001; Swaine 2003). The easier it is to exercise these clauses, the more the effective obligations of states are reduced.

For example, article 98 of the Rome Statute of the International Criminal Court provides that

> [t]he Court may not proceed with a request for surrender which would require the requested State to act inconsistently with its obligations under international agreements pursuant to which the consent of a sending State is required to surrender a person of that State to the Court, unless the Court can first obtain the cooperation of the sending State for the giving of consent for the surrender.[23]

In other words, a state can opt out of its obligations under the Rome Statute with respect to another state's citizens through a bilateral agreement with the other state. The United States has actively sought to conclude so-called Article 98 agreements (i.e., induce other states to lower their commitment level under the Rome Statute with respect to U.S. citizens) with a variety of states in order to reduce the exposure of U.S. citizens abroad (Helfer 2005). Reservations also serve to reduce the demands that agreements place on states by establishing conditions under which a state is exempt from some or all obligations or providing that certain obligations do not apply at all. In practice, reservations may dramatically curtail the impact of a treaty with stringent obligations. Syria, for example, is a party to the CEDAW but acceded to it subject to the reservation that Syria not be bound by provisions that are "incompatible with the provisions of Islamic Shariah."[24] Given the subject matter of the agreement, this reservation seems certain to amount to a significant opting out from the treaty's obligations.

To an international law skeptic, reservations, escape clauses, and exit clauses are unnecessary. After all, any agreement can be breached, terminated, or renegotiated at any time by either party, and there is, or course, no coercive scheme to sanction such conduct. The doctrinal rules of international law, on the other hand, make such clauses important. Article 56 of the Vienna Convention on the Law of Treaties, for example, states that a party is normally unable to exit a treaty that does not contain a termination clause.

The truth lies somewhere between these two extreme positions. It is correct to note that states are never truly locked into an agreement. As a practical matter, sovereign states are able to denounce a treaty and cease performing at any time, regardless of the legal allocation of rights. In 1997, for example, North Korea announced its intention to withdraw from the ICCPR, despite the fact that the treaty contains no provision for withdrawal and the Vienna Convention on the Law of Treaties states that in such a circumstance states are not able to withdraw from a treaty.[25] Similarly, Indonesia notified the UN on January 20, 1965, that it intended to withdraw from that organization, despite the lack of authorization for withdrawal in the UN Charter. (On September 19, 1966, Indonesia announced its intention to resume membership and participation in the UN.) In this sense, every agreement includes an implicit and nonderogable exit clause. States can also suspend their performance (as they would under an escape clause) as long as they can discourage other parties to the agreement from abrogating the agreement in response. Finally, even under traditional international law rules it is always possible to terminate or amend an agreement if all parties agree. There are, therefore, unavoidable mechanisms for states to adjust the bargain either unilaterally or collectively.

That states can unilaterally change the terms of the agreement, however, does not mean that they can do so costlessly. That agreements often include explicit exit and escape clauses demonstrates that these provisions deliver some value beyond what would be present without them. They indicate that many agreements are more valuable to states if they allow for temporary or permanent suspension of obligations under specified conditions.

Why might these additional provisions add value relative to the options of renegotiation or unilateral defection? Two main reasons suggest themselves. First, reservations, exit clauses, and escape clauses may increase the total value of an agreement by encouraging nonperformance in instances where performance would be inefficient. Second, such provisions may serve to reduce the cost to the parties in instances where nonperformance is inevitable. "Legalizing" nonperformance prevents negative-sum sanctions from being imposed. I will consider each of these explanations in turn.

Some exit and escape clauses are explained by states' efforts to identify substantive terms that maximize the value of the agreement. That is, the value-maximizing substantive terms may include promises that are contingent on some set of events or that are suspended in certain situations. For example, the UN Convention on the Law of the Sea (UNCLOS) provides that ships of all states enjoy the right of innocent passage through territorial waters.[26] Consider for a moment the negotiation dynamic that leads to this result. Coastal states have an interest in preserving as much control over their territorial waters as possible. Maritime states, on the other hand, have an interest in the greatest possible freedom on the seas. All states have an interest in reaching some form of agreement that allows for the peaceful and orderly movement of ships. In the course of negotiations, coastal states are prepared to consent to the right of innocent passage in exchange for some other concession, such as, for example, restrictions on what qualifies as innocent passage. This point of agreement comes about because the right of passage is worth more to maritime states than the right to exclude is worth to coastal states. This can be seen by imagining a state that is both a maritime and a coastal state (as are many key states). As a coastal state, there is an interest in exclusion, but as a maritime state there is an interest in free passage. The state will agree to a rule of innocent passage if that right is worth more to it than the right to exclude. Because states are collectively attempting to maximize the value of the agreement, they carry out a similar analysis—they will agree to a right to innocent passage if that has more value than the right to exclude.

The right to passage is not absolute, however. A coastal state is entitled to suspend that right temporarily for the protection of its security.[27] This provision can be described as an escape clause—if granting innocent passage generates a threat to the security of the coastal state, it can avoid its obligation. The presence of this escape clause is easy to explain as part of the effort to maximize the total value of the agreement's substantive terms. That is, it seems likely that coastal states would place a value on the ability to exclude on security grounds that exceeds maritime states' interest in passage. This escape clause, then, is fully consistent with what we would expect from parties negotiating an agreement.

A similar analysis could be conducted for reservations and exit clauses. Reservations may simply be a convenient way to tailor an agreement to the needs of individual states without cumbersome negotiations, and exit clauses provide a way for states to terminate an international obligation without suffering the costs of breach.[28]

Sykes (1991) offers a public-choice explanation for the escape clause present in the GATT that resembles the argument advanced here, but that also considers the costs and benefits generated by domestic politics. He argues that the escape clause of the GATT (article XIX) maximizes the expected payoffs to the parties by allowing breach when the cost of compliance is greater to the parties than the cost of breach. Sykes's analysis of the relevant costs focuses on the costs to the political decision-makers. He argues that the GATT escape clause requirements— increased imports and serious injury (or threat thereof) to domestic industries—identify circumstances in which trade obligations are likely to impose large political costs on the importing state and violation is likely to impose only small costs on the exporting state. Import competing groups in the importing state will value protection the most when they are facing financial hardship, and the injury requirement identifies that circumstance. Exporting groups in the exporting state are likely to tolerate protection abroad when their exports are increasing, as provided for by the increased imports requirement. The escape clause, Sykes argues, carves out circumstances in which escape from the obligations of the GATT yields a net gain to the parties.

Sykes presents his theory in the context of the GATT, but it could be applied in a similar way elsewhere. The challenge in applying the theory to other agreements would be to identify the political costs and benefits in the relevant context to determine whether they offer a plausible explanation of a particular escape clause. Sykes' theory relies on costs and benefits felt by political leaders. This is in contrast to the approach I use in most of this book, which treats states as unitary actors. The two approaches can be reconciled if one assumes that when we refer to the "preferences of the state" what we mean are the preferences of those who make the relevant decisions.

In some contexts, however, reservations, escape clauses, and exit clauses are difficult to explain with reference to the value-maximizing conditions of performance. Members of the WTO, for instance, can ban the importation of products that represent a threat to plant, animal, or human health. The agreement, combined with the jurisprudence of the WTO's dispute resolution system, further provides that decisions about the level of risk a state will tolerate and judgments about the validity of science are left, to a considerable degree, in the hands of states and are generally not reviewed by the dispute resolution organs of the WTO. There is little doubt that the right to exclude unsafe products is consistent with maximizing the value of the agreement—the exclusion of such products will normally be worth more to an importing state than the sale of such products will be to an exporting state. Leaving judgments about risk and science in the hands of individual states, however, is more difficult to explain in this way. Giving that much discretion to states seems to open the door to abuse and protectionism—forms of inefficient nonperformance of the primary WTO obligations. In terms of the preferred substantive rules, it seems to make more sense to have a review of such decisions, either by WTO panels and the WTO's Appellate Body or by competent panels of experts, and have trade policy turn on those decisions.

Consider how this sort of delegation of policy decisions would play out, however. Specifically, think about the recently decided case regarding the importation of genetically modified organisms (GMOs) into Europe. Europe established significant restrictions on the importation of such products, citing health concerns. The United States, Canada, and Argentina complained about these rules at the WTO. As the rules of trade currently stand, there is quite modest review of the scientific judgments made by European authorities. Suppose, however, the inquiry was more detailed. Suppose the WTO was charged with forming its own judgment regarding the safety of these products. And suppose that, like the United States, the WTO concluded that they were safe and must be admitted. What would happen then? Most likely, Europe would continue to resist the importation of the products. Assuming that European concerns about health are legitimate (even if amplified by the interests of the agricultural industry), it is hard to imagine that a WTO decision would be sufficient to open the borders. It seems much more likely that Europe would accept WTO sanctions rather than open its markets to products it perceives to be dangerous. Indeed, that is exactly what happened in the analogous *Beef Hormones* case, in which, despite having lost at the WTO in 1998 and despite sanctions having been imposed by the United States and Canada, Europe has refused to admit the beef in question.

A WTO ruling followed by noncompliance and the imposition of sanctions serves only to reduce trade flows. Instead of a single trade barrier (the European ban, in the example given), there are two (the European ban and the trade sanctions imposed by the complaining parties). If one could identify instances in which there will be noncompliance, it is sensible to exempt those instances from the relevant rule—to create an escape clause.

So even though the first best situation might be compliance, there are times when that is not possible because the available sanctions for a violation provide insufficient incentives for the violating party to change its behavior. The second best outcome in that situation is to declare the relevant behavior to be legal because doing so avoids the negative-sum sanctions that would follow a violation.

This argument is really the same as the one made earlier in this chapter. The inclusion of reservations, escape clauses, and exit clauses has two effects. First, it reduces the overall level of compliance by allowing noncompliance to take place (under certain conditions) at lower cost. This may be costly to the parties if compliance in those situations is preferred to noncompliance. Second, it reduces the total costs imposed in the event of noncompliance. This increases the value of the agreement in those instances where there would be noncompliance with or without the reservation, escape clause, or exit clause. In drafting an agreement, then, states face a trade-off between increased compliance and reduced costs in the event of noncompliance. In some instances, this will provide them with a reason to permit reservations or include exit and escape clauses.

Reservations, Exit, Escape, and Participation

Though it is commonly argued that reservations, exit clauses, and escape clauses increase states' willingness to enter into agreements (Helfer 2005), that need not be true. Excessive use of these design elements would reduce the total value of the agreement and, therefore, the incentive of (at least some) potential signatories to join. It is true that reducing a state's commitment normally makes it more attractive for that state to join, but the same action also reduces the benefits the agreement offers to all other participants, thereby reducing their incentive to join. The presence of a liberal exit or escape provision in a treaty may be attractive to states because it gives them the option of avoiding the obligations of the treaty (temporarily or permanently) if they later conclude that the treaty or some aspect of it does not serve their interests. But the same provision may also dissuade a state from joining because it fears that others will exit the regime and attempt to free ride on the policies of those that remain.

Another problem is that exit clauses make it more difficult for states to rely on the treaty and the behavior of other states. If exit allows other states to avoid their obligations, it makes less sense to invest in reliance on the treaty remaining in force. A state may be reluctant to join a treaty if it fears that its treaty partners will decide to exit after it has made wholesale changes to its environmental laws and regulations.

The simple but poorly understood point is that reducing the obligations of one party will normally have a negative impact on other parties to the agreement. The impact of exit, escape, and termination provisions on the willingness of states to sign, then, will differ from agreement to agreement, depending on whether they increase or decrease the value of the agreement to the potential parties.

Permitting and Prohibiting Reservations

Reservations differ from escape and exit clauses in one important respect. A state typically submits its reservations after the final version of the treaty has been negotiated. Permitting a state to introduce a reservation in this way gives it a final opportunity to avoid any part of the obligation that it does not like. The rules on reservations (arts. 19–23, Vienna Convention on the Law of Treaties) give each state the opportunity to make take-it-or-leave it amendments to the treaty. However, this ability to make reservations is or can be limited in a number of ways. First, the treaty itself may prohibit reservations. Such is the case in the Rome Statute of the International Criminal Court, which states in article 120 that "[n]o reservations may be made to this Statute."[29] Second, reservations are not permitted if they are "incompatible with the object and purpose of the treaty" (Vienna Convention on the Law of Treaties, art. 19.c). Third, other parties to the treaty are free to accept or reject each reservation (with silence being construed as acceptance).[30] If a state objects to a reservation, the relevant provisions of the treaty do not apply as between the reserving and the objecting party, unless the objecting party also objects to the entry into force of the treaty as between these two states, in which case the treaty does not bind either of them with respect to the other.[31] Finally, all of these rules are default rules, so the parties to an agreement can, if they choose, create some alternative regime to govern the use of reservations.

The benefit of allowing reservations in this way is that it allows states to negotiate multilateral treaties that are tailored to states' individual needs without cumbersome negotiations about each state's detailed demands. There may also be informational benefits from permitting states to make reservations (Helfer 2006; Swaine 2006). A reservation tells other states that they should not rely on the reserving state's compliance with a specific obligation. The obvious problem is that reservations allow states to opt out of portions of the treaty. Doing so may upset the balance of concession included in the agreement. Ultimately, the trade-off between the costs and benefits of allowing reservations is something the states involved can evaluate. They can then have reservations governed by the rules they prefer. We remain, however, unable to anticipate with any confidence when reservations will be permitted and when they will be forbidden.

The Interaction of Form and Substance

Trade-offs between Form and Substance

It is useful to distinguish between the form and substance of an agreement to help isolate and understand specific features of international agreements. That is what this chapter has done up to this point.

Ultimately, however, there is no avoiding the fact that questions of form and substance interact in important ways. I have alluded to that interaction several times already, and it is now time to confront it head-on.

To get a sense of how form and substance affect one another, consider the following stylized description of how states use international agreements to resolve cooperative problems. Imagine that a group of states faces a multilateral prisoner's dilemma. For concreteness, assume they are concerned about global warming. All states agree that some cooperation is needed, but they disagree on how that cooperation will take place.

At the negotiation stage, each individual state is only concerned with how its own payoffs will be affected. An agreement impacts payoffs in two ways: (1) it imposes costly obligations on the state (e.g., reducing certain emissions), and (2) it affects the aggregate level of harmful emissions (which in turn impacts the state's payoffs). Notice that the state is not concerned with the particular content of the agreement as such. The state is only interested in the words written on the page to the extent that they impact its payoffs, either directly by imposing obligations on it, or indirectly through their effect on emissions. Every state, as it discusses the language to be included in the agreement, has in mind the relationship between that language and these two concerns.

Now consider what it means to say that states negotiate toward an agreement that maximizes their joint payoffs, subject to transaction costs. Suppose a draft agreement is proposed that includes a set of substantive obligations to reduce harmful emissions, as well as provisions governing the form of the agreement, including dispute resolution, whether the agreement will be a treaty, rules governing reservations, exit, and escape, monitoring, reporting and verification procedures, and perhaps some other provisions. An individual state is concerned about all of these variables, but again, only to the extent that they impact its payoffs. In other words, the state must evaluate how the various provisions affect its interests.

Now imagine that an alternative proposal is put forward. The new proposal provides for weaker substantive obligations (e.g., it increases the permitted levels of emissions) but also provides for stricter monitoring and dispute resolution. How will a state evaluate the appeal of this new proposal relative to the older draft? To begin with, one can consider each of the changes between the old and new proposals separately.

A weakening of the substantive provisions will, all else equal, reduce the burden on the state, but it will also reduce the impact of the agreement on global emissions. The stricter monitoring and dispute resolution provisions, however, will have the opposite effect. They will tend to improve compliance with whatever obligations are entered into and, therefore, increase the burden on the state and the impact of the agreement on global emissions. Without more information, there is no way to know if the new agreement will lead to a higher or lower global level of emissions and no way to know if it generates higher or lower payoffs for the state.

One possible outcome is that a lower level of obligation coupled with stricter monitoring and dispute resolution will lead to both a higher payoff for the state and a lower level of emissions worldwide. Furthermore, the new proposal may also be better for all other states (perhaps with some transfers). If so, the states will agree to replace the older draft with the new proposal.

The point here is that by adjusting the form of the agreement, the parties can affect their future behavior in a way that is analogous to changes in substantive provisions. Once this is recognized, it is clear that form and substance must be considered together when examining international agreements. Each of the variables present in an agreement affects, in one way or another, the payoffs of the parties and for that reason interacts with the other variables. Increasing the cost of a particular action, whether this is done through a change in the substantive provisions or through changes in the form of the agreement, makes that action less likely.

Nor is the trade-off only between matters of form and of substance. All of the features of an agreement can be traded off against one another. Commentators have examined some of the potential interactions. Raustiala (2005) focuses on the choices regarding hard and soft law; shallow and deep cooperation (reflecting the degree to which an agreement demands changes to behavior); and monitoring and enforcement provisions. Gilligan (2004) focuses on breadth and depth, pointing out that a trade-off between breadth and depth can be avoided by adjusting the substance of the agreement—specifically by allowing different parties to take on different obligations. A variation on Gilligan's insight is that more liberal use of reservations will weaken the trade-off between depth and breadth.

How Is the Trade-off Made?

Recognizing the basic trade-off between form and substance leads to a new question. How do states choose from the many possible combinations of formal and substantive design elements? How do they navigate the interaction of all the relevant variables? How do they choose a single agreement from the enormous (and perhaps infinite) number of potential ones?

The simple answer is that they weigh the costs and benefits of each design element and select a combination that provides the greatest possible net benefit. Thus, for example, states might agree to a higher level of substantive obligation but a lower level of dispute resolution if the former combination delivers the same benefits (e.g., the same level of global emissions and impact on each state) at lower cost (e.g., the costs in the event of a violation are lower).

A more complete answer considers how states weigh the various design elements and the inference we can draw from the decisions states make. Each design element has different advantages and disadvantages, costs and benefits. These will depend on the particulars of the situation, so it is difficult to say anything definitive at this level of generality. No single design yields the highest value agreement in all contexts. Recognizing that the various design elements offer different costs and benefits in different situations helps to explain why international agreements come in such a wide range of forms.

Viewing the construction of international agreements in this light, two basic strategies for drawing inferences from observed agreements suggest themselves.

The first is to group agreements into categories by subject matter and compare across categories. For example, international regulatory cooperation seems to be dominated by soft law agreements rather than treaties (e.g., Basel Accord, informal agreements on competition policy, memoranda of understanding on securities law) but cooperation in human rights is dominated by treaties (e.g., ICCPR, CAT, Genocide Convention).[32] This suggests that regulatory cooperation features a set of trade-offs that differ from those in human rights. Perhaps the incentive to defect is smaller in the former than in the latter, making the need for commitment less powerful. Alternatively, it may be that the domestic law implications of treaties are important in the human rights context but less so for regulatory matters.

What is clear is that some difference between these two areas has created distinct approaches to resolving problems of cooperation. One can imagine an enormous number of such comparisons. Few agreements seem to use formal dispute resolution, yet such provisions are relatively common in trade agreements. Investment agreements are almost exclusively bilateral (or occasionally multilateral but with very few states) while others, such as human rights agreements, often aspire to universal membership (or perhaps membership of all states in a region). This sort of comparative analysis promises to yield significant insights into the decisions states make when they create agreements.

Providing for private rights of action is another example. Such rights are quite rare in international agreements, and seem to be present in only certain kinds of agreements. The most conspicuous agreements that give private parties the right to seek legal remedies for violations are bilateral investment treaties (virtually all of which include a private right of action for investors) and some human rights agreements. Human rights agreements providing such a right include: the European Convention on Human Rights;[33] the Optional Protocol on Civil and Political Rights;[34] the Optional Protocol to the CEDAW;[35] the CAT;[36] the American Convention on Human Rights;[37] and the International Convention on the Elimination of all Forms of Racial Discrimination.[38] Of these, all but the European Convention and the American Convention make the provision of private rights of action optional for state parties.[39] Why might this be? One possibility is that these agreements are asymmetric, in the sense that the obligation represents a much more important de facto commitment for some of the parties than for others. In general, for example, Western democracies (among others) are already in compliance with human rights agreements and so can join without taking on significant obligations beyond what they are already doing. One conspicuous exception is the European Convention on Human Rights, which has created the most procedural rights (in terms of access and enforcement of judgments), thus permitting the development of substantive human rights case law. The Convention establishes the ECHR, which resolves hundreds of cases a year brought and submitted directly by individuals against states parties. Furthermore, judgments of the ECHR are forwarded to the Committee of Ministers of the Council of Europe (comprised of the foreign ministers of each member state), which monitors enforcement of the remedies the ECHR prescribes. Such remedies may include the modification of offending domestic laws to comply with the ECHR's interpretation of the rights granted by the Convention.[40]

Bilateral investment treaties (BITs) impose similarly asymmetric burdens. These treaties are predominantly signed between rich and poor states, and although both states promise to provide certain protections for investors, in practice it is the developing state that is entering into a significant commitment, because much more investment flows from north to south than from south to north. Developed states, then, take on little risk that they will have to defend themselves against a private party (though NAFTA has provided some well-known instances of private parties complaining about the actions of the United States and Canada). Developing states, on the other hand, expose themselves to a much larger risk of being a defendant in an international arbitration under a BIT.

Why would developing states expose themselves to a private right of action in this context and not in others? One possibility is that they are unable to resist the pressure from their developed treaty partners, which is especially strong in the investment area. Or it may be that developing states benefit more from the additional credibility that comes with the presence of private rights of action and so are happy to take on this obligation in an area where credibility is of great importance to their effort to attract foreign investment. A third possibility is that developing states have more modest power in interstate disputes and so lose less than their developed counterparts by allowing private rights of action to substitute for such disputes. There are no doubt other possible explanations that can be considered and evaluated using the general theoretical framework of this chapter and this book. These possibilities are, in principle, testable. One could investigate, for example, whether private rights of action are more common in subject–matter areas and between partners where pressure from developed parties is especially likely, how the need for credibility correlates to the presence of private rights of action, and whether they arise in situations where developing states are least likely to be able to violate and to resist pressures to correct their violation. Though a proper empirical evaluation would be required to draw firm conclusions, the last of these explanations does not seem, at least at first glance, especially likely, because one of the common areas in which we see private rights of action is investment. When a state expropriates an investment (including partial or regulatory expropriation) it seems that it is relatively well positioned to resist pressure to reverse course. The developing state, after all, is acting within its own territory, so it is insulated from legal actions elsewhere. In addition, other states will normally have very little ability to engage in a reciprocal expropriation, precisely because of the asymmetric burdens involved.

The second approach that seems likely to yield useful insights into the design of international agreements is to examine behaviors, mechanisms, or patterns of agreements that seem consistent across and within different forms of agreements. The most obvious examples in this category are features that are present in treaties but not in soft law agreements. Soft law agreements tend to omit formal sanctions, dispute resolution, exit clauses, escape clauses, and other devices that serve to amplify the costs of a violation or allow states to avoid an obligation while remaining in compliance with the precise language of the agreement.[41]

One might react by pointing out that soft law agreements are not "binding" under traditional international law principles and, therefore, there is no sense in which a state can be said to have violated international law. This argument would then assert that there is no need for either enforcement mechanisms such as dispute resolution or for escape and exit provisions because there can be no violation. This line of reasoning is consistent with traditional notions under which the category of international "law" is different in kind from other promises. From a rational choice perspective, however, this binary notion of whether or not an agreement is "binding" is problematic. States enter into agreements—whether treaties or soft law—to enhance cooperation. Both forms of agreement facilitate cooperation among states because they impose some form of cost (reputation, reciprocity, retaliation) on states that fail to comply. The choice between soft law and treaties represents just one of the ways states adjust the magnitude of those costs. For these reasons, this book rejects the traditional distinction between soft law and treaties.[42] They are more accurately viewed as choices along a spectrum of commitment. It follows that it makes as much sense to include exit clauses, escape clauses, and dispute resolution provisions in soft law agreements as in treaties. There is, therefore, no obvious reason that, for example, dispute resolution should only be associated with treaties and not with soft law. States certainly could draft a soft law agreement that included provisions for a tribunal to determine if one party had acted inconsistently with the terms of the agreement. Sanctions could even be provided for if the states so desired. In practice, however, this is not generally done, which presents us with a puzzle.

A better explanation for the absence of certain design elements from soft law agreements turns on the relative costs and benefits of those elements. That we do not generally see dispute resolution and sanctions provisions in soft law agreements suggests that states consistently prefer hard law agreements without these elements to soft law agreements with them. In other words, as states add credibility to their commitments, they prefer to increase the reputational stake in an agreement by moving from soft law to hard law, rather than by moving, for example, from soft law without dispute resolution to soft law with dispute resolution. The main implication is that the choice of hard law offers a more attractive cost-benefit trade-off than does the inclusion of dispute resolution. Similarly, that soft law agreements normally do not contain exit or escape clauses suggests that states prefer weaker substantive rules within the soft law agreement to stronger substantive rules combined with an escape or exit clause.

The Scope of Agreements

International agreements vary widely in their scope from extraordinarily narrow (e.g., The Load Line Convention Between the United States and Canada, which exempts certain ships operating exclusively on the joint Canada—U.S. coast from the requirements imposed by the International Load Line Convention) to the extremely broad (e.g., the UN Charter).[43] Under what circumstances will states choose the former, and when should we expect them to choose the latter?

The Narrowest Possible Scope

In considering this problem, it is helpful to make an additional assumption that will be relaxed in short order. I assume for the moment that the transaction costs of entering into a treaty grow larger as the scope of the treaty increases. Indeed I assume that the transaction costs of a treaty rise at an increasing rate as the range of issues included grows.[44] These costs may be offset by benefits. Broadening the scope of an agreement may improve the effectiveness of the agreement, may allow states to negotiate transfers across issue areas, and may yield economies of scope. For the moment, assume that the increase in transaction costs outweighs these benefits. It follows that it is easier for states to enter into two independent agreements than to enter into a single agreement that covers the same topics.

The intuition behind this result is straightforward. As the number of issues addressed by an agreement increases, so do the number of potential deals and the number of relevant interests. Indeed, the number of possible deals increases geometrically with the number of issues on the table. This increase in complexity can be expected to make agreement more difficult in many situations.

In addition to reducing the complexity of negotiations, narrowing the scope of an agreement makes it easier to use experts in discussions of policy issues. This can be seen in virtually any specialized international organization. These bodies bring in (or develop their own) experts on the relevant issue to assist parties to the agreement in negotiation and in policy-making. To take just one example, within the World Intellectual Property Organization (WIPO) is the WIPO Policy Advisory Commission, described as "a Commission of eminent international experts drawn from a broad range of fields, including politics, diplomacy and administration, which have bearing on intellectual property cooperation."[45] Similar examples can be found in the International Labor Organization, the Codex Alimentarius Commission, the Chemical Weapons Convention Technical Secretariat, and the "expert review teams" the Kyoto Protocol provides for, among others. To be sure, a less specialized organization could have experts on specific topics, but there would remain a need to make decisions about how reports from these experts should influence the overall organization. Within a more specialized organization (or in the context of a more specialized negotiation) experts can speak directly to the policy concerns of the organization (or negotiators).

The implication of the foregoing is that states will craft their agreements as narrowly as possible. Though the assumptions made to yield this prediction are significant (and will be relaxed later), many international agreements appear to be explained by this simple preference for narrower scope. Many regulatory agreements among states, for example, are quite narrow in scope. Rather than enter into a single agreement that establishes the way states cooperate in antitrust, securities, criminal law, and the like, states tend to enter into separate agreements in each area. For example, the United States and Canada have an enormous number of agreements with one another, including separate agreements in antitrust,[46] securities,[47] criminal law,[48] and the environment,[49] to name just a few areas of cooperation. Indeed, these two states often have multiple agreements within a single subject area.

Both theory and practice, then, suggest that states' default instinct is to have a single agreement address the narrowest possible scope of issues. Any observer of international affairs will immediately protest that there are many examples in which the scope of the agreement seems much broader than whatever would be the "narrowest possible." One obvious example is the WTO, the product of a complex set of agreements all adopted simultaneously as a "single understanding." The organization is concerned not only with trade but also health and safety matters, domestic subsidies, internal taxation and regulation, environment, intellectual property, and many other issues. So it is certainly correct that some agreements have a broader scope than would be predicted by the foregoing discussion. Why would states expand the scope of an agreement in this way? What are the benefits that sometimes outweigh the increase in transaction costs likely to accompany a broader scope? The next three subsections offer three reasons why states may do so: to improve the effectiveness of the agreement, to generate transfers among the parties, and to capture economies of scope.

Once these three potential reasons to broaden the scope of agreement are understood, one would predict that states will select the scope of the agreement such that the marginal cost of greater scope (increased transaction costs) equals the marginal benefit (improved effectiveness, transfers, economies of scope).

Broadening the Scope to Ensure Effectiveness

Some problems can only be addressed effectively if cooperation takes place on a range of issues. Consider the example just mentioned—the WTO. The goal of liberalizing trade requires, most obviously, cooperation on the elimination of tariffs. But a simple agreement on tariffs would be ineffective, because a state can achieve precisely the same level of protection by adopting an appropriately chosen quota on imports. To liberalize trade, then, also requires the regulation of quotas and, for the same reason, other nontariff barriers such as discriminatory internal taxes. Even if states accept obligations with respect to both tariff and nontariff barriers, access to foreign markets can still be frustrated by subsidies, and so some regulation of those is sensible as well. As states negotiated WTO agreements, then, it is not surprising that they included tariffs,[50] nontariff barriers,[51] and subsidies.[52] Once the general obligations were established, states sought exceptions of various kinds, and this further broadened the scope of the agreement, generating individual clauses on exceptions[53]—as well as a range of agreements that in one way or another cabin the obligations states are taking on.[54]

Recognition of the relationship between liberalized trade and the nontrade issues addressed in the WTO agreements explains a great deal of what we observe at the WTO. It is true that the original GATT, entered into in 1947, was intended to liberalize trade and yet omitted some of the features of the WTO, most notably the detailed agreements on health and safety, agriculture, antidumping, subsidies, and safeguards (for the moment we put aside the dispute resolution provisions, which are discussed later in this chapter). But each of these issues was, in fact, addressed in the original GATT, though in an incomplete way. The WTO represented an attempt to build on the GATT experience with these issues. With the experience of the GATT behind them, negotiators were able to arrive at terms that address these problems more comprehensively.

Two additional subject matter categories remain, however, that cannot easily be explained by a close connection between those subjects and trade in goods. These are services and intellectual property, each of which is the subject of its own agreement within the WTO system. To understand why these agreements would be included within the WTO, we must turn to other explanations, and I will do so in the next subsection.

Before moving on, however, consider another example: the United Nations Convention on the Law of the Sea (UNCLOS), which covers rights of passage, rights of access to economic resources, jurisdiction of states over ships in their water, rules governing warships, piracy, and more. At first glance, many of these issues could be addressed through their own separate agreements. A moment's thought, however, reveals that the various issues addressed in UNCLOS are closely related and are best considered as a group. An agreement governing jurisdictional issues related to the law of the sea, for example, must also address rights of access to the sea's economic resources. It makes no sense to consider the jurisdictional question divorced from the right of passage because each impacts the other. Similarly, the right of innocent passage through territorial seas confers a benefit on maritime states, but the value of that benefit (and therefore what they are prepared to concede in exchange) is closely connected to the rules governing passage through straits. In much the same way, the right of passage can only be understood if the relevant rules governing warships are also specified.

Broadening the Scope to Generate Transfers

A second reason that states may choose to broaden rather than narrow the scope of an agreement is to facilitate agreement by linking two or more (possibly unrelated) issues. (Koremenos et al. 2001; Raiffa 1982). This point is really a relaxation of the prior assumption that greater scope increases transaction costs.

An agreement is only possible (putting aside coercion) if every party to the agreement is better off joining it rather than refusing to do so (or creating some other agreement with a subset of the parties). In economic parlance, the agreement must be in the core of the bargaining game. At times, the interests of the parties on a particular issue are such that there is no agreement that all prefer to the status quo.

Theories of negotiation tell us that when parties cannot find any bargaining space over a particular set of issues, broadening the scope of the negotiation and bringing in additional issues may allow them to reach an agreement. Consider, for example, the problem of reaching an international agreement on the subject of intellectual property rights. For many years the United States and other developed states sought such an agreement without success. The basic problem is easy to see. Research and development of intellectual property is disproportionately located in developed states, and they have the most to gain from international intellectual property protection. When determining their preferred policy, they consider the profits their local producers of intellectual property earn and ignore the benefits that faster and cheaper access to existing technologies may provide for other states. Though they take into account the benefits of greater access for their own citizens, that population represents only a small fraction of the global set of consumers. States that engage in very little innovation, in contrast, have different concerns. They are only interested in the impact of a global intellectual property regime on their own citizens. Accordingly, they ignore the profits of foreign producers of intellectual property. They prefer a relatively weak regime that would give their citizens better access to existing technologies. Though they get some benefits from a faster pace of innovation to the extent that this provides benefits to their citizens, they will, nevertheless, prefer a weaker set of global protections than will innovating states.

This basic divergence between the interests of states made it impossible to reach agreement on the terms of a multilateral agreement, despite many years of effort. Developed states, led by the United States, sought a regime with strong protections for intellectual property, while developing states rejected proposals to increase standards. As long as negotiations were limited to the subject of intellectual property, the effort to reach an agreement was doomed. There was simply no common ground.

In conventional theories of negotiation, an impasse of this sort can be addressed through the construction of transfers to compensate the losers in an agreement. Thus, for example, a buyer and a seller will agree on a quality level that equates the marginal cost of increased quality to the seller with the marginal benefit of that increased quality to the buyer. This quality level will be chosen because it maximizes the total value of the contract for the parties. Once the quality level is chosen, a price will be set to divide the surplus from the agreement. The precise division of the surplus will depend on the bargaining position of the parties, but will be chosen so that all parties prefer the agreement to the status quo. By negotiating over both the quality level and a cash payment, the parties can reach an agreement even if they each have a different preferred quality level.

The same principle applies in international negotiations. Once the value-maximizing agreement is identified, parties that prefer the status quo (or some alternative agreement) can be compensated with a transfer of cash or something else. In the international context, however, cash payments are rare (though not unheard-of). This is likely a product of the fact that states are reluctant to use money as a mechanism to construct transfer payments. This may be explained by the fact that cash payments go from the general treasury of one state into that of another, and may therefore not have enough political salience to be practical. If money is not available (or easily available) to construct transfers, states must look to other mechanisms for transferring value from one party to the other. The obvious candidate, and the one states normally use, is concessions in other areas.

Because negotiating across issue areas imposes costs (which is part of what motivated my initial assumption that states will seek narrower rather than broader agreements), states will attempt, in the first instance, to identify concessions in a particular issue area. So, for example, when negotiating over the harmonization of income and capital gains taxes across international borders, the United States and the United Kingdom reached agreement by exchanging concessions within that subject area.[55] In the intellectual property context, however, states' interests were sufficiently divergent as to make this impossible.[56] Developing states preferred the status quo to a regime of stronger intellectual property protections, so there was very little within the intellectual property arena that they wanted from their developed counterparts.

When intellectual property was brought into the WTO, however, the scope of the negotiations changed. There was suddenly an array of potential concessions that could generate value for developing states. As it happened, the key concessions granted market access, agricultural subsidies, and protection from unilateral sanctions by the United States (Abbott 1996a; Bronkers 1999). In exchange for these concessions, developing states agreed to the TRIPs agreement. By widening the scope of intellectual property negotiations, states were able to generate transfers that in turn made agreement possible.[57]

One caveat is necessary at this point. If one assumes that states negotiate to the efficient agreement (subject to transaction costs) and that a consensual agreement yields a Pareto improvement, it follows that the Uruguay Round must have increased the welfare of all states, or at least must have been expected to do so. If states are able to coerce one another and if transfers are costly, however, the assumption of an efficient agreement cannot be sustained. This point was made in chapter 2 in exactly the same context—the Uruguay Round negotiations. If those negotiations were coercive, there is no guarantee that developing states are better off under the current system than they were under the prior one.

Koremenos, Lipson, and Snidal reach a similar conclusion about the scope of international agreements, but tie their prediction to the number of actors involved.[58] They state that "[a]s the number of actors increases...the heterogeneity within the group will typically also increase.... When states have heterogeneous interests, issue linkage may generate new opportunities for resolving conflicts and reaching mutually beneficial arrangements" (Koremenos et al. 2001, p. 25). This claim appeals to issue linkage in a way that is similar to my own discussion, but focuses on the number of actors rather than the strategic interests of those actors. The number of actors, however, is not directly relevant to the question of whether there exists a bargaining space among a group of states. Adding actors may increase the heterogeneity within the group, but it also increases the set of possible agreements (because each new actor can offer its own concessions within the relevant subject area). There is, therefore, no necessary connection between the number of actors and the scope of the agreement. By way of example, consider the Montreal Protocol on Substances That Deplete the Ozone Layer. This is a multilateral agreement with (initially) 30 parties, yet it addresses a single relatively narrow issue. Its narrow focus was possible because all the parties to the agreement shared at least some basic interest in increasing the level of protection for the ozone layer—there was bargaining space. Reaching consensus did not require a broadening of the scope.

What ultimately determines whether the scope of an agreement must be broadened to facilitate transfers is not the number of actors, but rather whether one or more potential agreements exist that will make all parties better off. This, in turn, is determined by the nature of the problem and the availability of transfers within a particular issue area. For example, parties could not have more divergent or heterogeneous interests than they do in border negotiations. But agreement is nevertheless possible because concessions of territory by one party can be offset by concessions by the other party in other locations. In other areas, such as intellectual property prior to its inclusion in the WTO, there may be no way to compensate a party that makes a concession, so it is difficult to reach agreement.

Broadening the Scope to Generate Economies of Scope

The final reason that states may choose to broaden the scope of negotiations is to take advantage of economies of scope: some institutional features of an organization may be useful for more than just one agreement. Rather than re-creating these features from scratch, states may choose to have one set of institutional features serve more than one issue.

Consider another example taken from the WTO context—the General Agreement on Trade in Services (GATS). Rather than including the GATS in the WTO, states could have established a separate, stand-alone agreement to deal with services. Doing so would have had the advantage of allowing negotiation over services to take place by itself in a more simplified context and presumably with fewer distractions.

The negotiation of the services agreement was made easier by the fact that it was bundled with the rest of the Uruguay Round negotiations and concessions in other areas could be made to encourage the adoption of the GATS. This is partly explained by the ability of a larger negotiation to generate transfers. Like the TRIPs agreement, the GATS was favored by developed countries, and the consent of developing countries might not have been possible in a stand-alone services agreement.

Regardless of whether transfers were necessary to reach an agreement on GATS, however, the institutional structure of the WTO made the inclusion of the agreement on services practical. If the GATS had been negotiated on its own, many features of the WTO would have had to be reproduced within whatever institution was charged with managing the services agreement. The most obvious of these is the dispute settlement mechanism that exists in the WTO. Building a separate dispute settlement process for the services agreement not only would have been duplicative and wasteful but also would have made dispute settlement less effective. Trade disputes in the services area do not come neatly packaged and cabined off from other trade issues.[59] Having two tribunals deal with these issues (one for the services dispute, another for the dispute as it affects other issues) would generate a host of problems, including jurisdictional battles among tribunals, conflicting rulings, confusing precedents, and so on. It is much simpler to fold the entire dispute process into a single tribunal. There is also interaction between trade in goods and trade in services that made it convenient to negotiate over both at once and address both within a single institution. Finally, including the GATS in the Uruguay Round negotiations offered other economies of scope, including a single place for future negotiations, a single secretariat, a common set of institutional resources and personnel, and so on.

Most of these reasons for including the GATS with the rest of the WTO speak to the economies of scope to be had by using a single institution. One might ask why the GATS could not have been negotiated on its own (to reduce transaction costs) and then included in the WTO, along with the GATT and the TRIPs agreement, to take advantage of the economies of scope. The answer is that there are also economies of scope in the negotiation itself. Though negotiation on services involves a somewhat different set of issues than does negotiation on goods, and although the positions of an individual country may be different on the two subjects, there is nevertheless considerable overlap in the relevant negotiating teams and the skill set required to consider the relevant issues. The GATS also borrows language and principles from the other WTO agreements, making it sensible to consider them all at one time.

Membership in International Agreements

Federalism, Treaties, and Membership

Theories of federalism teach that jurisdiction over a problem should be allocated to the lowest level of government capable of internalizing the relevant externalities (Inman and Rubinfeld 1997; Oates 1972). When applied to international problems, the lesson is that international agreements should include all states (and only those states) that are significantly affected by relevant externalities. If all such states are included, the resulting agreement will internalize the costs and benefits of the relevant rules and, therefore, represent a more efficient regime. An agreement to regulate the use of a river that crosses national borders, therefore, is most sensibly addressed in an agreement that includes all states in which that river is present. Global warming issues, in contrast, implicate all states in the world, and so agreements to address this issue should be universal.

Because states are assumed to be rational, the foregoing normative statement—that the relevant externalities should dictate optimal membership size—is also a positive statement. That is, a model of rational states predicts that membership, at least as a first cut, will be determined by the presence and reach of externalities. All else equal, then, the number of participants in an agreement will increase with the number of states affected by the externalities associated with the problem at hand. This prediction is hardly surprising and might even be considered obvious, but it is worth making because it offers a plausible explanation for the level of participation in many of the agreements we observe.

The United Nations was established to address issues of global concern, including matters of peace and security, and so it not surprisingly aspires to universal membership. Over the last 60 years or so, human rights issues have been characterized as matters of universal concern, and it is therefore not surprising that many human rights agreements, such as the ICCPR, seek universal participation. In contrast, agreements that address problems whose effects are largely limited to two states are often bilateral. Bilateral tax treaties provide an obvious example.

This lesson of federalism, however, has significant limits when applied to international law. Assigning jurisdiction within a federal system is a matter of identifying the level of government that will handle a particular matter. When a matter is addressed at the international level, however (regardless of how many states are implicated), a fundamentally different dynamic is at work. The most important difference is that in international negotiations, there is no power to "legislate" rules that will bind states that have not consented.[60]

International agreements bind only those that consent to them, so they only come into being if they represent a Pareto improvement over the status quo for all participating states (putting coercion aside).[61] In a world without transactions costs, this difference would be inconsequential because any Kaldor-Hicks-efficient agreement (i.e., one that increases the overall surplus) could be made to be Pareto efficient as a result of transfers among states. In international negotiations, however, such transfers can be costly, and so Pareto efficiency may be difficult to obtain.

The result is that principles of federalism are likely to serve only as an upper bound on the membership. Despite the merits of including all affected parties, there will be instances in which, for any number of reasons, only a subset of affected parties will participate in an agreement. The United States, for example, ultimately decided not to be bound by the Kyoto Protocol. This decision reflected a judgment by the United States that the costs of the agreement (to the U.S.) exceeded the benefits. It may be that the gains from U.S. participation would have been sufficient to justify a transfer (in the form of concessions in other areas, cash, or something else) from other states to the United States, but there may not have been any available transfer that was acceptable to other states and sufficient to induce U.S. participation. A similar discussion could be had with respect to regional human rights agreements, such as the American Convention on Human Rights, which implicate universal concerns (at least under a universalist vision of human rights). Generalizing, transaction costs may cause some states to remain outside an agreement even if their participation would increase the total surplus.

Agreements may also feature fewer participants than are affected because the parties to the agreement are able to extract rents by excluding others. The clearest example of this behavior is the Organization of the Petroleum Exporting Countries (OPEC), an organization that is effective precisely because it only allows producers to participate. It is clear that a more efficient global outcome would allow greater competition in the market for oil, but producer states have succeeded in forming a cartel and extracting monopolistic rents. In the absence of transaction costs, all states of the world (including OPEC states) could negotiate an agreement that would feature competitive pricing and production and would compensate OPEC states for abandoning their cartel. Doing so would maximize the total surplus and would therefore allow all states, including producers, to do better than they do under the status quo.

To understand membership in international agreements and organizations, then, requires that one first consider the number and identity of states affected by the relevant externalities in order to identify the maximum number of likely participants. This inquiry establishes a ceiling on the likely membership. The next step is to consider what forces might prevent some subset of these states to resist an agreement or, conversely, what might cause one group to exclude another group.

Substance, Form, and Membership

When negotiating an agreement, states interested in a relatively strong set of substantive commitments and broad membership often face a trade-off. On one hand, they can prioritize a large membership, but if transfers are difficult to arrange, this may require a watering down of the substance of the agreement. On the other hand, they may insist on stringent substantive standards in the agreement. This would establish rules that more closely approximate their preferred outcome, but would also cause some affected states to opt out of the agreement.

By way of example, consider the International Convention on the Protection of the Rights of Migrant Workers and Members of Their Families, which at present has 34 parties.[62] While some of the requirements of the Convention are perhaps redundant with other human rights agreements (the right to life, liberty, and security), the Convention calls on signatories to extend certain relatively stringent due process protections to migrant workers, including providing an interpreter free of charge when a worker or a member of his family is arrested and providing compensation to migrant workers who are the victims of unlawful arrest. Furthermore, the Convention calls for migrant workers to be treated equally with nationals in a number of issue areas, including eligibility for social security benefits. The advantage of this approach is that it creates strong and comprehensive standards governing the treatment of migrant workers, presumably in ways that are close to the preferred policies of the members. However, the cost of this approach is that many states, including the United States, have chosen not to subject themselves to the Convention's obligations.

Contrast this example with the ICCPR, which has over 125 members. The terms of the agreement, while sweeping, are also fairly vague. Furthermore, because nations can opt out of the provisions permitting review of violations alleged by individuals, there is no entity capable of developing specific, substantive standards. The result is the Covenant's broad membership, at the cost of weak substantive commitments.

Why would states choose one of these strategies (broad membership with weak substance or narrower membership with stronger substance) over the other? States may judge that they would prefer to have a small impact on many states rather than impose stronger obligations on a few states. Negotiating an agreement that includes high human rights standards might attract a small set of countries, and those countries may already be in compliance. The agreement, then, would lead to little or no change in the behavior of states and in that sense would serve no purpose.[63] For states seeking to improve human rights, then, it might be preferable to agree to weaker substantive obligations if doing so will expand the membership to include states whose behavior may change to come into compliance. This can, of course, go too far, in the sense that an agreement that is so lacking in substance as to allow any state to join without fear of noncompliance would have no value.

Notice how this discussion of the relationship between substance and membership is analogous to the prior discussion of form and substance, in the sense that substance and membership can be traded off against one another in much the same way that form and substance interact. If a large membership is important to states, the agreement can be made less credible by reducing or eliminating monitoring provisions, making it soft law, adding more generous escape clauses, and so on. Each of these changes will reduce the cost of membership for states.

Externalities and Membership

One of the few analytical discussions of membership in international agreements is provided by Koremenos, Lipson, and Snidal (2001). They conjecture that there will be fewer members in agreements that address more difficult "enforcement problems." They use the term "enforcement problem" to refer to the incentive individual states have to defect from a cooperative arrangement. In other words, if the incentive to defect is greater, there will—all else equal—be fewer members. The theoretical underpinnings of this conjecture go back to Olson's work (1965) on collective action (i.e., the pursuit of a goal by a group of people).

When one applies a rational choice model of compliance, there are in fact two collective action problems at work. The incentive to defect from a cooperative arrangement, noted earlier, is the primary problem. This problem could at least be mitigated if defecting states were sanctioned by other states. Collective sanctions, however, present a secondary collective action problem. Among the points Olson makes is that it is difficult to make collective sanctions work, a problem that exists for the same reason that there is an incentive to defect from the primary agreement: every participating state has an incentive to free ride with respect to sanctions. And as the number of actors increases, the incentive to free ride increases.[64] The near-total absence of collective sanctions for violations of international legal commitments is largely consistent with Olson's claims about free riding.

The sanctions international law provides, which I described in chapter 2, include reputational sanctions, the reciprocal withdrawal of compliance, and retaliation. None of these necessarily call on collective sanctions. Nor is it accurate to suggest that adding members is dangerous because a breach by one member leads to the suspension of the treaty with respect to all members (Downs and Rocke 1995, p. 126). Under the rules of international law, a breach of a multilateral treaty by one state normally allows "specially affected" states to "suspend the operation of the treaty . . . in the relations between itself and the defaulting State."[65] One might think that, notwithstanding the law of treaties, a breach by one party will provoke other parties to terminate their own compliance. This is certainly possible, but such an action would only be taken if the remaining states are better off with no agreement than they are with the existing agreement still in place as to the nonviolating parties. But if this is so, it is difficult to explain why the agreement was ever entered into. Perhaps the violator was essential to the agreement (in which case, other states prefer to be a party to the agreement if and only if the violator is also a party), but if so, it would not have been possible to get consent to an agreement that excluded the violator in the first place.

Ultimately, the threat of reciprocal noncompliance can function even in a multilateral agreement, to the extent that it is possible to exclude the violating state from the benefits of the agreement. This most commonly happens bilaterally between the offended and violating states, as is the case at the WTO, where an offended state can suspend its own concessions (in a limited fashion) in response to an ongoing violation by another state. Where an offending state cannot be excluded from the benefits of an agreement, however, reciprocity obviously will not work well. Should one party to the Kyoto Protocol violate its obligations, it makes little sense for other states to suspend their own compliance in response.

The conclusion one can draw, then, is that smaller membership may have an advantage when dealing with true public goods problems. This is so because with fewer members, the threat of reciprocal noncompliance is more credible. There is a greater chance that persistent violation by one party will generate payoffs for the other parties that cause them to violate. If one violation causes the agreement to collapse, of course, the incentive to free ride disappears, which in turn helps enforcement.

Barrett (2003) makes this precise point in explaining why environmental treaties generally cannot hope to attain universal membership. Because each member state pays a cost for complying but all states affected by an externality reap the benefit of a state's compliance, agreements will only be self-enforcing at the point at which the marginal member's defection makes it in every other member's self-interest to cease complying. In other words, reciprocal noncompliance is effective in deterring violations when a member's compliance determines whether the cooperative surplus is greater or less than the cost to individual states of compliance. Bilateral agreements represent the most obvious version of this point. For example, the Great Lakes Water Quality Agreement of 1972 (renewed in 1978), a bilateral agreement to address a public good, sets out a series of guidelines and objectives for governing the chemical, physical, and biological integrity of the Great Lakes Basin ecosystem. This agreement presents no free-riding problem because an attempt to free ride will trigger the agreement's termination.

Unfortunately, many public goods problems simply cannot be addressed with an agreement that includes just a few parties, and so the desire to include all states affected by the problem will typically override the desire to strengthen the role of reciprocity, assuming an agreement is reached at all.

All of this seems to suggest a conclusion that is the opposite of the conjecture Koremenos, Lipson, and Snidal. Problems with externalities that affect many states should be addressed through agreements with more, rather than fewer, members.

The incentive to defect from an agreement is closely related to the level of externalities present. If a state is able to push costs off on others while enjoying benefits for itself then what Koremenos and her colleagues refer to as the enforcement problem is severe. To the extent that this situation corresponds to one in which there are many affected countries, one should expect more rather than fewer members. I have already mentioned the reason for this: an optimal agreement will include all countries affected by a problem, so that the relevant externality can be internalized.

It should be added that large externalities affecting many states will make it more difficult to reach agreement at all. Where many states have an incentive to free ride, for example, agreement may be elusive. This goes to the likelihood of *reaching* an agreement, however, not the number of members that should be expected *conditional on an agreement being put in place.*

This theoretical conclusion has some empirical support. As Mitchell and Keilbach say in their study of several environmental agreements, "membership is not a design choice reflecting enforcement problems . . . but a parameter dictated by the number of actors who must be included to resolve the problem" (2001, p. 897).[66] Similarly, Richards, in his discussion of the series of bilateral and multilateral agreements that emerged after World War II to govern international aviation markets, in large part through price fixing, notes: "Institution builders sought to include all countries of the international aviation community in order to stem the potential for cheating" (2001, p. 995). In other words, if nations outside the price-fixing arrangement set prices lower than those the regime set for its members, the regime would collapse. Thus, the success of the regime depended on inclusive membership that engaged all the relevant nations.

Signing Treaties

Up to this point, the discussion has assumed that states elect either to be a party to a treaty or to remain outside its regime. In the context of multilateral treaties, however, a third option exists for states. In modern multilateral treaties, the initial decision states make is normally not whether to be parties to the agreement but whether to sign it. A state that has signed a treaty is normally not considered to be bound until it has ratified the treaty. There is, therefore, a period of time—sometimes short, sometimes long, and sometimes indefinite—when the state has signed but not ratified. To illustrate, the United States signed the UN Charter at the close of the San Francisco Conference on June 26, 1945, and the Senate gave its advice and consent to ratification on July 28, 1945, making it the third state to ratify the UN Charter. In contrast, the United States signed the ICCPR on October 5, 1977, but did not ratify it until June 8, 1992. Even more extreme, the United States signed the Kyoto Protocol in 1998 but, at least for the moment, shows no sign of planning to ratify it.[67]

The reality that many treaties have signatories that have not ratified raises the question of the legal significance, if any, of signing a treaty. The Vienna Convention on the Law of Treaties provides that a party that has signed a treaty must refrain from "acts which would defeat the object and purpose of the treaty."[68] Swaine (2003) provides a good discussion of this rule and the arguments both for and against it. The most persuasive justification of the rule (though surely not the reason it was initially adopted) is that states will be more prone to invest in reliance on a signed (and not yet ratified agreement) if it at least provides some assurance that the signatories will not undermine the treaty. This reduces the temptation, for example, to wait until others have ratified a multilateral agreement before expending domestic political capital to do so.

Requiring that signatories refrain from defeating the object and purpose of the treaty is, as Swaine points out, an imperfect solution to the foregoing problem. It also suffers from additional weaknesses, including a lack of clarity and the absence of a formal enforcement scheme. There remains, however, a certain good sense to the rule. Discouraging signatories from undermining the treaty increases the probability that it will be implemented successfully. This is so in part because signatories will refrain from (or at least will have an incentive to refrain from) actions that frustrate the treaty. Signatories that decide to work against the treaty are obviously able to do so, but must violate a rule of international law (specifically the Vienna Convention on the Law of Treaties). There is, then, a disincentive to signing and then working against the treaty.

More important, perhaps, the rule turns the act of signing into a useful signal. Because signing raises the cost of opposing the treaty, signing can serve to distinguish supporters from opponents. This gives the signatories a better sense of the true support that exists. Conversely, it makes it more difficult for opponents to pose as supporters in order to frustrate the treaty.

More could be said about the status of states that have signed a treaty without ratifying it, but the key point for present purposes is that it can be seen as a sensible first step toward joining a treaty. Given that states do not typically accept the full obligations of a treaty when they sign (for reasons related to history and domestic political realities), and given that the treaty-making process demands that political leaders invest in the ratification process, the act of signing represents a pledge of reputational capital regarding the agreement. It seems correct that the law should view this more as a promise not to undermine the treaty than as a pledge to ratify—since such a pledge would lack credibility in states where the person signing the treaty does not have full control over ratification (as in the United States) and would render the ratification process less significant or, if one takes the obligation to ratify seriously, would make the actual ratification irrelevant (since the obligation to ratify implies that the obligations of the treaty apply).

Signatories, then, can be seen as having consented to a more modest obligation than have those that have ratified. The former simply must refrain from defeating the object and purposes of the treaty, while the latter are bound by the treaty's terms. States may, of course, be prepared to accept the obligations of a signatory (perhaps because they support the goals of the treaty but are not prepared to comply fully, or perhaps because they receive something in exchange for signing) but not the obligations of a party to the treaty, and the existing rules governing signings largely allow states to do so.

This discussion, then, suggests that article 18 of the Vienna Convention on the Law of Treaties, which defines the consequences of signing, serves the interests of states and the international law system. One aspect of that article, however, is problematic, at least at first glance. Both the practice of states and the foregoing analysis seem to support a rule under which states could be signatories yet never ratify the agreement. Doing so would allow them to commit to a certain level of support for the treaty without taking on its obligations. The Vienna Convention on the Law of Treaties, however, provides that a state must refrain from acts that would defeat the object and purpose of the treaty "until it shall have made its intention clear not to become a party to the treaty."[69] This rule establishes a connection between the obligations of a signatory and ratification. The discussion so far suggests that it would be preferable to simply provide that signatories must refrain from acts that defeat the object and purpose of the treaty (the first clause of article 18[a]) without requiring that they "intend" to become a party.

Two observations may explain why the Vienna Convention on the Law of Treaties retained the implicit requirement that a state intend to become a party when it signs. First, allowing a state to simply sign an agreement without ratifying it expands that state's choice set. This is good for the state, but need not be good for states as a group. In some circumstances, it will be preferable from a systemic perspective to require that states either join the treaty or remain entirely outside of it. By removing the option of partial participation (signing without ratifying) this strategy can increase the number of states that join. The Vienna Convention on the Law of Treaties, then, may reflect a judgment that it is better overall to force states to choose between full participation and nonparticipation than to give them the option of signing without ratifying.

In some instances, for the reasons discussed, it may be better to allow for partial participation, which raises the second possible explanation for the existing language in the Vienna Convention on the Law of Treaties. The rules governing signing are default rules. States could create different rules in a particular treaty. This implies that any inefficiencies the existing default rules generate cannot be larger than the transaction costs of changing them. There is, therefore, a limit to the costs that can be attributed to undesirable signing rules. From this, one can infer that whatever the imperfections in the rules governing signature and ratification, they impose only modest costs on states.

Conclusion

International agreements cover many different substantive issues and come in many different forms. To understand the way states exchange promises with one another, however, requires some sort of framework within which to analyze this behavior. Though states have many objectives when they make agreements, rational states are able to assess the value of any particular agreement and compare alternative agreements to one another. In other words, they can calculate the payoff they receive from agreements, and then select the available agreement that maximizes that payoff.

It follows that all the choices states make when they negotiate an agreement are part of the effort to get the greatest possible benefits. Though this may seem obvious, it has important implications for how we think of the resulting agreements. It allows us to understand more clearly that form and substance are closely connected. More stringent substantive provisions increase the burden placed on states, but so do credibility-enhancing formal provisions. This is so because what matters to the state in the end are the costs and benefits of behavior. Both tougher substantive terms and stronger formal terms increase the costs of certain behaviors. States seeking to maximize the benefits of an agreement, then, are able to trade off substance and form to maximize the value of the agreement.

One of the ways states trade off substance and form is by choosing to enter into soft law agreements. These agreements represent less of a commitment than treaties, and at times offer a higher payoff to states. They are, nevertheless, agreements. They are intended to, and in fact often do, influence state conduct. Furthermore, the Three Rs of Compliance make both treaties and soft law effective. Because the same forces are at work for both types of agreement, it makes sense to study them using the same tools and at the same time. Soft law is not and should not be considered something apart from other forms of international law. It should instead be recognized as one option on the spectrum of commitment that states face.

With respect to the substantive terms of agreements, it is difficult to draw precise conclusions at this level of generality about what one should expect beyond what the discussion about trade-offs between form and substance implies. It is possible, however, to gain some sense of how states will choose the scope of an agreement. In general, states prefer agreements that are narrower rather than broader in scope. Incorporating more issues increases the transaction costs of negotiation and makes it more difficult to take advantage of specialized expertise. But beyond a certain point, a narrower agreement will fail. This may be because it is too narrow to effectively constrain states, because additional topics must be included in the negotiation in order to construct transfers necessary to reach agreement, or because increased scope leads to economies of scope. Needless to say, it is not possible to make strong predictions about the scope of a given agreement without more detailed information about the context, but when that information is available, this analysis can help us to anticipate and understand why a particular set of issues is or is not addressed within a single agreement.

This chapter also sheds light on membership in international agreements. There is an incentive for states to increase membership up to the point where the parties capture all relevant externalities. This effort may be frustrated, however, by states that are unwilling to join on terms that other parties can accept or because a subset of all affected parties can form their own agreement and capture the benefits of cooperation while imposing negative externalities on excluded states. Membership also interacts with substance, in the sense that strong substantive terms may reduce membership. States, therefore, will sometimes trade off substance for membership (or vice versa) in order to maximize their payoffs.

5

CUSTOMARY INTERNATIONAL LAW

Our basic theory of compliance is relatively easy to apply to consensual agreements such as treaties and soft law. Through an exchange of promises, states and their representatives make explicit pledges of reputational capital, establish reciprocal commitments, and identify situations in which retaliatory actions may be taken. Because the states themselves control the form and content of their promises, they can specify every aspect of the commitment. They can, for example, indicate how much reputation they wish to stake on a particular promise.

One important source of international law, however, does not operate based on this sort of explicit consent. Customary international law (CIL) arises more organically out of the actions of states. Can we understand CIL within the book's theory of international law, or is it somehow a distinct legal institution that requires some wholly separate theory and explanation? This chapter describes how the theory of compliance developed in this book is able to make sense of CIL. Like soft law and treaties, the force of CIL arises from states' desire to protect their reputations and the threat of reciprocal noncompliance or retaliation by other states.

Though CIL is often criticized, and occasionally said to be irrelevant, a coherent theory of CIL is important to an understanding of international law for several reasons. First and foremost, CIL is foundational, both as one of the two main traditional sources of international law and as the basis for obligations that undergird the entire international legal system, such as the rule that treaties must be obeyed. Second, a good deal of universal law comes in the form of CIL. Although treaties have taken over some areas of law that were formerly governed exclusively by custom, CIL continues to play a role in such crucial areas of law as state responsibility, state immunity, jurisdiction to apply law, foreign direct investment, and human rights. Where treaties do exist in these areas, rules of CIL can make obligations binding on all states, including nonsignatories. The Vienna Convention on the Law of Treaties, for example, codifies much of the customary law of treaties, but it is generally accepted that these rules apply, through customary international law, to states that have not joined the Vienna Convention on the Law of Treaties (including the United States). Some treaties also rely on rules of CIL in the sense that they incorporate them by reference. For example, the WTO's dispute resolution procedures provide that interpretations of WTO obligations should be "in accordance with customary rules of interpretation of public international law."[1] Finally, CIL provides a set of default rules that help to order the interactions of states when no relevant treaty applies.

The development of the theory of CIL requires some adjustments to the conventional way we understand CIL. Traditional notions of CIL are heavily doctrinal and largely atheoretical. Some of the standard views of CIL cannot be reconciled with the theory presented here or any other theory of rational states. These elements of CIL, therefore, must be rethought or discarded if we are to understand how CIL influences states.

The Traditional Definition of CIL

Before getting too far along, we should be clear about definitions. There is a lively debate in the legal literature about the existence or relevance of CIL, and different authors use different terminology. To begin with, it is important to understand what traditional international law scholars mean when they refer to CIL, and how I use the term in this chapter. For reasons that I will explain, there is some difference between the two definitions.

The traditional definition of CIL is strictly doctrinal, in the sense that a particular norm is said to be a rule of CIL if it satisfies a two-part doctrinal test. The most commonly cited version of this definition is provided by article 38 of the Statute of the ICJ, which defines CIL as "international custom, as evidence of a general practice accepted as law."[2] A slightly different formulation is provided by the Restatement (Third) of Foreign Relations Law of the United States, which defines CIL as that "resulting from a general and consistent practice of states followed by them from a sense of legal obligation."[3]

The first element that is said to be necessary for a rule of CIL, then, is sufficient state practice. The ICJ statute requires "a general practice" and the Restatement requires "a general and consistent practice." The second element, sometimes referred to as the "subjective element," is known as *opinio juris*. This part of the test requires that the practice be accepted as law or followed from a sense of legal obligation.

This traditional definition is problematic in any number of ways, as is well documented in the literature. The classic critique is D'Amato (1971), but there are many others. These complaints address both the practice and *opinio juris* elements of the foregoing definition, as well as the practical difficulties with applying it. I will mention just a couple of the problems with it, which should be sufficient to illustrate why an alternative approach is needed.

With respect to state practice, there is no agreement on how much state practice is required to satisfy this portion of the test. It is clear that it is not necessary for every state to engage in the practice, but beyond that there is no way of knowing how many states are required. The same is true with respect to the duration and consistency of the practice. How long must it have been going on? It seems to be accepted that a single inconsistent act is not enough to undermine a claim of consistent state practice, but it is unknown how much inconsistency is sufficient. Furthermore, there is no agreement on the question of what "counts" as practice. At first glance, one might think that "practice" refers to states' actual actions. This approach, however, is unworkable because states do not "act" often enough to base a meaningful assessment of practice on actions alone. But if something other than actions must be considered, what counts and what does not? One could include statements (defined somehow) on the grounds that they represent an expression of a state's views, but this has the obvious problem that states speak strategically and will routinely misrepresent their beliefs and intentions. The same question arises with respect to votes in international organizations, which are at least arguably more of an act than simple statements. Some commentators, such as D'Amato, prefer a relatively narrow definition, whereas others are much more expansive (Akehurst 1974–75). The ICJ itself has used diplomatic correspondence as evidence of state practice.[4] Finally, it is difficult to know what it means to require widespread practice in a world of close to 200 states. For most problems, many states will have no relevant practice, at all in the sense that they will simply not be dealing with the issue or problem in question. Most other states will not have any kind of documentation or record-keeping to reveal their practice, and for those that do, the practical difficulty of collecting and reading relevant documents from countries with widely divergent legal traditions and many different languages will create an additional bar to comprehensive research on practice. As a practical matter, then, the evaluation of state practice is fairly ad hoc and heavily favors powerful countries with easily accessible records in a commonly spoken language.

The *opinio juris* requirement suffers from equally serious problems. One such problem relates to the way *opinio juris* is identified. We are not able to observe states' sense of legal obligation, and so must rely on actions and statements. This raises the same basic set of problems present with respect to the practice requirement. State actions are more likely to reflect beliefs (though they may not even do that much) but are less frequent. Statements are more common but are quite likely to be made strategically and less reliably offer information about state beliefs.

In addition to the aforementioned problems with the concepts of *opinio juris* and practice, the doctrinal definition of CIL is problematic because it offers little guidance with respect to the relative importance of the two factors. Some commentators take the position that the practice requirement is the more important of the two elements, or even that *opinio juris* is not required at all if there is sufficient state practice (Mendelson 1998).[5] The most extreme version—in which *opinio juris* is not required—is of course difficult to reconcile with the basic doctrinal definition of CIL that virtually all commentators share, and raises the problem of how to distinguish "mere" behavioral regularities from CIL. In contrast, other prominent observers argue that *opinio juris* is the more important of the two requirements (Roberts 2001). A focus on *opinio juris* is appealing to those who want to expand the set of norms that are considered CIL. If one can ignore or downplay the practice requirement, it is possible to argue for the inclusion of any number of moral rights on the roster of CIL rules. The most conspicuous example is torture, which CIL is generally said to prohibit, despite its widespread use. This position has sufficient purchase among international legal writers that the CIL rule against torture is reflected in the Restatement of Foreign Relations[6] as well as in American case law.[7]

One particularly flexible interpretation would allow *opinio juris* and practice to be traded off against one another. Under this view, if there is consistent state practice, less weight is put on the *opinio juris* requirement, and if the practice is less consistent or less widespread, a higher level of *opinio juris* is needed (Kirgis 1987).

The foregoing brief discussion should make it clear why CIL is so often viewed as unsatisfactory. The basic definition has two prongs, but has failed to clearly define either one or provide guidance on how they relate to one another. The primary problem with conventional explanations of CIL follows directly from this poorly specified doctrine. Existing views on the subject are normally based on the foregoing definition of CIL. Because the definition is incomplete, however, the resulting debates lack a strong foundation on which to build.

An alternative way of describing the central problem with the traditional literature on CIL, and the reason the doctrinal weakness is not addressed more effectively, is that so much of the academic work is atheoretical. Our understanding of CIL has emerged and evolved over many years with almost no attempt to provide theoretical underpinnings. The wide range of positions on the doctrine of CIL arise in part because there are no underlying first principles one can turn to in an effort to resolve these questions.

This lack of a coherent and disciplined theory is a serious problem for any consideration of CIL. It makes it difficult to address the doctrinal problems and fails to explain how CIL might influence state conduct. As is true in much of the discussion of international law, it is simply asserted or assumed that CIL binds states in some meaningful way. Without an explanation of the mechanism through which state behavior is affected, however, there is no way to understand when states will comply with these rules and when they will violate them.

The theory of CIL that exists today tends to be viewed with skepticism. The simplest explanation of CIL, and one that enjoyed considerable currency at one time, relied on natural law.[8] Defenders of this approach are difficult to find today. The other possible theory that can be extracted from current writing on CIL is a consent-based approach. The notion here is that states are only subject to international law to the extent that they consent to it. On this view, compliance stems from consent, though why consent should subsequently generate compliance is left unexplained.[9] Beyond the question of how consent can lead to compliance, consent is problematic because CIL is, by its nature, not the product of explicit consent. If consent were required for CIL, a state could escape the application of a rule by providing evidence that it had not consented. Such an approach is inconsistent with existing CIL doctrine, according to which CIL applies to all states unless they are "persistent objectors." Persistent objectors are excused from a rule, but only if they have openly and consistently objected to a rule of CIL from the moment the rule began to emerge. This high standard implies that states can be subject to the rule without their consent. This problem has not been lost on scholars of CIL, and they have responded with the notion of "inferred consent." The idea here is that states are assumed to have consented to a rule unless they object. There is, of course, a big difference between consenting to a rule and failing to object to it (Byers 1999, p. 143).

An alternative attempt to reconcile CIL with notions of consent argues that states have consented to a "secondary" rule of CIL formation under which rules satisfying the aforementioned doctrinal requirements become binding. The most obvious problem with this approach is the complete absence of evidence that states have in fact consented to such a secondary rule. Furthermore, there is no apparent way for an existing state to withdraw or a new state to withhold its consent. So the rules of CIL formation, according to this view, apply to all states whether they support the rules or not. Needless to say, this is a curious notion of consent, and one that is quite distant from any standard understanding of the term.

Rational Choice Critics

In recent years, a new breed of CIL critics has emerged, led by Jack Goldsmith and Eric Posner (1999, 2000, 2005). Methodologically, these critics adopt a rational choice approach much like the one I use in this book. Their conclusions, however, differ from those I advance here, in that they dismiss the possibility that CIL can affect state behavior.

To understand the position Goldsmith and Posner take, one must first take some care in understanding the way they use the relevant terminology. They accept that certain norms have come to be called customary international law, but the core of their argument is that this is simply a label that has no effect on the conduct of states. Put differently, they acknowledge that behavioral norms arise, but they do not believe that there is any sense in which "law" affects state behavior. In their own words:

Although most international law scholars acknowledge that states are more likely to violate customary international law as the costs of compliance increase, they insist that the sense of legal obligation puts some drag on such deviations. Our theory, by contrast, insists that the payoffs from cooperation or deviation are the sole determinants of whether states engage in the cooperative behaviors that are labeled as customary international law. This is why we deny the claim that customary international law is an exogenous influence on states' behavior. (2005, p. 39)

Implicit in this passage is the view that CIL does not affect the payoffs of states or, at least, does not do so because it is law.[10]

The discussion that follows shows that there is no theoretical basis for the conclusion that CIL cannot have an independent influence on state behavior. Before turning to that discussion, however, it is worth considering these critics' arguments. The simplest claim that CIL does not matter is a version of the one-shot prisoner's dilemma discussed in chapter 2. Because there is no coercive enforcement mechanism, there is obviously no way to cooperate in such a game. Once the assumption of a one-shot game is relaxed, however, a theoretical claim that CIL cannot matter is unsustainable.[11]

To dismiss the relevance of CIL, then, requires additional assumptions about the practice of states. One might, for example, assume that the number of states in existence is too large to support cooperation through CIL (Goldsmith and Posner 1999; Olson 1965). The problem with this assumption is that the number of states required to establish a rule of CIL is clearly not terribly large (Norman and Trachtman 2004). Schacter claims, for example, that "States with navies—perhaps 3 or 4—made most of the law of the sea" (1996, pp. 536–37). Though this may be an extreme claim, it remains the case that even under traditional interpretations of CIL, a modest number of powerful states have been responsible for much of the formation of CIL.

Furthermore, the theory of CIL that emerges from rational choice assumptions does not rely on organized multilateral cooperation in the development of legal rules or in their enforcement. As developed here, CIL emerges instead from a process in which individual states develop beliefs about the reputation of other states and about the norms that amount to legal obligations. Each state then updates its beliefs about other states on the basis of observed behavior. Critically, each state acts on its own and seeks to maximize its own payoffs. There is no need for collective action and an increase in the number of states need not reduce the efficacy of CIL.

Compliance and CIL

I begin by clarifying the definition of CIL that I use. The question that is ultimately of interest is how international law affects state behavior. In other words, we would like to know how international law affects state payoffs. In the context of CIL, one major issue is separating the effect of law from the effect of mere norms. With this in mind, CIL should be defined as those norms that, because they are considered to be law, affect state payoffs. Notice that this is a functional rather than a doctrinal definition, and as such is distinct from the traditional definitions of CIL. These traditional definitions, putting aside the many disagreements they engender, identify norms as CIL if they have certain characteristics (*opinio juris* and consistent state practice) without much concern for whether they affect state behavior.

The proposed definition admittedly creates an identification problem. Because the definition limits CIL to those norms that, because of their legal status, affect incentives, it does not provide a way to test the claim that the status of CIL makes a difference to outcomes. For this reason, it would be preferable to have some other way to determine when a particular norm is considered a rule of CIL. Unfortunately we have few, if any, such options. The formation of CIL does not generally come with some identifiable event, in contrast to treaty signings and ratifications. Instead, it is formed through the formation of beliefs and expectations over time, making it difficult, and perhaps impossible, to identify its creation.

The traditional definition avoids this identification problem by identifying distinct criteria that are said to bring about a rule of CIL. As the foregoing discussion points out, however, and as is familiar to students of international law, this traditional definition does not seem to correspond with those norms that are commonly thought to be rules of CIL (e.g., torture) and is sufficiently vague as to undermine any attempt to identify CIL norms for the purpose of evaluating their impact on behavior.

To address this identification problem, one might look to the decisions of prominent tribunals such as the ICJ, on the theory that when they pronounce the existence of a CIL rule, there is a convergence of beliefs among states. This might allow one to test the proposition that legal status affects outcomes. This would not suffice as a definition of CIL, however, since many international norms do not get adjudicated before any such tribunal—yet they arise through some process.

The identification problem that is built into the definition I provide here, then, is inherent in the study of CIL and, therefore, unavoidable. Despite this problem, we can consider how rules of CIL might influence states; a task to which I now turn.

Having defined CIL as the set of customary norms that affect payoffs because they are considered "law," the next step is to identify the mechanism through which customary rules can affect payoffs. As has been true in earlier chapters, the key is to recognize that states interact repeatedly over time. If states interacted in a one-shot game, the absence of a coercive enforcement system would make it impossible for customary legal norms to affect outcomes in a rational choice model. But when states interact repeatedly over time, violations in one period generate costs in future periods.

In a repeated game, customary rules can affect behavior in much the same way international agreements do. A failure to abide by a rule today signals a willingness to ignore international legal obligations and thus makes future cooperation more difficult. If a state has a single reputation that affects all international legal obligations, violations of CIL rules will have a negative impact on its ability to extract concessions from others in exchange for its own promises in future agreements.

If a state has a reputation for compliance with CIL that is separate from its reputation for compliance with agreements (as seems likely), this relationship between CIL and treaties will not exist.[12] A state that violates a CIL rule will, nevertheless, face costs as a result.

The costs of violating a CIL rule come about in much the same ways as they do with respect to treaties. A sense of reciprocity, for example, supports some CIL norms. If one state fails to honor the rules regarding the treatment of diplomats, other states may decide to cease their own compliance with respect to the violator's diplomats. This imposes a cost on the violating state and, therefore, generates an incentive toward compliance.

A violation may also provoke retaliatory action by another state. A failure, for example, to honor CIL human rights norms may cause another state to impose sanctions in the form of trade measures or some other form of punishment. The most familiar version of such action would be retaliation for a failure to protect the rights of an ethnic group as was the case when international sanctions were applied against South Africa's apartheid regime. The imposition of such sanctions may be costly to the sanctioning state, but as discussed in chapter 2, a state may nevertheless be willing to sanction a violator to develop a reputation for being tough on those that violate international law.

Finally, violations of CIL may also impose a reputational cost because other states will be reluctant to rely on compliance from a state that has violated CIL rules in the past. Consider, for example, the evolution of sovereign immunity doctrine in the twentieth century. Under the traditional rule of sovereign immunity, states were completely immune from suit for acts undertaken in either a sovereign or commercial capacity. After World War II, however, states increased their involvement in commercial activities, and the inability of private parties to seek legal redress for the violation of commitments by state-owned enterprises hurt those enterprises' ability to operate efficiently. As a result, states began to adopt a "restrictive" view of sovereign immunity, under which states were not immune from suit for commercial actions. The restrictive view had the effect of protecting private parties who contracted with state-owned enterprises in the event of breach by those enterprises, and therefore of increasing the credibility of the state's commercial commitments. Adoption of the restrictive view of sovereign immunity implied not only that a nation's domestic courts could hear cases against foreign state-owned commercial enterprises, but presumably that a state would honor judgments against it in other nations' courts for actions taken in a commercial rather than sovereign capacity. This move to restrictive immunity thus involved costly reliance by each state on other states' behavior. Any individual state would presumably be better off under a regime in which it invoked absolute immunity, and thus refused to pay judgments based on commercial liability, while all other states adopted the restrictive view, honoring judgments. However, because states generally found it in their interest to induce reliance on their promises made in a commercial context, they chose to submit to liability in foreign courts under the restrictive view.

The way I have defined CIL, and the way costs come about in response to violations, blurs the line between legal rules and "mere" norms—at least as compared to traditional definitions under which there is a sharp distinction between that which is CIL and that which is not. The ambiguity created by this definition seems entirely appropriate. Both norms and CIL, after all, encourage states to engage in behavior that can be termed cooperative, even in the absence of formal sanctions. Both norms and CIL can affect the payoffs states receive. Both norms and CIL generate costs for those that do not comply.

If CIL has any impact on behavior because of its status as law, however, it must be different in some way from norms. There must be something about CIL that, all else equal, makes it stronger than "mere" norms. In fact, my definition of CIL is such that a norm can only be called CIL if it has some separate impact as a result of its legal character.

Chapters 1–4 explained how a legal commitment can influence pay-offs, and focused mainly on agreements. The same approach applies to CIL. Payoffs are affected when one state adjusts its estimate of another state's willingness to comply. Both CIL and mere norms operate in this way. In both cases, a failure to honor the relevant norm causes other states to reduce their expectations about the dishonoring states' will-ingness to honor the norm in the future, and this generates costs, as already discussed. The difference between CIL and norms is not the way they work but rather the magnitude of the consequences. Mere norms impose relatively modest costs when they are violated. It is understood that norms have a limited hold on states, and expectations about "compliance" are modest. Rules of CIL, however, come with a height-ened expectation of compliance. Notice that this is really a definitional claim. Rules of CIL, by definition, come with a higher expectation of compliance—that is why they generate higher costs in the event of a violation. If such higher costs are not present, then there is no sense in which an obligation affects states. Norms that acquire additional force because they are legal obligations will be rules of CIL under my defi-nition. Other norms will not.

All of this means that when a norm comes to be seen as a legal norm, states' expectations of compliance increase. This is analogous to the way the signing of a treaty increases the expectation that a state will comply with the rules specified in the treaty, even if these reflect existing norms. In other words, CIL and mere norms occupy different locations on a spectrum of commitment. States have an incentive to comply with both, but that incentive is stronger for CIL. It follows the there is no easy way to distinguish mere norms from rules of CIL. This is the inevitable result of the fact that both operate in essentially the same way and that they differ primarily with respect to how states perceive them. Among other things, this has the unfortunate effect of increasing the challenge of empirically testing the relevance of CIL.

Opinio Juris

The assumptions that states are rational rules out the possibility that a state complies with a rule of CIL because it somehow feels an obligation to comply or has a preference for compliance. To the extent that state behavior is influenced at all, it must be as a result of a change in payoffs. To understand how behavioral norms that acquire a legal character can influence behavior, then, we need to consider how the acquisition of that legal character influences payoffs. I focus initially on the reputational consequences of a breach of CIL. I discuss the role of retaliation and reciprocity later in the chapter.

Consistent with the model of state behavior and compliance developed in earlier chapters, imagine that a state must choose between two actions. The first is consistent with a rule of CIL, and the second is a violation of that rule. If the state violates the rule, it faces reputational sanctions. These sanctions arise as other states adjust their beliefs about the acting state. In other words, the reputational sanctions come about only if other states believe that the acting state has violated a rule of CIL (and reputational benefits come about only if other states believe that the acting state has acted consistently with a rule of CIL). Only then will they update their beliefs about the state on the basis of the violation. From the perspective of the acting state, then, what matters is not its own attitude or beliefs about the rule, but rather other states' beliefs. If these other states believe a rule of CIL exists, then actions contrary to that rule will generate a reputational cost.

This perspective gives us a sensible interpretation of the *opinio juris* element. The traditional view of this requirement is that it corresponds to a "sense of legal obligation." Existing scholarship, however, fails to explain how this sense of obligation translates into changed behavior.

The discussion up to this point shows that when others believe that a state has a legal obligation, a failure to behave consistently with that expectation can be costly.

Opinio juris, then, can be viewed as the belief of other states that the acting state has a legal obligation. When such a belief exists, the state pays a price if it acts inconsistently with that expectation. This satisfies our definition of CIL—the beliefs of states generate a legal obligation that affects payoffs.

Notice that there is no role for consent here. If other states believe that there is a legal rule, there is little an acting state can do about it. It can choose to violate the rule, of course, but this brings with it the attendant reputational costs. Consent is not relevant to the existence or effectiveness of the rule.

Two other aspects of the foregoing description of *opinio juris* are worth noting. First, all states do not have to share the sense of legal obligation that generates the rule of CIL. In fact, even a single observing state might believe that a rule of CIL exists. In that case, the decision to "violate" the rule would generate costs, but the costs would be limited to the reputational impact from a single state updating its beliefs. Semantically, in situations in which the group of states that believes there is a legal obligation is too small to qualify the rule as general custom, we refer to it as "special custom" (more on this below). Regardless of the label, the fact remains that such rules generate incentives for compliance. If even a single state believes that a rule applies, that state may update its beliefs about the acting state. A rule, therefore, may arise between as few as two states.

Obviously, if more states have a belief that a legal obligation exists, the cost of violation will be larger. Nevertheless, the way CIL affects payoffs can be thought of as largely bilateral. Each observing state updates its beliefs on the basis of its own view of the legal rules. In this respect, reputational sanctions are much like direct sanctions. Each state takes individual action against a violator, whether that action takes the form of direct sanctions or merely an updating of beliefs about the violating state's intention to comply with a rule of CIL. Unlike retaliatory sanctions, however, reputational sanctions are not costly to the state imposing them. Rather, they are beneficial to it because they reflect a more accurate estimate of another state's behavior, thus permitting more efficient reliance. Because each state independently updates its beliefs in reaction to a violation, multilateral sanctions are possible without multilateral cooperation.

That said, there remains a collective way in which expectations are formed. After all, beliefs about the legal rules are not formed in a vacuum. They represent conclusions about the collective behavior of states and its legal implications. For example, a given state may believe that there is a rule of CIL with respect to diplomatic immunity. In determining whether or not another state, state B, will comply with a rule of CIL such as diplomatic immunity, state A will estimate the costs and benefits facing state B in its compliance decision. Because the costs facing state B will certainly depend on the beliefs of states generally as to whether there is a norm, and whether that norm has attained the level of a rule of CIL, state A cannot help but include the beliefs of other states in its estimation of whether state B is likely to comply. Thus, state A's expectation about state B's compliance with the rules of CIL governing diplomatic immunity necessarily depends on what it observes the expectations of other states to be, even though the reputational sanctions resulting from what state A believes to be a violation by state B will act independently of other states.

This theory of how CIL affects states relies on what are termed beliefs (or expectations) of states. It is important to note that states cannot choose their beliefs; these are not policy variables that states can manipulate to achieve a desired outcome. Rather, a state's beliefs or expectations are formed by its interactions with the international community and reflect its perspective.

Understanding that CIL is the result of the expectations of states and that these expectations are in turn formed by the interaction of states and nonstate actors on the international scene helps us to understand the energy that goes into disputes about CIL. Feuds over the content of CIL are, in fact, battles to influence the beliefs of states. Human rights activists, for example, have succeeded in making human rights a part of the CIL discourse. Thus, in *Filartiga v. Pena-Irala*, the Second Circuit held that deliberate torture perpetrated under the color of official authority violated universally accepted norms of the international law of human rights and created a cause of action in U.S. courts against foreign nationals.[13] And when states debate whether a particular rule of CIL exists—as was done for many years with respect to the rules governing expropriation, for example—they are similarly attempting to influence the beliefs of other states.

The way CIL affects payoffs makes this "enforcement mechanism" effective in a way other mechanisms cannot be. For example, explicit punishments such as trade sanctions are subject to a free-rider problem. They are costly to impose, and thus there is an incentive for each state to wait for another state to incur the costs of punishing a violating state. Because the reputational sanctions described are themselves the result of rational and self-interested actions by states, there is no risk of free riding.

This discussion of *opinio juris* leaves open the question of whether a state can avoid a rule of CIL or at least reduce its force by objecting to it. Under traditional notions of CIL, the persistent objector doctrine provides that a state can exempt itself from a rule of CIL by persistently and openly dissenting from that rule from the time the rule begins to emerge. The theory presented here does not speak directly to the question of whether this sort of objection will succeed. It is possible, however, to get a sense of what would be necessary for a persistent objector to succeed. The act of objecting can only affect the impact of CIL if it affects the expectations of states. If objecting is enough to persuade other states that a particular norm is not a legal norm, at least as it applies to the objecting state, then the consequences of a violation are reduced and may even be eliminated entirely. On the other hand, if objecting does not alter the beliefs of other states, then the persistent objector doctrine is a fiction.

As a descriptive matter, then, the role of the persistent objector exception is difficult to judge. What seems likely, though, is that objecting to what would otherwise be a rule of CIL is itself costly. Objecting to a rule in a conspicuous way signals a reluctance to be bound by a norm that is emerging or that has emerged as a rule of CIL. Though this is not itself a violation of CIL, other states may be reluctant to rely on the objector's compliance with the rule and may themselves refuse to comply when dealing with the objector. It is possible for these costs associated with objecting to a rule of CIL to be sufficiently large, relative to costs of actually violating the same rule at some future date, that states may choose not to become persistent objectors. This conclusion is consistent with the observation that states rarely make use of the persistent objector exception (Stein 1985).

From a normative standpoint, there is a reason to think that the persistent objector doctrine is underutilized. To see why this is so, notice first that in at least some instances CIL will be unable to deter a state from taking a particular action. This observation follows from the fact that CIL is a relatively weak form of law and that states at times face powerful incentives to violate it. Furthermore, states will sometimes know that a particular norm of CIL will be insufficient to affect their behavior—presumably because the state's other interests swamp any incentive effect created by CIL. In these instances where CIL cannot affect behavior, it is inefficient to wait for the state to violate the law and then to penalize it through formal or reputational sanctions. To the extent that the sanctions at issue are costly, the punishment is wasteful in the sense that it has no impact on behavior and no deterrence effect. Furthermore, to the extent that it is possible to have states declare in advance that they intend to disregard a particular CIL rule, other states can adjust their conduct to take this into account, reducing and perhaps eliminating any costs associated with the violation.

The persistent objector principle allows states that cannot be deterred by a rule to exempt themselves from its application and to avoid a reputational sanction when they act inconsistently with that rule. Furthermore, use of the persistent objector doctrine permits other states to rely on more accurate expectations about a state's behavior, because states that know they will violate a rule provide notice ahead of time when they object to the rule.

There is, of course, a concern about the opportunistic use of the persistent objector doctrine by states wishing to selectively avoid the application of a rule of CIL, but this concern is mitigated by the requirement that states must declare their objection as the rule is forming. This early declaration of an objection raises the cost of using the doctrine by forcing states to announce their objection to the rule generally, rather than as it applies in specific situations, and thus separates states that are willing to bear that cost from those that are not.

The foregoing rationale for the persistent objector doctrine suggests that there are efficiency gains to be had by exempting states that simply cannot be deterred. The same reasoning suggests that there should be an analogous exception for states that wish to opt out of a rule after the rule is in place. A "subsequent objector" doctrine would permit states that are undeterrable to object to a rule even after the rule has coalesced into a rule of CIL. This rule does suffer from one problem that the persistent objector doctrine does not: if states no longer have to declare their intentions at the time the rule is forming, the danger of opportunistic use of the rule increases. To avoid this difficulty, a subsequent objector doctrine should require that a state object to a rule as soon as the state has a significant interest in the rule. Under the current doctrine of CIL, states are bound by a rule that they may have had no interest in objecting to at the time the rule formed. In this circumstance, however, the failure to object was predicated not on an intention to comply, but rather on disinterest. As soon as the state develops an interest in complying with or violating the rule, the state should be able to declare its intentions. This would allow the efficiency gains discussed earlier while at the same time alleviating concerns about opportunistic use.

Similar logic would apply to new states. Under current doctrine, new states are bound by existing rules of CIL, despite the fact that they have obviously not had the chance to object to those rules. The theory of CIL offered here suggests that new states should have the opportunity to declare their objections to any existing rules of CIL, not out of any concern about the state having consented to the rule, but because of the efficiency gains to the legal system as a whole if states are able to escape sanctions for actions that are undeterrable.[14]

The analysis also clarifies the relationship between what is known as "general custom" and "special custom." Under conventional international law doctrine, CIL that applies worldwide is known as "general custom." It is also possible, however, for CIL to apply to some subset of states such as, for example, a region. When CIL appears in this form, it is referred to as "special custom." If we view CIL as the product of the beliefs of individual states, it is clear that the doctrinal bright line distinction between these two forms of CIL makes little sense. As already mentioned, even a single observing state may believe that a rule of CIL exists, and that belief generates a (perhaps small) cost for other states. If more states have this belief, the cost of acting inconsistently with the perceived rule of CIL increases. One can call such a custom a "general custom" if enough states share the relevant belief, and special custom otherwise.

Within the existing literature on CIL, there is a debate about the possibility of what has come to be known as "instant custom" (Bin Cheng 1965). As the name suggests, the notion of "instant custom" is that rules of CIL do not always require any particular period of time to change but rather can sometimes change instantly. The majority view among commentators is hostile to the notion of instant custom, and with good reason. As long as state practice is a necessary condition for the establishment of CIL, the changing of a rule necessarily takes time. Weil has correctly noted that instant custom is "no mere acceleration of the custom-formation process, but a veritable revolution in the theory of custom" (1983, p. 435). This is so because instant custom cannot be reconciled with a definition of CIL that requires consistent state practice. The ICJ, though it does not require a long period of consistent state practice, rejects the possibility of instant custom, stating that "the passage of only a short period of time is not necessarily . . . a bar to the formation of a new rule," but:

> an indispensable requirement would be that within the period in question, short though it may be, State practice . . . should have been both extensive and virtually uniform . . . and should moreover have occurred in such a way as to show a general recognition that a rule of law or legal obligation is involved.[15]

Because the practice of many states cannot change instantly, the requirements that practice be "extensive and virtually uniform" and that it "show a general recognition" that a rule exists precludes instant custom.

Under the theory of CIL developed in this chapter, however, practice plays no role. Once the practice element is discarded (except as evidence of *opinio juris*), instant custom is possible. If CIL requires only *opinio juris*, then customary rules can change as quickly as *opinio juris* changes. And because *opinio juris* is a set of beliefs, these can change instantly. Notice that this insight helps to illuminate the role of another controversial aspect of CIL—UN General Assembly resolutions. It is understood that UN resolutions do not act as a form of legislation, but there is debate about exactly what they do mean. In particular, are they a form of state practice relevant to the formation of CIL, and can they generate a rule of CIL? As I will discuss, practice is best considered as evidence of *opinio juris,* and to the extent that UN resolutions (or any other form of speech) provide evidence of *opinio juris,* it too can be used as evidence. United Nations resolutions may also serve another function. To the extent that they themselves affect the attitudes and beliefs of states, it is possible that they are, in fact, able to generate a form of instant custom.

To illustrate, Bin Cheng examined two UN resolutions pertaining to outer space—resolutions 1721A and 1962—and concluded that such resolutions could be evidence of *opinio juris* (1965). In essence, he argued that while General Assembly resolutions lack any legislative power, the General Assembly performs a function similar to that of a traditional common-law judge: namely, it "finds" the law that already exists. Thus, in Bin Cheng's view, a clear statement by the General Assembly asserting a principle of customary international law, while it lacks binding force in and of itself, indicates that the requisite *opinio juris* is present. While Bin Cheng believed that the two resolutions he examined fell short of meeting this standard, this idea can be logically extended to resolutions that fail to meet his clear statement rule. Because states impose reputational sanctions independently from one another, statements made during the course of passing a resolution may indicate that certain states consider a norm to be binding, even if the resolution fails to clearly indicate that all states so believe. Furthermore, having passed a resolution that indicates some support for a rule of CIL, states that formerly did not believe that a rule existed may come to consider themselves bound by the rule because they are now more accurately able to judge what other states expect of them.

State Practice

The traditional definition of CIL includes, of course, a practice requirement in addition to the *opinio juris* requirement. Though all commentators agree that the requirement exists in some form, there is considerable disagreement about its precise contours. The failure of the legal literature to reach consensus on the practice required to create CIL should not surprise us. Scholarship on CIL (and international law in general, for that matter) has been largely atheoretical. Without some theoretical basis on which to debate alternative conceptions of this requirement, commentators have no common principles from which to derive conclusions. Their claims, therefore, cannot easily be evaluated.

The rational choice approach I adopt in this book provides the theoretical foundation necessary to discuss international law, including CIL, in a systematic way. When we apply this theory to the practice requirement, however, it turns out that there is no room for practice in the definition of CIL. Practice may remain relevant, as I will discuss, as evidence of *opinio juris*, but it does not itself contribute to the existence of a rule of CIL.

This conclusion follows from the foregoing discussion of *opinio juris*, which demonstrates that *opinio juris*, defined as a belief among states that another state faces a legal obligation, is sufficient to generate a reputational sanction in the event of a violation and, therefore, sufficient to affect payoffs. The payoffs are affected because the belief that a legal rule exists leads states to adjust their beliefs about a violating (or complying) state's willingness to honor the legal rules. This relationship between *opinio juris* and payoffs does not hinge in any way on the actual practice of states.

Though this discussion explains why practice cannot be part of the definition of CIL, it does not follow that practice has no relevance to custom. In particular, practice can serve as evidence of *opinio juris*. It is, of course, not possible to observe *opinio juris* directly, so it must be inferred on the basis of other evidence. This is true for adjudicatory bodies (both domestic and international) that must interpret CIL rules, as well as an individual country that must assess the attitude of other states toward CIL rules in order to know what rules apply to its actions. If, for example, Morocco is considering an action that is arguably a violation of CIL, it will want to know the costs of that action. It will be less costly for Morocco to take the action if European states view it as legal rather than illegal. To determine the costs of its action, then, Morocco must try to determine European states' beliefs. Because it cannot observe those beliefs directly, it must rely on other clues. These include statements government leaders make, reactions to similar actions that other states have taken, and the practice of European states themselves. The practice of European states, then, represents valuable evidence as Morocco attempts to determine the rules of CIL to which it is subject.

This understanding of practice helps to resolve debates among traditional scholars about what should count as state practice. In the existing literature, it is clear that states' actions are relevant but the importance of other types of behavior is unsettled. In particular, there is no consensus on the question of whether statements count as practice. Some commentators prefer to limit the notion of practice to physical acts (D'Amato 1971, p. 88) while others would include not only statements made in appropriately formal contexts but also domestic laws, resolutions of international organizations, states' instructions to officials, and more (Akehurst 1974–75, pp. 5–10).[16] As I discussed earlier in this chapter, the dilemma for evaluating state practice is straightforward. States engage in physical actions rarely enough that it is often not possible to draw credible inferences about state practice from those actions. Is there a state practice against the use of force? The vast majority of states refrain from the use of force every day, but this can hardly be evidence of a meaningful state practice. The failure to use force is more an omission than an act, and it seems far-fetched to draw conclusions from that failure to act. But then how is a traditional international lawyer to evaluate the practice element with respect to an alleged CIL rule governing the use of force? Even the fact that force is sometimes used need not undermine the claim that such a rule exists, because if force is used rarely enough then it may simply represent a violation of the rule, not an erosion of it. When physical acts provide only inconclusive evidence with which to evaluate the practice element, it is tempting to turn to statements. There is no shortage of statements to the effect that the prohibition on the use of force (subject to exceptions) is a rule of CIL, including article 2(4) of the UN Charter. The problem with turning to statements, however, is that states often speak strategically and there is no reason to think that governments' statements bear a close relationship to what they actually believe or do. States almost universally condemn the use of torture, for example, but it is clear that actions are often inconsistent with this rhetoric.

Once one recognizes that practice is not itself a requirement for the existence of a rule of CIL capable of influencing states, the proper way to interpret practice becomes clear. If practice is used to demonstrate the existence of *opinio juris*, then one should obviously give greater weight to practice that sheds greater light on *opinio juris*. So explicit state action that seems contrary to the short-term interests of the state and that is accompanied by a claim that the state is acting in compliance with a CIL obligation would represent strong evidence of *opinio juris*. Similarly, criticism by one state that the actions of another have violated CIL norms is credible evidence of *opinio juris* if the complaining state has no other reason to issue the criticism. In both these cases, the actions and statements are more probative because they are costly to the state and there is no reason, other than CIL, that the state would behave in this way. Other actions or statements will often be more difficult to categorize, of course. Speeches given in international organizations, for example, might offer evidence of *opinio juris*, but might also be strategic talk. More generally, actions are likely to carry greater weight than omissions. Ultimately, the evaluation of practice (whether acts or speech) will turn on the extent to which it credibly evidences *opinio juris*. Though this inquiry is not simple and considerable vagueness remains, it is an improvement over the current debate about practice because it at least explains the role practice plays.

Interestingly, though the doctrinal definition of CIL continues to include the practice element, it is not unusual for commentators to overlook that definition when they argue in favor of a particular rule. The most conspicuous example of this sort of behavior is the already mentioned claim that there exists a CIL ban on torture. Though it is generally understood that enough nations use torture to undermine any serious claim about such a rule satisfying the practice requirement, many authoritative sources consider torture to be a violation of CIL (Restatement (Third) of Foreign Relations Law of the United States, 702(d) (1987); *Filartiga v. Pena-Irala*, 630 F.2d 876, 878 (2d Cir. 1980)). This perception cannot be reconciled with the traditional definition, but is consistent with the theory of CIL I develop in this chapter. If states believe that other states have a legal obligation to refrain from engaging in torture (even if those states engage in it themselves), a rule of CIL can emerge in the absence of state practice.

Removing the practice element from the definition of CIL clarifies debates about this sort of modern CIL claim. In particular, a range of human rights norms (including torture) are now said to be CIL rules. Without passing on the question of whether these norms are in fact rules of CIL, the objection that state practice is lacking is clearly insufficient once one recognizes that it is *opinio juris* and not practice that affects payoffs and state behavior.

An Example of CIL: *Pacta Sunt Servanda*

To illustrate how CIL works under a rational choice theory, consider one of the foundational rules of international law, the rule that treaties are to be obeyed (*pacta sunt servanda*). Although the notion that a treaty is "binding" in a way that soft law is not is reflected in the Vienna Convention on the Law of Treaties, it is also said to be a rule of CIL and is consistent with my definition of CIL—states expect one another to follow this rule even if, like the United States, they are not party to the convention. Because this rule meets my definition of CIL, it is binding on states in the sense that it imposes costs on states that ignore the rule.

It is difficult to think of legal obligations that are more universally accepted than this one. General acceptance of the fact that treaties are the most formal pledge a state can make seems likely to influence state behavior and seems likely to do so *because* of the perception that there is a legal obligation. It is, after all, precisely this legal obligation that states call on to lend credibility to their commitments when they sign a treaty rather than a soft law instrument.

Given that treaties are used as commitment devices, it must be the case that there is some cost associated with violating that commitment. In the case of treaties, a violation signals a willingness to ignore the customary international law that treaties are to be obeyed. By leveraging the legal obligation created by custom, states can make their treaty commitments more credible. This would not be effective if CIL had no impact on state behavior.

One might respond that the treaty is simply the way states signal seriousness, and that a rule of CIL that treaties must be obeyed adds nothing to this explanation of behavior. But the creation of a treaty does more than simply signal seriousness. In particular, it usually triggers a set of domestic law procedures that can be cumbersome for negotiators and heads of state. If states simply wanted to signal their seriousness, one can think of many simpler ways to do so that would not require these domestic procedures. States (or their leaders) could, for example, enter into agreements printed on red paper when they are very serious, yellow when they are slightly less serious, and green when they are least serious. Or they could title the agreement "A very serious commitment between the state of X and the state of Y."[17] States could then enter into "treaties" when they (or their leaders) want the associated features of treaties, including the aforementioned domestic procedures and the default rules of the Vienna Convention on the Law of Treaties. This approach would allow states to separate the seriousness of their commitment from these other issues and, therefore, give them greater flexibility. The most plausible reason states do not operate in this way is that the Vienna Convention on the Law of Treaties and CIL require compliance with treaties, and this rule gives states a greater ability to make credible commitments.

CIL and Other International Law

If one accepts the interpretation of CIL presented here, there remains the question of how CIL fits in with the rest of the international legal landscape. Conventional international legal thinking and scholarship presents CIL as a world unto itself, largely unrelated to treaties or other forms of international commitment. We are left, in this traditional account, with separate and distinct explanations for CIL, treaties, soft law, and so on.

The rational choice approach adopted in this book, however, demonstrates that a single theory of international law can encompass the various forms of international legal cooperation and can do so more effectively than the traditional approaches. Confronted with a norm of CIL, states must take into account the fact that there are consequences for violating that norm. The same basic forces are at work in CIL as in other areas of international law. On the spectrum of commitment, CIL occupies a different position—virtually everybody agrees that CIL has less impact, all else equal, than treaties—but is not a conceptually distinct phenomenon.

Though treaties surely present a more credible and powerful commitment device, they are costly to negotiate and require all participating states' consent. As discussed, no agreement between states is necessary under the *opinio juris* requirement of CIL, because reputational costs depend on the independent beliefs of states, although states' beliefs may be formed interdependently.

Customary international law can also emerge through repeated interactions over time, which gives states another mechanism (in addition to agreement) to manage cooperation. In particular, CIL can bind states without their explicit consent, giving it the potential to help create cooperation even when the result is not a Pareto improvement. To illustrate, imagine a rule of CIL that generates benefits to states as a group, but imposes modest costs on one state. To be more concrete, suppose the rule imposes a cost of 10 on state A but yields a benefit of 50 to all other relevant states. If consent were required for the establishment of a rule of law, an agreement on the rule could only come about if the state for which the rule is costly received some form of transfer payment in exchange for compliance. Such payments are often difficult to negotiate, and so it may be impossible to reach agreement. If, however, the relevant norm becomes a rule of CIL and if the reputational sanctions of violating that rule are larger than 10, all states will choose to comply, and the higher total payoff will be achieved. The rule still imposes a cost on state A, but yields benefits to other states that outweigh those costs. In this example, CIL has allowed cooperation to take place that would not have been possible through an international agreement.

All of this discussion is a product of theory rather than empirical investigation. One limit of a theoretical approach is that it does not speak directly to the strength of CIL and the instances in which it will affect behavior and outcomes. I have shown that it is possible for CIL to affect state behavior in a model of rational states, but this does not mean that it actually does so, let alone that it does so frequently. At least some of the debate over CIL suffers as a result of confusing the theoretical question of whether CIL can exist with the empirical question of whether it does exist.

Because we do not have any reliable empirical evidence about the actual impact of CIL, virtually all inquiries into CIL, including this chapter, have focused on the theoretical side. Both sides of the CIL debate marshal anecdotal evidence to support their claims, but the conclusions to be drawn from such stories are often themselves subject to debate, and in any event, one cannot generalize from these individual accounts.

It is thus important to be clear about what can and what cannot be shown. There is no doubt that in a model of rational states, it is possible for a rule of CIL to influence state behavior and to do so because it is perceived to be a legal obligation.

The next step is to consider, in an admittedly somewhat speculative way, the force CIL is likely to have on states. One conclusion we can safely reach is that rules of CIL will have less impact on behavior, all else equal, than will rules contained in treaties or even soft law agreements. One key difference between rules that are the subject of an agreement and CIL is the clarity of the agreement. In most cases, rules of CIL will be imprecise, and states may disagree as to their content. Agreements, in contrast, are able to specify states' particular obligations in an explicit way. Though there is no denying that international agreements are always somewhat imprecise, they normally offer greater clarity than do rules of CIL.

For example, it is generally said that there is a rule of CIL with respect to transboundary harms, particularly environmental harms. The ICJ confirmed this in the Nuclear Weapons Advisory Opinion, stating that "the existence of the general obligation of States to ensure that activities within their jurisdiction and control respect the environment of other States or of areas beyond national control is now part of the corpus of international law relating to the environment."[18] However, the bounds of this rule are unclear. While liability has been found on the basis of transborder environmental harm, it is surely not the case that all, or even most, externalized environmental harms result in liability.[19] With severely limited case law available to define the contours of this obligation, determining what constitutes a violation is largely a matter of guesswork.

In addition to uncertainty with respect to content, CIL rules are often imprecise because there is disagreement about whether they represent legal rules at all. When a state acts, observing states that believe the action is a violation of the CIL will adjust their beliefs accordingly. This will impose costs on the acting states, and the threat of this cost represents a deterrent to the action in the first place. States that view the act as legal, however, will not update their beliefs. The net result is that the violation imposes costs, but those costs are smaller as a result of the disagreement with respect to the content and/or the existence of the rule.

Customary international law is likely to be weak relative to international agreements for an additional reason. Recall that when a state violates a norm of international law, the reputational sanction comes about because future efforts at cooperation become more difficult. This is most obvious in the treaty context, where one can imagine that past failures to honor treaties will hamper a future effort to resolve a similar problem through a treaty. States do not engage in explicit negotiation about CIL, however, and so the reputational sanctions for a violation of a CIL rule are more subtle and likely smaller. That is, a violation of CIL does not compromise a state's ability to enter into future cooperative arrangements in the way a treaty violation does. It is conceivable that a CIL violation can harm a state's reputation even in the treaty-making context, but, as discussed in chapter 3, it seems likely that there is some compartmentalization of reputation and that a state's reputation for compliance with treaties is substantially independent of its reputation in CIL.

Other factors affecting the relevance of CIL will be essentially the same in the CIL context as in the treaty or soft law context. The sanctions for a violation of CIL may take the form of an unwillingness on the part of other states to rely on compliance with CIL by the violating state (reputation), a reluctance on the part of other parties to comply with that same norm (a form of reciprocity), or the imposition of a direct sanction (a form of retaliation).

What does all of this add up to? Once again, without empirical evidence, it is difficult to draw any definitive conclusions about the importance of CIL. One relevant source of evidence is the behavior of the states themselves. They and their leaders seem to invest considerable resources in an attempt to influence perceptions about CIL. To illustrate, the European Union claims that the "precautionary principle," drawn from CIL, governs state behavior with respect to the regulation of meat and meat products.[20] It is difficult to explain why the European Union would do so if CIL did not influence its payoffs. The same is true of NGOs, many of which go to great lengths to advance their view of CIL. For example, Human Rights Watch, among others, mounted a campaign to pressure the United States to stop executing child offenders. A central claim of groups like Human Rights Watch was that the practice of executing children was illegal under customary international law.[21] It is hard to explain why states and sophisticated nonstate actors, assumed to be rational, would invest resources and energy in trying to influence the perception of others as to the content of CIL if they did not expect such an investment to affect the payoffs faced by states.

Having said all of the foregoing, I should also note that although CIL can generate cooperation, there are clearly significant limits to its ability to do so. Because the reputational sanctions from violation are likely to have no more than a small effect on a state's reputation for compliance with treaties, the real reputational cost is probably limited to a state's reputation for compliance with CIL. Indeed, even within the set of all CIL rules, a state might have several reputations, as discussed in chapter 3. This suggests that the costs of violating a rule of CIL are likely to be small, which in turn implies that CIL can only generate cooperation when the gains from violation are small.

6

UNDERSTANDING
INTERNATIONAL LAW

The study of international law is undergoing a transformation from a discipline focused on practice and doctrine into one putting greater emphasis on theory and social science methodology. International law scholars are rapidly adopting more sophisticated analytical techniques and applying these tools to study how states use law to promote cooperation in our anarchic international system.

This book seeks to contribute to our growing theoretical understanding of international law by developing a general rational choice theory capable of explaining the subject. The basics of the theory are simple and rely on the three ways a violation of international law can generate costs for a state (the Three Rs): reputation, reciprocal noncompliance, and retaliation. A state that does not comply with its international legal obligations may suffer because it finds it more difficult to make credible international commitments or benefit from international law in the future (reputation); because other states terminate their own compliance (reciprocity); or because other states punish it, even when doing so is costly (retaliation). Each of the Three Rs of Compliance can increase the costs of violation and, therefore, promote cooperation.

Though both reciprocity and retaliation have a certain intuitive appeal, they each rely on some notion of reputation, as discussed in chapter 2. Reciprocal noncompliance will only follow a breach if the violating state is unable to credibly promise compliance in the future; and a rational state has no incentive to retaliate unless doing so helps it to develop a reputation for punishing violators or helps it end an ongoing violation.

Some forms of international cooperation will feature all of the Three Rs, but others will feature only one or two of them. Of particular note is the challenge multilateral agreements pose for reciprocity and retaliation. Threats of reciprocal withdrawal of compliance will often fail to promote cooperation in multilateral agreements because they lack credibility or are simply inappropriate, as is the case, for example, in many multilateral human rights and environmental agreements. The threat of retaliation will often be no more effective at promoting co-operation because retaliation faces a serious free-rider problem. Of course, some multilateral agreements and institutions attempt to address the free-rider problem. The UN Charter, for example, states that UN member states will "accept and carry out the decisions of the Se-curity Council."[1] Similarly, article 5 of the North Atlantic Treaty states that if an armed attack should occur in Europe or North America against one NATO member, each member agrees to "assist the Party or Parties so attacked by taking forthwith, individually and in concert with the other Parties, such action as it deems necessary, including the use of armed force, to restore and maintain the security of the North Atlantic area."[2] This sort of attempt may help to counter the free-rider problem, but certainly does not eliminate it. Where neither reciprocity nor re-taliation is effective, cooperation must rely on reputation.

In contrast to reciprocity and retaliation, reputation can work—indeed will often work better—in multilateral agreements. Reputational sanctions are the product of a rational updating of beliefs by non-violating states, so there are no free-rider or credibility concerns. Fur-thermore, they come about in a decentralized way without the need for organization or cooperation among the sanctioning states. Reputation may work especially well in multilateral agreements if the presence of many states within the agreement increases the flow of information regarding the rules and the behavior of states.

Developing a reputation for compliance with international law al-lows states to capture larger gains from international cooperation. When states enter international agreements and when they make decisions about compliance, they take the relevant reputational consequences into account. Because compliance with international obligations improves a state's reputation, an incentive toward compliance is generated. This incentive toward compliance represents the value added by interna-tional law.

An immediate implication of this theory is that there is no stark distinction between agreements that are formal treaties and those that are not. Though treaties represent a more serious commitment and a greater pledge of reputational capital, all else equal, than do other agreements, this is a difference of degree. All agreements, whether treaties or not, affect state behavior through the same mechanisms. If one thinks of an agreement as a tool to constrain states' behavior, and if one thinks of the extent to which an agreement "binds" a state as lying on a spectrum, then the choice of a formal treaty rather than some other less formal agreement moves the promises made along that spectrum, but it does not represent a wholly different kind of agreement.

Just as the distinction between hard and soft law is less stark than traditional international legal scholars have claimed, there is only a fuzzy line between "mere norms" and customary international law. Both CIL and norms affect state behavior through the same mechanisms. The key difference is that when a norm comes to be seen as a rule of CIL, expectations about compliance increase. The costs of violation are therefore higher, and, all else equal, states are more likely to comply. The mechanism that generates an incentive to comply with CIL, however, is essentially the same as that which encourages compliance with other norms. Relative to other norms, CIL represents a move along a spectrum and binds a state more thoroughly.

One can also consider the relative force of all of the aforementioned legal forms. Treaties generally represent the strongest form of international legal commitment. This is so for reasons that are familiar to all students of international law. They are consent based, are reduced to writing (usually), and are relatively precise representations of each state's commitments. They are also understood to be the most solemn pledge a state can make, which is what we mean when we refer to treaties as "legally binding." Soft law has all the same traits, with the exception that it is a less serious commitment of reputational capital. On the other hand, CIL is not the product of an individual country's consent, is typically unwritten (though it may be codified in a treaty or soft law instrument), and is often vague. It is true that it is referred to as "legally binding," but that label serves primarily to distinguish it from norms rather than to deliver the reputational implications of a treaty. Customary international law is further weakened by the fact that, depending on the extent to which reputation is compartmentalized, a violation of CIL comes with a smaller cost than is the case with treaties. That is, a violation of CIL may only affect a state's reputation for compliance with custom—in which case the state's ability to enter into valuable treaties will be unaffected. All that said, CIL still has the potential to impact state behavior, both because it sets expectations and because a loss of reputation for complying with custom can be costly for states. Finally, all observers agree that international norms also affect states. Such norms are very much like CIL —they lack explicit consent, are unwritten, and are often vague. In addition, they lack the "bindingness" of custom. As such, the consequences of failing to honor them, while often real, are less than is the case for custom.

The foregoing discussion makes it possible to identify a hierarchy of international law rules, with treaties the most likely to affect behavior, norms the least, and soft law and customary international law in between, as shown in figure 6.1.

Of course, this simple representation can be amplified with a host of relevant details. Treaties, for example, can include dispute resolution or not (and indeed can provide different forms of dispute resolution), and can include stronger or weaker monitoring provisions, more or less burdensome substantive rules, and so on. All these things will affect the extent to which treaties affect state behavior. Soft law is no different—a soft law agreement could, in principle, have all the same features. Soft law agreements themselves also come in an endless variety of forms, such as memoranda of understanding, informal pledges, detailed written declarations, codes of conduct from international organizations, and much more. These different forms can also be used to modulate the level of commitment states make. Among other possibilities, a rule of CIL may apply to a simple or a difficult cooperation problem, may enjoy the support of all powerful states or may be opposed by some of them, and may be more or less controversial (e.g., there is widespread agreement that the rules in the Vienna Convention on the Law of Treaties represent customary law, but disagreement remains about whether the precautionary principle—which permits decision-makers to take anticipatory action to avoid or minimize risks whose consequences are uncertain but potentially serious, and which has been incorporated into many international environmental treaties—has become a customary rule). Norms

Figure 6.1

are subject to similar variations. All these factors, and many more, affect the ability of a rule to influence states. The relevance of these other factors implies that the ranking of sources, then, is conditional on all other factors being equal. There is no claim here that, for example, every treaty is more effective than every example of soft law. In fact, recognition that these sources lie on a continuum makes it easier to understand why no such claim can be made.

Like any theoretical discussion, this book has made simplifying assumptions. Such assumptions are a necessary part of understanding our complex world (a 1:1 map is of no use), but it is important to remember that alternative approaches are possible. The rational choice assumptions I use throughout the book allow development of a theory of international law in a relatively organized and disciplined way and help to generate predictions. Other approaches, however, can usefully add to this model. Liberal theory can shed light on the relationship between international law and domestic politics and help us to understand how the competition among domestic interest groups can generate state preferences. To give just one example, liberal theory may contribute to our understanding of reputation by exploring how (if at all) domestic constituencies punish leaders who violate international obligations. Constructivist theory may yield insights into how state preferences are formed. The rational choice model takes preferences as given, but it would enrich our thinking to have a better grasp on how they come about, how stable they are over time, and so on. The focus in this book on rational choice does not imply that these other methods lack value or that a rational choice model is the only proper approach. Rather it reflects the fact that developing a theory of international law requires us to make certain initial assumptions and to stick with them as much as possible. At times a slavish commitment to assumptions undermines rather than advances the inquiry, and so even in this book the explicit and intentional reliance on rational choice assumptions is relaxed in a few places. When one should stick to assumptions and when one should relax them is more art than science, and reasonable people may differ on the correct approach. I have tried to remain true to the basic rational choice assumptions as much as possible and have relaxed them only when some alternative approach seemed like a critical part of the explanation of some observed phenomenon such as the use of soft law rather than treaties. This approach could be criticized as either overly reliant on formal assumptions (and insufficiently willing to introduce alternatives as needed to explain observed behavior) or undisciplined (and unnecessarily willing to introduce ad hoc assumptions). There really is no one true way to balance the benefits of theoretical rigor with the pragmatic application of theory to facts. The hope here is that being clear about the approach and as transparent as possible regarding assumptions will enable the book's claims to be examined and tested against states' observed behavior and to be used for further theoretical inquiry.

Regardless of one's model of state behavior, a study of compliance must consider what factors beyond international law might motivate states to comply. This inevitably brings into play the international relations literature, which is concerned with the question of how states interact in the international arena. Engagement with the political science literature reminds us that international political forces affect state behavior, including in matters of international law.

The traditional doctrinal categories of international law (treaties, CIL, general principles of law, judicial decisions, and teachings) offer an artificially crisp distinction between the legal and the political. That definition would exclude, for example, the Helsinki Final Act, which despite the fact that it was negotiated at a high level and takes the form of a written document, is soft law. But surely that agreement is within the scope of the study of international law. Or consider the UDHR. This is a foundational document without which it would be difficult to properly study subsequent human rights agreements or the human rights system, yet it is soft law. Surely no student of international law would argue that it somehow falls outside of the boundaries of what we look at when we study "law."

How, then, can we distinguish these two examples of soft law from other practices that do not seem to implicate the same obligation on the part of states? When Soviet and American dignitaries visited one another, for example, the flags of both countries were often displayed, yet it hardly makes sense to speak of this practice in terms of an obligation under international law. The same question can be posed with respect to the distinction between law and politics. If political compromise can often be described as soft law, and if (as this book has argued) soft law is considered part of international law, how can we separate law from politics? Where does the inquiry of the international legal scholar give way to that of the political scientist?

Though legal scholars may have reasons to wish for a clear boundary between international law and international politics, it is clear that no such boundary exists. There is no easy or clear way to distinguish international law from either politics or mere norms. International politics affects every international legal obligation, including formal treaties and CIL, just as it affects quasi-legal agreements (i.e., soft law) and norms. That does not make international law irrelevant or uninteresting, but it does require an acknowledgment that other forces are also at work. Put another way, international law has the potential to influence state behavior, but always does so in a political context.

International legal scholars, therefore, have little choice—they must encounter and engage the world of politics. Law, by itself, is insufficient. This should not be perceived as bad news for international legal scholars—in fact, it should not be news at all. Legal scholars have always recognized that politics matter for international law. The lesson here is simply that they must address this reality more directly and explicitly.

International law and international relations are similarly intertwined when one considers questions of compliance. International legal obligations can affect a state's actions, but the political payoffs are always relevant. As I discussed in chapter 3, we cannot even evaluate the reputational consequences of an action without an understanding of the nonreputational (including political) payoffs.

All this calls into question many conventional views about international law. For example, one of the many ways the theory developed in this book differs from traditional international law scholarship concerns the question of what it means for a state to be "bound" by international law. All agree that this means that the state faces a legal obligation. This book explains that international law may or may not cause a state to behave consistently with that obligation. Some international legal rules will have greater "compliance pull" than others and in that sense can be said to be "more" binding. This is contrary to claims made in traditional international legal scholarship to the effect that all rules of international law are all "equally binding" (Shelton 2006, p. 321). For the latter view to be accurate requires that the word "binding" be synonymous with having a legal obligation. It cannot be understood to qualify the power of that legal rule to influence states. It is more useful to think of bindingness as a characteristic that can vary over some range, with greater bindingness corresponding to legal rules that have a stronger impact on states.

Having said that international law can be understood using this theory, I must hasten to add that this book has barely scratched the surface of what we can learn from the theory of international law. It does not attempt to address every aspect of international law; no book could do so. For example, I have intentionally avoided a focus on any one substantive issue, despite the fact that there are important differences among the areas of trade, environment, human rights, use of force, laws of war, investment, and the many, many other areas where international law is applied. Nor have I attempted to engage any more than a handful of specific legal rules. Virtually any international law rule or set of rules could be analyzed through the rational choice model laid out in this book, and doing so would further advance our understanding of international law. Nor have I sought to contribute to the important and ongoing empirical debate about the impact of international law. It should be clear to everyone interested in international law that there is a critical need for empirical evidence on when and how international law affects state behavior.

What I do try to do in this book is lay the foundation for a theory of international law. Better theory will help us make better decisions about how and when to use international law and will give us a better sense of when it can be effective.

NOTES

Chapter 1

1. Vienna Convention on Consular Relations, art. 36.1(b).
2. Medellin v. Dretke, 371 F.3d 270 (2004).
3. See Case Concerning Avena and Other Mexican Nationals (Mex. v. U.S.), 2004 I.C.J. 1 (Mar. 31).
4. Petition for Writ of Certiorari at *11, Medellín v. Dretke, 544 U.S. 660 (2005) (No. 04–5928), 2004 WL 2851246.
5. Sanchez-Llamas v. Oregon, 126 S. Ct. 2669 (2006).
6. Sanchez-Llamas, 126 S. Ct. at 2672.
7. Ex parte Medellin, 223 S.W. 3d 315 (Tex. Crim. App. Nov. 15, 2006).
8. Adam Liptak, "Texas Court Rebuffs Bush and World Court," *New York Times,* November 16, 2006.
9. G. M. Filisko, "Texas Court Tells Bush to Back Off," *ABA Journal eReport,* November 2006.
10. 127 S. Ct. 2129 (April 30, 2007).
11. United States—Safeguard Measures on Imports of Certain Steel Products, WT/DS248, 249, 251, 252, 253, 254, 258, 259/AB/R (2003).
12. Mexico—Measure Affecting Telecommunications Services, WT/DS204/R (2004).
13. Allee and Huth (2006) identify 30 instances from 1919 to 1995 in which territorial disputes were submitted to international arbitration or adjudication. In only three of those cases was the arbitration or adjudication not fully successful in ending the dispute.
14. Smith & Grady v. United Kingdom, 29 Eur. H.R. Rep. 493 (1999); Lustig-Prean & Beckett v United Kingdom, 29 Eur. H.R. Rep. 548 (1999).
15. Sarah Lyall, "British, under European Ruling, End Ban on Openly Gay Soldiers," *New York Times,* January 13, 2000, A1.
16. Biological Weapons Convention, art. 1.

17. North American Free Trade Agreement Implementation Act, Pub. L. 103–182, 107 Stat. 2057 (1993), *codified at* 19 U.S.C. § 3301 et seq. Art. 1603 of NAFTA, which calls for the parties to admit on a temporary basis otherwise qualified business persons, is directly implemented by 19 U.S.C. § 3401.

18. 1997 Convention on the Prohibition of the Use, Stockpiling, Production, and Transfer of Anti-Personnel Mines and on Their Destruction, art. 9, September 18, 1997, 36 ILM 1507.

19. Landmine Monitor Fact Sheet, prepared by Human Rights Watch for the Ninth Meeting of the Intersessional Standing Committee on the General Status and Operation of the 1997 Mine Ban Treaty, Geneva, Switzerland, 9 February 2004; International Campaign to Ban Landmines website, www.icbl.org/content/download/20111/387737/file/art9_feb_2004.pdf.

20. Pub.L. 103–236, 103d Cong., 2d Sess. (1994).

21. Convention against Torture or Other Cruel, Inhuman, or Degrading Treatment or Punishment, Dec. 10, 1984, 14 UNTS 85, 23 ILM 1027.

22. 22 U.S.C. § 6725 (1998).

23. Basel Committee on Banking Supervision, International Convergence of Capital Measurement and Capital Standards, reprinted in 51 Banking Rep (BNA) 143, July 25, 1988. For more on the implementation of the Basel Accord, see Ho (2002).

24. For a more detailed discussion of this cheap talk theory see Guzman (2006).

25. Political scientists have called for a greater emphasis on compliance as a means to understanding cooperation; see Downs, Rocke, and Barsoom (1996). It is this theoretical line of reasoning that this book explores.

26. Chayes and Chayes (1993, p. 178).

27. This definition of soft law is the dominant one, but it does not enjoy universal support. Some authors prefer to label as "soft law" treaties that are vague or incomplete. See Weil (1983): "It would seem better to reserve the term 'soft law' for rules that are imprecise and not really compelling, since sublegal obligations are neither 'soft law' nor 'hard law': They are simply not law at all." Others use the term "soft law" to refer to international arrangements that are imprecise, that fail to delegate authority for interpreting and implementing law, or that are not binding under international law. See Abbott and Snidal (2000).

Chapter 2

1. Canada and the United States have signed mutual defense agreements, which arguably imply nonaggression, but these are motivated by concerns about the common defense of the countries against, for example, the Soviet Union

during the Cold War rather than worries about military conflict between these North American states. These countries are also bound by article 2.4 of the UN Charter, which forbids the use of force subject to exceptions only for self-defense and Security Council authorization. Like the imagined nonaggression treaty mentioned in the text, it is quite implausible that this obligation deserves any credit for the lasting peace between Canada and the United States.

2. Chapter 4 provides a similar discussion of why coordination games, even when addressed using international law, are not strong examples of international law at work.

3. The Warsaw Convention's most important contribution was the creation of international rules and limits for airline liability for accidents. The Convention was amended twice, and was modified and superseded with respect to its liability rules in 1999 by the Convention for the Unification of Certain Rules for International Carriage by Air (the "Montreal Convention"). In addition, the Convention on International Civil Aviation (the "Chicago Convention") established rules governing the legal status of airspace, airplane registration, and safety, and created the International Civil Aviation Organization, a UN agency charged with overseeing and coordinating international air travel. Additional agreements, such as the Convention on Offences and Certain Other Acts Committed on Board Aircraft (the "Tokyo Convention"), the Convention for the Suppression of Unlawful Seizure of Aircraft (the "Hague Convention"), and the Convention for the Suppression of Unlawful Acts Against Safety of Civil Aviation (the "Montreal Convention") govern criminal offenses committed on airplanes.

4. This assumes, of course, that states actually wish to compete against each other, and thus wish to be in the same place. When international politics have interfered with the Olympics, such has not always been the case. In 1980, nations boycotting the Moscow Olympic Games held an alternative competition in Fontainebleau, France. In 1984, as part of the Soviet-led boycott of the Los Angeles Summer Olympics, boycotting states held the Friendship '84 games in various venues throughout Eastern Bloc nations, most notably Moscow.

5. Another popular game of this sort, for example, is "stag hunt," in which both players prefer a certain strategy (strategy A), but another strategy (strategy B) is less risky in the absence of assurances that the other player will choose strategy A. Jervis (1985), for example, has suggested that victorious allies following a war sometimes play a stag hunt game. Continued cooperation among the allies can ensure that the defeated enemy will not rise again to threaten the system and can yield gains in trade, science, and cultural exchange. Though all states have an incentive to cooperate, that incentive is only present if each state expects the others to cooperate as well.

6. The absolute value of the payoffs chosen here are arbitrary. Only the relative payoffs matter.

7. For a different, related discussion of reciprocity, see Keohane (1986).

8. The theory is developed in the context of international agreements. Chapter 5 discusses how the model applies in the context of customary rules.

9. This calculation relies on the fact that $x + x/(1+r) + x/(1+r)^2 + \ldots = x(1+r)/r$.

10. If a state complies in the first period while the other state violates, it receives a payoff of -50. It then violates in subsequent periods, leading to a total payoff of $-50 + 80/(1+r) + 80/(1+r)^2 \ldots = 80\ (1+r)/r - 130$.

11. Cooperation can be achieved as long as $100R > 120 + 80R$, or simplifying, $R > 6$. Recalling that $R = (1+r)\ /\ r$, there can be cooperation as long as $(1+r)\ /\ r > 6$, which is equivalent to $r < .2$.

12. See Axelrod (1984, pp. 126–132); Oye (1986, pp. 16–18); Koremenos et al. (2001).

13. Vienna Convention on the Law of Treaties, art. 60.

14. Treaty Between the United States and Great Britain Relating to Boundary Waters Between the United States and Canada, Jan. 11, 1909, U.S.-Can., 36 Stat. 2448 (hereafter Boundary Waters Treaty).

15. The treaty provides two dispute resolution provisions. Article 9 provides that disputes shall be referred to the International Joint Commission established by the treaty, but the decisions of the Commission "shall not be regarded as decisions of the questions or matters so submitted either on the facts or the law, and shall in no way have the character of an arbitral award." Article 10 provides that disputes can be submitted to the Commission for a decision, but this requires the consent of both parties.

16. Treaty Banning Nuclear Weapons Tests in the Atmosphere, in Outer Space and Under Water, Aug. 5, 1963, 14 UST 1313, 480 UNTS 43.

17. Treaty on the Non-Proliferation of Nuclear Weapons, opened for signature July 1, 1968, 21 UST 483, 484, 729 UNTS 161, 169.

18. The use and impact of retaliation is not limited to the legal context, of course, but for my purposes it is sensible to focus on that situation.

19. Michael R. Gordon, "Clinton Considers a Tougher Policy to Halt the Serbs," *New York Times*, April 17, 1993, A1F.

20. Brazil–Export Financing Programme for Aircraft (WT/DS46/AB/R), Aug. 2, 1999, Brazil–Export Financing Programme for Aircraft, Recourse to Arbitration by Brazil Under Article 22.6 of the DSU and Article 4.11 of the SCM Agreement, Aug. 28, 2000 (hereafter Brazil–Aircraft [22.6]).

21. Brazil–Aircraft (22.6), para. 92.

22. See, for example, International Law Commission, Responsibility of States for Internationally Wrongful Acts, ch. IV.E.1, U.N. GAOR 56th Sess., Supp. No. 10, U.N. Doc. A/56/10 (November 2001).

23. One might add the European Court of Justice to this list. Because of the peculiar structure of the European Union, however, I put this sort of European cooperation to one side. As explained in chapter 1, cooperation among EU member states and the European Court of Justice is, in some ways, more akin to cooperation among the states of the United States than that among other sovereign states. I also omit the International Criminal Court because its focus is on the prosecution of individuals rather than states. Rome Statute of the International Criminal Court, art. 1. I include the European Court of Human Rights because its jurisdiction extends beyond the European Union.

24. Convention on the Prohibition of the Development, Production, Stockpiling, and use of Chemical Weapons and on their Destruction (Chemical Weapons Convention), 1974 UNTS 3, A/RES/47/391.

25. The Security Council has the authority, in principle, to authorize the use of force and could presumably do so to enforce some decisions of international courts. In practice this sort of enforcement does not take place, and even if it did, the Security Council itself does not have an enforcement arm and so would have to rely on individual states to take action.

26. In practice, advisory opinions from the ICJ sometimes do, notwithstanding their advisory status, assign blame and impose reputational costs on a state. The most obvious example of this is the Advisory Opinion on Israel's Wall, in which the ICJ concluded, in an advisory opinion, that Israel had violated international law in its construction of a security wall in the occupied Palestinian territories. See Legal Consequences of the Construction of a Wall in the Occupied Palestinian Territory, 2004 I.C.J. 131 (July 9).

27. Chayes and Chayes (1993, 1995) reach the same conclusion, though they use different assumptions and rely on a different causal mechanism.

28. Posner and Sykes (2006) provide an economic analysis of state responsibility.

29. Draft Articles on Responsibility of States for Internationally Wrongful Act, 53 UN GAOR Supp. (No. 10) at 43, U.N. Doc. A/56/10 (2001).

30. Chorzow Factory (Germany v Poland) (Jurisdiction) [1927] PCIJ (ser A), No. 9.

31. In fact, the Antarctic Treaty itself contains only a reference to "living resources," a phrase that suggests that the parties drafting the treaty were more mindful of the economic benefits to be derived from exploiting Antarctica than of the preservation of its environment. For more on the evolution of environmental protection under the Antarctic Treaty, see Blay (1992).

32. One could include in the list of "commitments" made by states a number of other acts that do not amount to agreements. These might include, for example, unilateral declarations, votes in international organizations, domestic

policy decisions, and so on. These have a more tenuous connection to this discussion of international law and so are put aside for the moment. They also raise an important question about where international "law" ends and "politics" begins, which I address in chapter 6.

33. Art. 51 states: "The expression of a State's consent to be bound by a treaty which has been procured by the coercion of its representative through acts or threats directed against him shall be without any legal effect." Art. 52 states: "A treaty is void if its conclusion has been procured by the threat or use of force in violation of the principles of international law embodied in the Charter of the United Nations."

34. See Abbott (1996a, 1996b). Bronkers (1999, p. 548).

35. Goldsmith and Posner (2005, p. 87). ("[W]e are skeptical that genuine multinational collective action problems can be solved by treaty.")

36. One might challenge the notion that parties to a human rights agreement benefit from the compliance of other parties to the agreement. I put that issue to one side for the purposes of this example.

37. The 1994 agreement is the Agreed Framework Between the United States of America and the Democratic People's Republic of Korea, October 21, 1994.

38. Treaty on the Non-Proliferation of Nuclear Weapons, opened for signature July 1, 1968, 21 UST 483, 729 UNTS 161.

Chapter 3

1. See, for example, Huth (1988); Nalebuff (1991); Walter (2006b); Press (2004–5); Powell (1990).

2. For example, Downs and Jones say: "No detailed justification of the traditional theory of reputation exists in the literature" (2002, p. 100).

3. My rational choice approach assumes that states care only about their own payoffs, but one can accommodate a concern for others by including that concern in the state's utility function. Though admittedly ad hoc, it is a possible way to account for other-regarding behavior by states.

4. I put aside for the moment how actions in one area might affect reputation in other areas.

5. Goldsmith and Posner (2005, p. 103). ("[T]here are methodological reasons for resisting the assumption that states incur a reputational cost whenever they violate a treaty.... Once one makes that assumption, it becomes more difficult to explain why some treaties generate more compliance than others.")

6. Treaty on the Non-Proliferation of Nuclear Weapons, opened for signature July 1, 1968, 21 UST 483, 729 UNTS 161.

7. For a brief account of the history of the development of South Africa's nuclear project, see Spence (1984).

8. Bayesian updating is simply the rational adjustment of existing estimates based on new information. Bayes's rule can be formally stated as follows: $P(C|E) = [P(C) \ P(E|C)] \ / \ P(E)$, where C denotes compliance with international law, E denotes new evidence such as observed compliance or observed violation, $P(C)$ is the probably of compliance, $P(E)$ is the probability of observing a given outcome, either compliance or violation, and $P(E|C)$ and $P(C|E)$ are conditional probabilities. Bayes's rule allows parties to estimate the future likelihood of an event on the basis of new information, $P(C|E)$, as the product of their prior belief about the likelihood of that event, $P(C)$, and the ratio of the probability of observing evidence in favor of that belief conditional on the belief being correct, $P(E \ | \ C)$, and the total (or marginal) probability of observing evidence in support of the belief, $P(E)$. In an iterative context, the estimated probability becomes the prior belief in the next round of updating.

9. The debate about the status of customary international law in the investment area is a longstanding one that I do not attempt to resolve here. My thoughts on this debate are presented in Guzman (1998b).

10. A. N. Sack (1927), in his treatise on public debt, contends that "odious debt" accumulated by a repressive regime and used for illegitimate purposes need not be repaid by successor regimes. In practice, the idea of odious debt has never been consistently applied (see Great Britain v. Costa Rica). Furthermore, the Russian Revolution predated this argument by some 20 years.

11. Downs and Jones reach a similar, though more tentatively stated conclusion: "the impact of reputation on [new states'] fortunes may be far greater than for more established states" (2002, p. 113).

12. According to Sagan, "during the debate in Kiev, numerous pro-NPT Ukrainian officials insisted that renunciation of nuclear weapons was now the best route to enhance Ukraine's international standing" (1996, p. 81).

13. I discuss the extent to which a state's reputation is compartmentalized by issue area (or in other ways) later in the chapter.

14. Uncertainty about nonreputational payoffs will also reduce the degree to which violations that are expected strengthen an existing reputation. Imagine that a state violates an obligation, and that observing states anticipated a violation given what they knew about the reputational and nonreputational payoffs. If they had a high degree of certainty regarding the nonreputational payoffs, the fact that the violating state behaved as expected reinforces the prior beliefs about reputation. If there was much more uncertainty about nonreputational payoffs, there is a greater chance that the estimate of the acting states' reputation is wrong (and too low) and that the violation came

about because the nonreputational payoffs provided a stronger incentive to violate than the observing states realized. Though the observing state's estimate of the violating state's reputation is reinforced by the violation, the uncertainty about nonreputational payoffs reduces the extent to which that reinforcement takes place.

15. See Helfer (2002).

16. See Amnesty International, "Unacceptably Limiting Human Rights Protection," press release, March 1, 1999; http://web.amnesty.org/library/Index/ENGAMR050011999?open&of=ENG-GUY.

17. Mutual Defense Assistance Agreement, May 23, 1950, 1 UST 420, TIAS 2071, 81 UNTS 3.

18. General Agreement for Economic Cooperation, December 21, 1961, 12 UST 3229, TIAS 4930, 433 UNTS 269.

19. Agreement for Financing Certain Educational Exchange Programs, October 24, 1963, 14 UST 1510, TIAS 5451, 489 UNTS 303.

20. Sanitary and Phytosanitary Agreement, annex B.1, 2.

21. See, e.g., Agreement Between the Government of the United States of America and the Government of the Federal Republic of Germany Relating to Mutual Cooperation Regarding Restrictive Business Practices, 27 UST 1956, signed June 23, 1976, entered into force September 11, 1976. The International Competition Network has a website: www.internationalcompetitionnetwork.org/.

22. For a discussion of this debate, see Guzman (1998b).

23. In fairness, Chayes and Chayes do not emphasize reputation in their book, and may have simply been referring to a state's reputation as a shorthand for its reputation with respect to any particular agreement or situation. Within the legal literature in general, there has been sufficiently little explicit discussion of reputation that it would be an overstatement to claim that there is a person or group advancing the claim that states have a single reputation in all areas. Even within the political science literature, though there are many discussions that seem to proceed on the implicit assumption that states have a single reputation, I am not aware of any explicit claim that states have a single reputation.

24. The state of the customary international law of investment was in dispute at the time (Guzman 1998b).

25. This is arguably in contrast to the United States' attitude toward decisions of the ICJ where the United States' record of compliance is fairly poor. It has, for example, resisted or refused compliance in the case of Military and Paramilitary Activities (Nicar. v. U.S.), 1986 I.C.J. 14 ¶ 188 (June 27); the Vienna Convention on Consular Relations (Paraguay v. United States of America); the LaGrand Case (Federal Republic of Germany vs. United States

of America), 2001 I.C.J. 466 (June 27); and the Case Concerning Avena and Other Mexican Nationals (Mexico v. United States of America), 2004 I.C.J. 128 (Mar. 31). The latter three cases all deal with U.S. law enforcement officials' failures to notify foreign nationals of their right to consular assistance. In Paraguay, the prisoner in question, Angel Breard, was executed in defiance of an ICJ order for a stay so that the ICJ might hear the case. Paraguay subsequently dropped the case. LaGrand followed a similar fact pattern, except that Germany successfully pursued its case against the United States following the execution of the LaGrand brothers in Arizona. Finally, following a determination by the ICJ that the United States had violated the VCCR in the cases of 51 Mexican nationals sentenced to death, President Bush ordered state courts to give "meaningful review" as a matter of comity to Mexican nationals who may not have been apprised of their rights under the VCCR. At the same time, the United States withdrew from the Optional Protocol to the VCCR, which conferred on the ICJ jurisdiction to hear disputes. The fate of the 51 Mexican nationals in Avena has not yet been determined by American courts.

26. "[T]he reputational implications of noncompliance are narrower and hence smaller than much of the literature suggests" (Downs and Jones 2002, p. S98).

27. Article 80 of the Treaty of Versailles explicitly forbade the unification of Austria and Germany, without the approval of the Council of the League of Nations.

28. Geneva Convention Relative to the Treatment of Prisoners of War, art. 126.

29. See, e.g., Douglas Jehl and Eric Schmitt, "Officer says Army Tried to Curb Red Cross Visits to Prison in Iraq," *New York Times*, May 19, 2004, A1.

30. India–Patent Protection for Pharmaceutical and Agricultural Chemical Products, WT/DS79, May 6, 1997.

31. See Sell (1995).

32. Status Report by India, Addendum, India-Patent Protection for Pharmaceutical and Agricultural Chemical Products, April 15, 1999, WT/DS50/10/Add.4 WT/DS79/6 (1999).

Chapter 4

1. As the authors note, "[w]e call these 'conjectures' to indicate that they represent generalizations based on a common rational-choice theoretical framework, although they are not formally derived here; however in presenting the underlying logic of each conjecture we identify close variants that have been formally derived by scholars working in the rational choice tradition" (Koremenos et al. 2001, p. 780).

2. See Koremenos, Lipson, and Snidal (2001, p. 782); Koremenos (2005, p. 550).

3. Though this discussion considers only international law, it may be possible for states to diversify the risks they face in other areas as well. If this is true the assumption of risk aversion is problematic in those areas as well.

4. Convention Against Torture, art. 2.2.

5. I have elsewhere analyzed an application of this notion that states will breach rather than comply when compliance costs are too high (Guzman 2004).

6. International Standards and Recommended Practices: Personnel Licensing, International Civil Aviation Organization, Annex 1 (Amendment 164), Convention on International Civil Aviation, December 7, 1944, 61 Stat. 1180, 15 UNTS 295.

7. Convention on International Trade in Endangered Species of Wild Fauna and Flora, March 3, 1973, 27 UST 1087, 993 UNTS 243 (entered into force July 1, 1975).

8. For an example of a well-crafted public choice analysis in international law, see Sykes (1991).

9. It is worth noting that this is certainly not the first discussion of how the problem of modeling domestic activities intersects with the study of international law. The practical outcome in virtually every analysis has been to treat the state as a unitary actor, as is done here. Elsewhere (Guzman 2002a, pp. 900–904) I provide a more detailed discussion of how one can and should handle public choice issues when writing on international law.

10. Though the illustration used is a bilateral one, it is easy to extend the discussion to a multilateral context.

11. ICCPR art. 9:1.

12. ICCPR art. 4:1.

13. It is true that compliance with an agreement subject to a valid reservation or compliance with escape and exit provisions leaves a state in compliance with its promise, but that fact does not make the promise to perform any more credible. That is, if it is relatively easy for the promisor to legally avoid performance, the promisees are less able to rely on the behavior of the promisor, and so the promise to perform is less credible.

14. One potential response is that customary law is sometimes said to require not only that states honor their legal commitments but also that they "make full reparation for the injury caused by [an] internationally wrongful act." Draft Articles on Responsibility of States for Internationally Wrongful Acts, adopted by the International Law Commission at its 53rd session (September 2001), Supp. No. 10 (A/56/10), chap. IV.E.1; www.un.org/law/ilc/convents .htm. It is clear that, for a variety of reasons, this purported rule of customary international law should not be viewed as a full substitute for other credibility-enhancing design elements. There is little evidence that there is a

practice of complying with a rule of this sort, and so it is not clear that there is, in fact, such a customary rule. Even if there were such a rule, it would affect treaties and not other forms of agreement. And if there were such a rule, one would expect much more use of dispute resolution, since this is the most sensible mechanism with which to determine the appropriate level of reparations owed. Finally, the rule advanced in the Draft Articles of State Responsibility often provides for quite modest compensation and under certain conditions may demand only "an acknowledgement of the breach, an expression of regret, a formal apology, or another appropriate modality." Draft Articles, art. 37.

15. In addition to the problems with flexibility arguments in general, this particular claim is flawed because dispute resolution does not prevent states from seeking a negotiated solution. It is true that it may change the threat points of the two sides, but it in no way prevents negotiation or removes control of the issue from the states involved.

16. Part of the story in the United States was that the Senate was hostile to a treaty and it would have been politically difficult for the president to enter into an executive agreement.

17. Morsink (1999) and Glendon (2001) provide detailed histories of the origins of the UDHR.

18. An alternative interpretation is that the United States sought broader participation in the declaration. This leads to the question of why other states (the ones that would join a nonbinding agreement but not a treaty) might care about the choice between hard and soft law, and the answer here is again reputation.

19. Similar views are expressed in Builder (2000) and Raustiala (2005).

20. I am grateful to Daniel Bodansky for this example.

21. Vienna Convention on the Law of Treaties, art. 1.

22. Note that the discussion here is concerned with agreements that are "treaties" under international law, as opposed to those that are considered "treaties" under the laws of the United States and, therefore, require the advice and consent of the U.S. Senate. Nothing here addresses the question of when the president of the United States will opt for a "treaty" under U.S. law or a congressional-executive agreement. On these issues see Ackerman and Golove (1995); Setear (2002); Martin (2003).

23. Rome Statute of the International Criminal Court, July 17, 1998, art. 98(2), 2187 UNTS 90.

24. Reservations of Syrian Arab Republic to the CEDAW Convention; www .un.org/womenwatch/daw/cedaw/reservations-country.htm.

25. Strictly speaking, the Vienna Convention on the Law of Treaties, art. 56(1), provides that a treaty without provisions governing termination,

denunciation, or withdrawal "is not subject to denunciation or withdrawal unless: (a) it is established that the parties intended to admit the possibility of denunciation or withdrawal; or (b) a right of denunciation or withdrawal may be implied by the nature of the treaty."

26. United Nations Convention on the Law of the Sea, 1833 UNTS 3 (1982), art. 17.

27. United Nations Convention on the Law of the Sea, 1833 UNTS 3 (1982), art. 25.

28. Koremenos (2005) considers an additional tool to limit the obligations of the parties to an agreement: the use of duration provisions or sunset clauses. In her model, risk-averse states prefer temporary agreements to protect against uncertainty over time. When an agreement sunsets, the parties are then able to renegotiate it, subject to renegotiation costs. The model predicts that greater risk aversion, greater uncertainty, and lower renegotiation costs each increases the probability of a finite agreement. The model relies heavily on the assumption of risk aversion, which for reasons already given seems inappropriate in the context of international agreements. If states are assumed to be risk neutral, an increase in uncertainty should not affect the appeal of agreements of limited duration. The cost of renegotiation when an agreement sunsets, instead of the cost of renegotiation when it is still in force, would determine its duration.

29. Rome Statute of the International Criminal Court, opened for signature July 17, 1998, art. 120, 2187 UNTS 90, 155.

30. Vienna Convention on the Law of Treaties, art. 20.

31. Vienna Convention on the Law of Treaties, art. 21. The Human Rights Committee, established by the ICCPR, has put forward a more radical view of the consequences of objecting to reservations, at least in the human rights context. The Committee asserts that "[t]he normal consequence of an unacceptable reservation is not that the [ICCPR] will not be in effect at all for a reserving party. Rather, such a reservation will generally be severable, in the sense that the [ICCPR] will be operative for the reserving party without benefit of the reservation." Human Rights Committee, General Comment 24, UN/Doc. A/50/40, vol. 1, p. 199 (1995).

32. There are, of course, exceptions. The UDHR and various International Labor Organization Recommendations, for example, address human rights issues and are not treaties.

33. Art. 34, European Convention for the Protection of Human Rights and Fundamental Freedoms, 312 UNTS 221 (November 4, 1950).

34. 999 UNTS 171 (1967).

35. 2131 UNTS 83 (October 6, 1999).

36. Art. 22.1, Convention Against Torture and Other Cruel, Inhuman, or Degrading Treatment or Punishment, 24 ILM 535 (1985).

37. Art. 44, American Convention on Human Rights, 9 ILM 673 (1970).

38. Art. 14, International Convention on the Elimination of All Forms of Racial Discrimination, 5 ILM 353 (1966).

39. The causes of action under these agreements also vary in terms of the available remedies. For example, the Optional Protocol to the ICCPR and art. 22 of the CAT both allow states to voluntarily submit to the jurisdiction of commissions established by the respective conventions to receive communications from individuals about violations. However, the commissions (the UN Commission on Human Rights and the Committee Against Torture) lack the ability to award relief to the individual should they determine that human rights violations have actually occurred.

40. See Sims (2004).

41. These broad statements are subject to exceptions, of course, and a more complete inquiry would have to start by evaluating whether the claim itself can withstand careful scrutiny. The Basel Accord, for example, includes at least modest reporting and monitoring provisions; and the Financial Action Task Force, an organization made up of experts from various government ministries, law enforcement authorities, officials, and bank regulatory agencies, has produced what are called the "Forty Recommendations," which are backed up by both monitoring and the potential for sanctions; Simmons (2000a). The forty recommendations were promulgated in 1990. They can be found on the FATF website, www.fatf-gafi.org.

42. See chapter 2.

43. The Load Line Convention Between the United States and Canada, Canadian Treaty Series 34/10 (Entered into force July 26, 1934).

44. In formal terms, if the cost C of a treaty is a function of its scope S, I am assuming that both the first and second derivative of C with respect to S are greater than zero: $C'(S) > 0$, and $C''(S) > 0$.

45. From WIPO website, www.wipo.int/about-wipo/en/pac/index.htm.

46. Agreement Between the Government of the United States of America and the Government of Canada Regarding the Application of Their Competition and Deceptive Marketing Practices Laws, August 3, 1995, U.S.-Can., reprinted in Trade Regulation Reporter (CCH) 4, par. 13, 503.

47. Canada–United States: Memorandum of Understanding on Administration and Enforcement of Securities Laws, 27 ILM 410 (1988).

48. Treaty on Extradition Between the United States and Canada of December 3, 1971, 27 UST 983.

49. North American Agreement on Environmental Cooperation, September 14, 1993, 32 ILM 1480.

50. For example, article II of GATT provides that states will not raise tariffs above the level agreed to on their negotiated schedules.

51. For example, GATT arts. IX and XIII address nontariff barriers.

52. Agreement on Subsidies and Countervailing Measures.

53. GATT, art. XX, for example, provides the primary list of exceptions to GATT obligations.

54. Among these are the Agreement on Sanitary and Phytosanitary Measures, the Agreement on Safeguards, the Agreement on Agriculture, the Agreement on Implementation of Article VI of the General Agreement on Tariffs and Trade 1994 (the "Antidumping Agreement").

55. Convention between the Government of the United States of America and the Government of the United Kingdom of Great Britain and Northern Ireland for the Avoidance of Double Taxation and the Prevention of Fiscal Evasion with Respect to Taxes on Income and on Capital Gains, July 24, 2001, as amended by a protocol signed July 19, 2002; entered into force March 31, 2003.

56. Elsewhere I make a similar claim about negotiations in the competition policy context (Guzman 1998a).

57. The TRIPs agreement was just one part of the very complex Uruguay Round negotiations, so the foregoing description is necessarily a highly simplified version of what took place. It is, however, broadly consistent with most commentators' views.

58. I refer here to what they term conjectures S1 and S2.

59. For example, the WTO case China–Value-Added Tax on Integrated Circuits, WT/DS309, addressed the GATS agreement as well as the GATT and China's accession to the WTO; Turkey–Certain Import Procedures for Fresh Fruit, WT/DS237, dealt with Agriculture, GATS, GATT, Licensing, and the Sanitary and Phytosanitary Measures Agreement.

60. I put to one side the primary exception to this rule, which is the Security Council's ability to adopt resolutions that are binding on all states.

61. This is something of a simplification, because the negotiations themselves (or events leading up to them) may cause the status quo to be unavailable going forward. So, for example, negotiations carried out in the shadow of a credible threat to withdraw from an existing agreement need not generate an outcome better than the status quo for all parties. Such negotiations only need to generate an outcome better than the no-agreement alternative.

62. International Convention on the Protection of the Rights of All Migrant Workers and Members of Their Families, G.A. Res. 45/158, U.N. GAOR, 45th Sess., Supp. No. 49A, p. 261, U.N. Doc. A/45/49 (1990) (entered into force July 1, 2003).

63. It is conceivable that some other purpose might be served, including delivering a political message to domestic constituents and changing global perceptions about acceptable human rights practices.

64. To be somewhat more precise, as the positive externalities from the production of the good grow less concentrated, the incentive to free ride increases.

65. Vienna Convention on the Law of Treaties, art. 60.2.b. A breach by one party only allows another party to suspend the operation of the treaty with respect to itself if the breach "radically changes the position of every party with respect to the further performance of its obligation under the treaty"; art. 60.2.c.

66. In their conclusion, Koremenos, Lipson, and Snidal acknowledge that their initial conjecture about membership was not borne out by the case studies included in Koremenos et al. (2001). They attribute this failure to find support for their conjecture to the fact that exclusion is rarely used as a punishment for noncooperators.

67. Other treaties signed but not ratified by the United States include the Biodiversity Treaty, the Comprehensive Test Ban Treaty, the Convention on the Rights of the Child, and the Convention on Race Discrimination in Employment.

68. Vienna Convention on the Law of Treaties, art. 18.

69. Vienna Convention on the Law of Treaties, art. 18(a).

Chapter 5

1. Understanding on Rules and Procedures Governing the Settlement of Disputes, art. 3.2.

2. Statute of the International Court of Justice, art. 38(1)(b).

3. Restatement (Third) of Foreign Relations Law of the United States, 102(2) (1987).

4. Right of Nationals of the United States of American in Morocco, 1952 I.C.J. Reports 176, 200.

5. Mendelson writes: "It is not necessary to demonstrate the presence of the subjective element in all, or perhaps even most, instances" (1998, p. 250). And "where there is a well established practice, the Court and other international tribunals, not to mention the States themselves, tend to conclude that there is a customary rule without looking for proof of opinio juris" (p. 289).

6. Restatement (Third) of the Foreign Relations Law of the United States, sec. 702 cmt. G. & rep. n. 5 (1987).

7. Filartiga v. Pena-Irala, 630 F.2d 876, 878 (2d Cir. 1980) (arguing that torture is a violation of customary human rights).

8. See Verdross and Heribert Koeck (1983).

9. Consent is sometimes offered as a general explanation of international law and compliance. Though the existence of consent is more evident in treaties, there remains no reason to think that the act of consenting to a rule causes a state to comply. I have discussed this issue in more detail elsewhere (Guzman 2002b, pp. 1833–1834).

10. Earlier writing by Goldsmith and Posner was more explicit: "The faulty premise is that CIL...influences national behavior" (2000, p. 640).

11. For ease of discussion, I will refer to the claim that CIL has no exogenous impact on behavior as equivalent to the claim that CIL does not matter. As mentioned, Goldsmith and Posner do not dismiss the relevance of behavioral norms, but they deny that viewing these norms as legal obligations has any relevance.

12. Treaties, after all, are a more serious pledge and commitment of reputational capital. Even soft law agreements are likely to be viewed as different from CIL for reputational purposes.

13. Filartiga v. Pena-Irala, 630 F.2d 876 (1980).

14. The same logic would also apply to new regimes, but would introduce the problem of determining when a change in regime is a sufficiently large break from the past as to provide an opportunity to repudiate existing rules of CIL.

15. North Sea Continental Shelf Case (F.R.G. v. Den.; F.R.G. v. Neth.), 1969 I.C.J. 3, para. 74 (Feb. 20).

16. The majority view among international law commentators would include a very broad range of statements within the definition of "practice" for the purpose of demonstrating CIL. The Report of the International Law Commission to the General Assembly of the United Nations, reprinted in [1950] 2 Y.B. Int'l L. Comm'n 364, stated that "[d]iplomatic statements (including protests), policy statements, press releases, official manuals (e.g., on military law), instructions to armed forces, comments by governments on draft treaties, legislation, decisions of national courts and executive authorities, pleadings before international tribunals, statements in international organizations and the resolutions those bodies adopt...are all forms of speech-act." In *Rights of Nationals of the United States of America in Morocco* case, 1952 I.C.J. Reports 176, 200, the ICJ appeared to agree with this approach, using diplomatic correspondence to evaluate a claim of state practice.

17. Though this sounds somewhat absurd, it is hardly more so than the current practice by which states sometimes enter into soft law agreements entitled "a nonbinding agreement on XYZ."

18. Legality of the Threat or Use of Nuclear Weapons, Advisory Opinion, 1996 I.C.J. 226, 241–42 (July 8). See also Corfu Channel (U.K. v. Alb.), 1949 I.C.J. 4, 22 (April 9), in which the ICJ said that it is "every State's obligation not to

allow knowingly its territory to be used for acts contrary to the rights of
other States."

19. See Trail Smelter (U.S. v. Can.), 3 R.I.A.A. 1905 (1941), finding Canada liable
    to the United States for damages done to land and water in the Columbia
    River valley by sulphur dioxide emissions from a zinc and lead smelter
    located in British Columbia.

20. See WTO Appellate Body Report, *European Communities—Measures Con-
    cerning Meat and Meat Products,* para. 120–125, WTO Doc. WT/DS26/AB/R,
    48 (January 16, 1998).

21. See Letter Brief to the Solicitor General on the *Domingues* Case, Human
    Rights Watch, September 24, 1999; www.hrw.org/children/domingues.htm.

Chapter 6

1. UN Charter, art. 25.
2. North Atlantic Treaty, art. 5.

BIBLIOGRAPHY

Abbott, Frederick M. 1989. Modern International Relations Theory: A Prospectus for International Lawyers. *Yale Journal of International Law* 14: 335–411.

———. 1996a. Commentary: The International Intellectual Property Order Enters the Twenty-First Century. *Vanderbilt Journal of Transnational Law* 29: 471–79.

———. 1996b. The WTO TRIPs Agreement and Global Economic Development. *Chicago-Kent Law Review* 72: 385–405.

Abbott, Kenneth W., and Duncan Snidal. 1998. Why States Act through Formal Organizations. *Journal of Conflict Resolution* 42: 3–32.

———. 2000. Hard and Soft Law in International Governance. *International Organization* 54: 421–56.

Abreu, Dilip, and Frank Gul. 2000. Bargaining and Reputation. *Econometrica* 68: 85–117.

Abreu, Dilip, David Pearce, and Ennio Stacchetti. 1986. Optimal Cartel Equilibria with Imperfect Monitoring. *Journal of Economic Theory* 39: 251–69.

Ackerman, Bruce, and David Golove. 1995. Is NAFTA Constitutional? *Harvard Law Review* 108: 799–929.

Akehurst, Michael. 1974–75. Custom as a Source of International Law. *British Yearbook of International Law* 46: 1–54.

Aldrich, George H. 2000. The Laws of War on Land. *American Journal of International Law* 91: 42–63.

Allee, Todd L., and Paul K. Huth. 2006. Legitimizing Dispute Settlement: International Legal Rulings as Domestic Political Cover. *American Political Science Review* 100: 219–34.

Alt, James, Randall Calvert, and Brian Humes. 1988. Reputation and Hegemonic Stability: A Game-Theoretic Analysis. *American Political Science Review* 82: 445–66.

Alter, Karen J. 2003. Do International Courts Enhance Compliance with International Law? *Review of Asian and Pacific Studies* no. 25: 51–78.

Axelrod, Robert. 1984. *The Evolution of Cooperation*. New York: Basic Books.

Axelrod, Robert, and Robert O. Keohane. 1986. Achieving Cooperation under Anarchy: Strategies and Institutions. In *Cooperation under Anarchy*, ed. Kenneth Oye. Princeton, N.J.: Princeton University Press, 226–60.

Barrett, Scott. 2003. *Environment and Statecraft: The Strategy of Environmental Treaty-Making*. Oxford: Oxford University Press.

Baxter, Richard. 1980. International Law in "Her Infinite Variety." *International and Comparative Law Quarterly* 29: 549–66.

Bernstein, Lisa. 1992. Opting out of the Legal System: Extralegal Contractual Relations in the Diamond Industry. *Journal of Legal Studies* 21: 115–57.

Blay, S. K. N. 1992. New Trends in the Protection of the Antarctic Environment: The 1991 Madrid Protocol. *American Journal of International Law* 86: 377–99.

Brewster, Rachel. 2006. Rule-Based Dispute Resolution in International Trade Law. *Virginia Law Review* 92: 251–88.

Bronkers, Marco C. E. J. 1999. A Warning against Undemocratic Developments in the WTO. *Journal of International Economic Law* 2: 547–66.

Builder, Richard B. 2000. Beyond Compliance: Helping Nations Cooperate. In *Commitment and Compliance: The Role of Non-binding Norms in the International Legal System*, ed. Dinah Shelton. New York: Oxford University Press: 65–73.

Busch, Lutz-Alexander, and Barbara Koremenos. 2001. *Negotiating the Bargaining Agenda*. Unpublished manuscript, University of California, Los Angeles.

Byers, Michael. 1999. *Custom, Power and the Power of Rules*. Cambridge: Cambridge University Press.

Carr, Edward Hallett. 1950. *A History of Soviet Russia: The Bolshevik Revolution*. Vol. 3. New York: Macmillan.

Chayes, Abram, and Antonia Handler Chayes. 1993. On Compliance. *International Organization* 47: 175–205.

———. 1995. *The New Sovereignty: Compliance with International Regulatory Agreements*. Cambridge, Mass.: Harvard University Press.

Cheng, Bin. 1965. United Nations Resolutions on Outer Space: "Instant" International Customary Law. *Indian Journal of International Law* 5: 23–112.

Coase, Ronald H. 1960. The Problem of Social Cost. *Journal of Law and Economics* 3: 1–44.

Coleman, James S. 1990. *Foundations of Social Theory*. Cambridge, Mass.: Harvard University Press.

Croley, Steven P. 1998. Theories of Regulation: Incorporating the Administrative Process. *Columbia Law Review* 98: 1–168.

D'Amato, Anthony A. 1971. *The Concept of Custom in International Law*. Ithaca, N.Y.: Cornell University Press.

Danner, Allison. 2006. When Courts Make Law: How the International Criminal Tribunals Recast the Laws of War. *Vanderbilt Law Review* 59: 1–65.

Downs, George W., and Michael A. Jones. 2002. Reputation, Compliance, and International Law. *Journal of Legal Studies* 31: S95–S114.

Downs, George W., and David M. Rocke. 1990. *Tacit Bargaining, Arms Races, and Arms Control.* Ann Arbor: University of Michigan Press.

———. 1995. *Optimal Imperfection? Domestic Uncertainty and Institutions in International Relations.* Princeton, N.J.: Princeton University Press.

Downs, George W., David M. Rocke, and Peter N. Barsoom. 1996. Is the Good News about Compliance Good News about Cooperation? *International Organization* 50: 379–406.

Dunoff, Jeffrey L., and Joel P. Trachtman. 1999. Economic Analysis of International Law. *Yale Journal of International Law* 24: 1–56.

Elkins, Zach, Andrew T. Guzman, and Beth Simmons. 2006. Competing for Capital: The Diffusion of Bilateral Investment Treaties, 1960–2000. *International Organization* 60: 811–46.

Farrell, Joseph, and Matthew Rubin. 1996. Cheap Talk. *Journal of Economic Perspectives* 10: 103–18.1.

Farrell, Joseph, and Garth Saloner. 1988. Coordination through Committees and Markets. *Rand Journal of Economics* 19: 235–52.

Fearon, James D. 1998. Bargaining, Enforcement, and International Cooperation. *International Organization* 52: 269–305.

Finnemore, Martha, and Kathryn Sikkink. 1998. International Norm Dynamics and Political Change. *International Organization* 52: 887–917.

Franck, Thomas M. 1995. *Fairness in International Law and Institutions.* New York: Oxford University Press.

———. 1988. Legitimacy in the International System. *American Journal of International Law* 82: 705–59.

Gilligan, Michael J. 2004. Is There a Broader–Deeper Trade-off in International Multilateral Agreements? *International Organization* 58: 459–84.

Ginsburg, Tom, and Richard H. McAdams. 2004. Adjudicating in Anarchy: An Expressive Theory of International Dispute Resolution. *William and Mary Law Review* 45: 1229–1339.

Glendon, Mary Ann. 2001. *A World Made New: Eleanor Roosevelt and the Universal Declaration of Human Rights.* New York: Random House.

Goldsmith, Jack L., and Eric A. Posner. 1999. A Theory of Customary International Law. *University of Chicago Law Review* 66: 1113–77.

———. 2000. Understanding the Resemblance between Modern and Traditional Customary International Law. *Virginia Journal of International Law* 40: 639–72.

———. 2005. *The Limits of International Law.* New York: Oxford University Press.

Goldstein, Judith, Miles Kahler, Robert O. Keohane, and Anne-Marie Slaughter, eds. 2001. *Legalization and World Politics.* Cambridge, Mass.: MIT Press.

Goodman, Ryan, and Derek Jinks. 2004. How to Influence States: Socialization and International Human Rights Law. *Duke Law Journal* 54: 621–703.

Grieco, Joseph M. 1988. Anarchy and the Limits of Cooperation: A Realist Critique of the Newest Liberal Institutionalism. *International Organization* 42: 485–507.

Guth, Werner, and Hartmut Kliemt. 1994. Competition or Cooperation: On the Evolutionary Economics of Trust, Exploitation, and Moral Attitudes. *Metroeconomica* 45: 155–87.

Guzman, Andrew T. 1998a. Is International Antitrust Possible? *New York University Law Review* 73: 1501–48.

———. 1998b. Why LDCs Sign Treaties That Hurt Them: Explaining the Popularity of Bilateral Investment Treaties. *Virginia Journal of International Law* 38: 639–88.

———. 2001. Antitrust and International Regulatory Federalism. *New York University Law Review* 76: 1142–63.

———. 2002a. Choice of Law: New Foundations. *Georgetown Law Review* 90: 883–940.

———. 2002b. A Compliance Based Theory of International Law. *California Law Review* 90: 1823–87.

———. 2002c. The Cost of Credibility: Explaining Resistance to Interstate Dispute Resolution Mechanisms. *Journal of Legal Studies* 31: 303–26.

———. 2004. Food Fears: Health and Safety at the WTO. *Virginia Journal of International Law* 45: 1–39.

———. 2005a. The Design of International Agreements. *European Journal of International Law* 16: 579–612.

———. 2005b. Saving Customary International Law. *Michigan Journal of International Law* 27: 115–76.

———. 2006. Reputation and International Law. *Georgia Journal of International and Comparative Law* 34: 379–91.

Guzman, Andrew T., and Beth A. Simmons. 2002. To Settle or Empanel? An Empirical Analysis of Litigation and Settlement at the WTO. *Journal of Legal Studies* 31: S205–S235.

Haggard, Stephan, and Beth A. Simmons. 1987. Theories of International Regimes. *International Organization* 31: 491–517.

Haas, Peter M. 1990. *Saving the Mediterranean: The Politics of International Environmental Co-operation.* New York: Columbia University Press.

Hathaway, Oona. 2002. Do Human Rights Treaties Make a Difference? *Yale Law Journal* 111: 1935–2042.

Helfer, Laurence R. 2002. Overlegalizing Human Rights: International Relations Theory and the Commonwealth Caribbean Backlash against Human Rights Regimes. *Columbia Law Review* 102: 1832–1911.

———. 2005. Exiting Treaties. *Virginia Law Review* 91: 1579–1648.

———. 2006. Response: Not Fully Committed? Reservations, Risk, and Treaty Design. *Yale Journal of International Law* 31: 367–82.

Helfer, Laurence R., and Anne-Marie Slaughter. 2005. Why States Create International Tribunals: A Response to Professors Posner and Yoo. *California Law Review* 93: 899–956

Henkin, Louis. 1979. *How Nations Behave: Law and Foreign Policy.* New York: Columbia University Press.

Ho, Daniel E. 2002. Compliance and International Soft Law: Why Do Countries Implement the Basel Accord? *Journal of International Economic Law* 5: 647–88.

Huth, Paul K. 1988. *Extended Deterrence and the Prevention of War.* New Haven, Conn.: Yale University Press.

———. 1997. Reputations and Deterrence: A Theoretical and Empirical Assessment. *Security Studies* 7: 72–99.

Inman, Robert P., and Daniel L. Rubinfeld. 1997. Rethinking Federalism. *Journal of Economic Perspectives* 11: 43–64.

International Law Commission. 2001. *Draft Articles on Responsibility of States for Internationally Wrongful Acts.* Adopted by the International Law Commission at Its Fifty-Third Session (September 2001), supp. no. 10. (A/56/10), chap. IV.E.1. www.un.org/law/ilc/convents.htm.

Jervis, Robert. 1985. From Balance to Concert: A Study of International Security Cooperation. *World Politics* 38 (10): 58–79.

Keohane, Robert O. 1983. The Demand for International Regimes. *In International Regimes*, ed. Stephen Krasner. Ithaca, N.Y.: Cornell University Press, 141–71.

———. 1984. *After Hegemony: Cooperation and Discord in the World Political Economy.* Princeton, N.J.: Princeton University Press.

———. 1986. Reciprocity in International Relations. *International Organization* 40: 1–27.

———. 1990. Multilateralism: An Agenda for Research. *International Journal* 45: 731–64.

———. 1997. International Relations and International Law: Two Optics. *Harvard International Law Journal* 38: 487–502.

Keohane, Robert O., and Lisa L. Martin. 1995. The Promise of Institutionalist Theory. *International Security* 20: 39–51.

Kirgis, Frederick. 1987. Appraisals of the ICJ Decisions: Nicaragua v. United States (Merits). *American Journal of International Law* 81: 146–51.

Koh, Harold Hongju. 1996. Transnational Legal Process. *Nebraska Law Review* 75: 181–207.

———. 1997. Why Do Nations Obey International Law? *Yale Law Journal* 106: 2599–2659.

Koremenos, Barbara. 2001. Loosening the Ties That Bind: A Learning Model of Agreement Flexibility. *International Organization* 55: 289–325.

———. 2005. Contracting around International Uncertainty. *American Political Science Review* 99: 549–565.

Koremenos, Barbara, Charles Lipson, and Duncan Snidal. 2001. The Rational Design of International Institutions. Special issue, *International Organization* 55: 761–99.

Krasner, Stephen D., ed. 1983. *International Regimes*. Ithaca, N.Y.: Cornell University Press.

———. 1999. *Organized Hypocrisy*. Princeton, N.J.: Princeton University Press.

———. 1991. Global Communications and National Power: Life on the Pareto Frontier. *World Politics* 43: 336–66.

Kydd, Andrew. 2000a. Trust, Reassurance, and Cooperation. *International Organization* 54: 325–57.

———. 2000b. Overcoming Mistrust. *Rationality and Society* 12: 397–424.

Lacarte-Muro, Julio, and Petinia Gappah. 2000. Developing Countries and the WTO Legal and Dispute Settlement System: A View from the Bench. *Journal of International Economic Law* 3: 395–401.

Lahno, Bernd. 1995. Trust, Reputation, and Exit in Exchange Relationships. *Journal of Conflict Resolution* 39: 495–510.

Lake, David A. 1996. Anarchy, Hierarchy, and the Variety of International Relations. *International Organization* 50: 1–34.

Lake, David A., and Robert Powell. 1999. International Relations: A Strategic-Choice Approach. In *Strategic Choice and International Relations*, ed. David A. Lake and Robert Powell. Princeton, N.J.: Princeton University Press, 3–38.

Leeds, Brett Ashley. 2003. Alliance Reliability in Times of War: Explaining State Decisions to Violate Treaties. *International Organization* 57: 801–27.

Leeds, Brett Ashley, and Sezi Anac. Alliance Institutionalization and Alliance Performance. *International Interactions* 31: 183–202.

Leeds, Brett Ashley, Andrew G. Long, and Sara McLaughlin Mitchell. 2000. Reevaluating Alliance Reliability: Specific Threats, Specific Promises. *Journal of Conflict Resolution.* 44: 686–99.

Legro, Jeffrey W., and Andrew Moravcsik. 1999. Is Anybody Still a Realist? *International Security* 24: 5–55.

Lipson, Charles. 1991. Why Are Some International Agreements Informal? *International Organization* 45: 495–538.

Lutz, Ellen L., and Kathryn Sikkink. 2000. International Human Rights Law and Practice in Latin America. *International Organization* 54: 633–59.

Maggi, Giovanni. 1999. The Role of Multilateral Institutions in International Trade Cooperation. *American Economic Review* 89: 190–214.

Martin, Lisa L. 2003. *The United States and International Commitments: Treaties as Signaling Devices.* Unpublished manuscript, Harvard University.

McGinnis, John O. 1996. The Decline of the Western Nation State and the Rise of the Regime of International Federalism. *Cardozo Law Review* 18: 903–24.

Mearsheimer, John J. 1995. The False Promise of International Institutions. *International Security* 19: 5–49.

Mendelson, Maurice H. 1998. The Formation of Customary International Law. *Recueil Des Cours* 272: 159–410.

Mercer, Jonathan. 1996. *Reputation and International Politics.* Ithaca, N.Y.: Cornell University Press.

Milgrom, Paul, Douglas C. North, and Barry R. Weingast. 1990. The Role of Institutions in the Revival of Trade: The Law Merchant, Private Judges, and the Champagne Fairs. *Economics and Politics* 2: 1–23.

Miller, Gregory D. 2003. Hypotheses on Reputation: Alliance Choices and the Shadow of the Past. *Security Studies* 12: 40–78.

Mitchell, Ronald B. 1994. *International Oil Pollution at Sea: Environmental Policy and Treaty Compliance.* Cambridge, MA: MIT Press.

Mitchell, Ronald B. and Patricia Keilbach. 2001. Situation Structure and Institutional Design: Reciprocity, Coercion, and Exchange. *International Organization* 55 (4): 891–917.

Moravcsik, Andrew. 1997. Taking Preferences Seriously: A Liberal Theory of International Politics. *International Organization* 51: 516–53.

———. 2000. The Origins of Human Rights Regimes: Democratic Delegation in Postwar Europe. *International Organization* 54: 217–252.

Morgenthau, Hans J. 1973. *Politics Among Nations: The Struggle for Power and Peace.* 5th ed. New York: Knopf.

Morrow, James D. 1994. Modeling the Forms of International Cooperation: Distribution versus Information. *International Organization* 48: 387–423.

———. 2000. Alliances: Why Write Them Down? *Annual Review of Political Science* 3: 63–68.

———. 2001. The Institutional Features of the Prisoners of War Treaties. *International Organization* 55: 971–91.

———. 2006. *Patterns of Compliance with the Laws of War.* Unpublished manuscript, University of Michigan, available at http://weber.ucsd.edu/~jlbroz/PISA/morrow.pdf.

Morsink, Johannes. 1999. *The Universal Declaration of Human Rights: Origins, Drafting, and Intent.* Philadelphia: University of Pennsylvania Press.

Nalebuff, Barry. 1991. Rational Deterrence in an Imperfect World. *World Politics* 43: 313–35.

Neumayer, Eric, and Laura Spess. 2004. *Do Bilateral Investment Treaties Increase Foreign Direct Investment to Developing Countries?* Unpublished manuscript, London School of Economics.

Norman, George, and Joel P. Trachtman. 2005. The Customary International Law Game. *American Journal of International Law* 99: 541–78.

Oates, Wallace. 1972. *Fiscal Federalism.* New York: Harcourt Brace Jovanovich.

Olson, Mancur. 1965. *The Logic of Collective Action: Public Goods and the Theory of Groups.* Cambridge, Mass.: Harvard University Press.

Oye, Kenneth A., ed. 1986. *Cooperation under Anarchy.* Princeton, N.J.: Princeton University Press.

Polinsky, A. Mitchell. 1989. *An Introduction to Law and Economics.* 2nd ed. Boston: Little, Brown.

Posner, Eric A. 2000. *Law and Social Norms.* Cambridge, Mass.: Harvard University Press.

Posner, Eric A., and Alan O. Sykes. 2006. *An Economic Analysis of State and Individual Responsibility under International Law.* Unpublished manuscript, University of Chicago.

Posner, Eric A., and John C. Yoo. 2005. Judicial Independence in International Tribunals. *California Law Review* 93: 1–74.

Powell, Robert. 1990. *Nuclear Deterrence Theory: The Search for Credibility.* New York: Cambridge University Press.

Press, Daryl G. 2005. The Credibility of Power. *International Security* 29: 136–69.

Raiffa, Howard. 1982. *The Art and Science of Negotiating.* Cambridge, Mass.: Harvard University Press.

———. 2002. *Negotiation Analysis.* Cambridge, Mass.: Harvard University Press.

Raustiala, Kal. 2005. Form and Substance in International Agreements. *American Journal of International Law* 99: 581–614.

Richards, John E. 2001. Institutions for Flying: How States Built a Market in International Aviation Services. *International Organization* 55 (4): 993–1017.

Risse, Thomas. 2000. Let's Argue! Communicative Action in World Politics. *International Organization* 54: 1–39.

Roberts, Adam. 1994. The Laws of War in the 1990–91 Gulf Conflict. *International Security* 18(3): 134–81.

Roberts, Anthea Elizabeth. 2001. Traditional and Modern Approaches to Customary International Law: A Reconciliation. *American Journal of International Law* 95: 757–91.

Rose, Andrew K. 2004. Do We Really Know That the WTO Increases Trade? *American Economic Review* 94: 98–114.

Rosendorff, Peter B., and Helen V. Miller. 2001. The Optimal Design of International Trade Institutions: Uncertainty and Escape. *International Organization* 55: 829–57.

Rovine, Arthur W. 1976. The National Interest and the World Court. In *The Future of the International Court of Justice*, ed. Leo Gross. Dobbs Ferry, N.Y.: Oceana: 462–73.

Sack, Alexander N. 1927. *Les Effets Des Transformations des Etats sure Leurs Dettes Publiques et Autres Obligations Financieres*. Paris: Receuil Sirey.

Sagan, Scott. 1996. Why Do States Build Nuclear Weapons? Three Models In Search of a Bomb. *International Security* 18: 54–86.

Sartori, Anne E. 2002. A Reputational Theory of Communications in Disputes, *International Organization* 56: 121–49.

Schacter, Oscar. 1996. New Custom: Power, Opinio Juris, and Contrary Practice. In *Theory of International Law and the Threshold of the Twenty-First Century: Essays in Honour of Krzysztof Skubiszewsk*, ed. Jerzy Makarczyk. Boston: Kluwer Law International, 531–40.

Schelling, Thomas. 1960. *The Strategy of Conflict*. Cambridge, Mass.: Harvard University Press.

Schwartz, Warren F., and Alan O. Sykes. 2002. The Economic Structure of Renegotiation and Dispute Resolution in the World Trade Organization. *Journal of Legal Studies* 31: S179–S204.

Scott, Robert E., and Paul B. Stephan. 2006. *The Limits of Leviathan: Contract Theory and the Enforcement of International Law*. New York: Cambridge University Press.

Sell, Susan. 1995. Intellectual Property Protection and Antitrust in the Developing World: Crisis, Coercion, and Choice. *International Organization* 49: 315–49.

Setear, John K. 1997. Responses to Breach of a Treaty and Rationalist International Relations Theory: The Rules of Release and Remediation in the Law of Treaties and the Law of State Responsibility. *Virginia Law Review* 83: 1–126.

———. 2002. The President's Rational Choice of a Treaty's Preratification Pathway: Article 2, Congressional-Executive Agreement, or Executive Agreement? *Journal of Legal Studies* 31: S5–S39.

Shelton, Dinah. 2006. Normative Hierarchy in International Law. *American Journal of International Law* 100: 291–323.

Shepsle, Kenneth. 1986. Institutional Equilibrium and Equilibrium Institutions. *The Science of Politics*, ed. Herbert Weisberg. New York: Agathon, 51–82.

———. 1989. Studying Institutions: Some Lessons from the Rational Choice Approach. *Journal of Theoretical Politics* 1: 131–47.

Shihata, Ibrahim F. I. 1965. The Attitude of New States toward the International Court of Justice. *International Organization* 19: 203–22.

Simmons, Beth. 2000a. International Efforts against Money Laundering. In *Commitment and Compliance: The Role of Non-Binding Norms in the International Legal System*, ed. Dinah Shelton. New York: Oxford University Press: 244–63.

———. 2000b. International Law and State Behavior: Commitment and Compliance in International Monetary Affairs. *American Political Science Review* 94: 819–35.

Sims, John Cary. 2004. Compliance without Remands: The Experience under the European Convention on Human Rights. *Arizona State Law Journal* 36: 639–60.

Slaughter, Anne-Marie. 1995. International Law in a World of Liberal States. *European Journal of International Law* 6: 503–38.

———. 2004. *A New World Order*. Princeton, N.J.: Princeton University Press.

Sobel, Joel. 1985. A Theory of Credibility. *Review of Economic Studies* 52: 557–73.

Spence, J. E. 1984. South Africa: The Nuclear Option. *African Affairs* 80: 441–52.

Spence, Michael. 1973. Job Market Signaling. *Quarterly Journal of Economics* 87: 355–74.

Stein, Ted L. 1985. The Approach of the Different Drummer: The Principle of the Persistent Objector in International Law. *Harvard International Law Journal* 45: 457–82.

Swaine, Edward T. 2002. Rational Custom. *Duke Law Journal* 52: 559–627.

———. 2003. Unsigning. *Stanford Law Review* 55: 2061–89.

———. 2006. Reserving. *Yale Journal of International Law* 31: 307–66.

Sykes, Alan O. 1991. Protectionism as a "Safeguard": A Positive Analysis of the GATT "Escape Clause" with Normative Speculations. *University of Chicago Law Review* 58: 255–303.

———. 2004. *The Economics of Public International Law*. John M. Olin Law and Economics Working Paper no. 216, 2nd series, unpublished manuscript, University of Chicago Law School.

Tobin, Jennifer, and Susan Rose-Ackerman. 2004. *Foreign Direct Investment and the Business Environment in Developing Countries: The Impact of Bilateral Investment Treaties*. Unpublished manuscript, Yale Law School Center for Law, Economics, and Public Policy, research paper no. 293.

Tomz, Michael. 2007. *Reputation and International Cooperation: Sovereign Debt Across Three Centuries*. Princeton, N.J.: Princeton University Press.

Tomz, Michael, Judith Goldstein, and Douglas Rivers. 2005. *Membership Has Its Privileges: The Impact of GATT on International Trade*. Unpublished manuscript, Stanford University.

UNCTAD. Occasional Note: International Investment Disputes on the Rise, 29 Nov. 2004. UNCTAD/WEB/ITE/IIT/2004/2.

Verdross, Alfred, and Heribert Koeck. 1983. Natural Law: The Tradition of Universal Reason and Authority. In *The Structure and Process of International Law: Essays on Legal Philosophy, Doctrine, and Theory*, ed. Ronald Macdonald and Douglas Johnston. The Hague: Martinus Nijhoff, 17–50.

Von Stein, Jana. 2005. Do Treaties Constrain or Screen? Selection Bias and Treaty Compliance. *American Political Science Review* 99: 611–22.

Walter, Barbara F. 2006a. Building Reputation: Why Governments Fight Some Separatists but Not Others. *American Journal of Political Science* 50: 313–30.

———. 2006b. *War as a Reputation Problem*. Unpublished manuscript, University of California, San Diego.

Waltz, Kenneth N. 1979. *Theory of International Politics*. Reading, Mass.: Addison-Wesley.

Watson, Joel. 1999. Starting Small and Renegotiation. *Journal of Economic Theory* 85: 52–90.

Weil, Prosper. 1983. Toward Relative Normativity in International Law. *American Journal of International Law* 77: 413–42.

Wendt, Alexander. 1999. *Social Theory of International Politics*. New York: Cambridge University Press.

Wilson, Bruce. 2007. Compliance by WTO Members with Adverse WTO Dispute Settlement Rulings: The Record to Date. *Journal of International Economic Law* 10 (2): 397–403.

Yarbrough, Beth V., and Robert M. Yarbrough. 1992. *Cooperation and Governance in International Trade: The Strategic Organizational Approach*. Princeton, N.J.: Princeton University Press.

INDEX

Note: Page numbers in *italics* indicate charts and graphs.

and scope of agreements, 169; and soft law, 160; and types of agreements, 119–20, 131, 133, 155–56, 157, 158

diversity of international agreements, 119–20, 120–21, 122–26

doctrinal issues, 10, 184, 204

domestic context: and contracts, 135, 137; and courts, 49; and customary international law, 202, 205; and domestic unrest, 79; and enforcement of agreements, 139; and escape clauses, 148; and form and substance of agreements, 157, 158–59; and national crises, 113; and objective of agreements, 128; and soft law, 146–47; and treaties, 145–46

Dominican Republic-Central America Free Trade Agreement (DR-CAFTA), 67, 106, 108

Draft Articles of State Responsibility, 55, 228–29n. 14

due process, 172

duration of agreements, 230n. 28

dyad-specific reputations, 107–8

EC–Hormones case, 53

economic agreements: antitrust agreements, 59, 123; and capital standards, 7, 67, 142, 157, 231n. 41; and compliance decisions, 56, 73; and customary international law, 192–93; and development programs, 108; economic cooperation agreements, 95, 99, 104, 105, 149–50, 166–67, 176–77; incentives, 81–82; investment agreements, 11, 50, 60, 88–89, 158–60, 184; and monopolies, 172; and multiple reputations, 103; and neoliberal economics, 103; and protectionism, 6, 151; and subsidies, 163–64. *See also* trade agreements

economies of scale and scope, 64, 163, 168–70, 181. *See also* transaction costs

educational assistance, 95

efficiency: and acceptable nonperformance, 149–51; and breaches of agreements, 136; and compliance levels, 138; and coordination problems, 27–28; and customary international law, 198–99; and design elements of agreements, 133, 136–37;

economies of scale and scope, 64, 163, 168–70, 181; and exclusionary agreements, 171–72; and externalities, 170; Kaldor-Hicks efficiency, 171; and membership of agreements, 170–71; and monitoring, 130; and multilateral agreements, 196; Pareto efficiency, 60, 62, 167, 171, 206–7; and reputational sanctions, 44; and signing agreements, 179; and sovereignty issues, 192; and the Uruguay Round, 167

empirical testing, 120. *See also* methodological issues

enforcement of agreements: contract model of agreements, 135; and customary international law, 196–97, 203; and domestic context, 139; and flexibility, 137; and international tribunals, 49–54; and membership in agreements, 174; and multilateral agreements, 65; strategies over time, 57; and types of agreements, 119–20

environmental issues and agreements: and case studies, 10–12; and collective action problems, 64–65; and compliance decisions, 16, 74–75; and customary international law, 207–8; and exit clauses, 153; and externalities, 175–76; and flexibility, 137; and form and substance of agreements, 155–56; and global warming, 65, 155–56, 170; and the Kyoto Protocol, 64–65, 78–79, 114–15, 162, 171, 175, 177; and membership in agreements, 170; and monitoring, 114–15; and multilateral agreements, 68, 212; and multiple reputations, 102, 103, 106, 109–10; negotiating, 129–30; and nonreputational payoffs, 82; and other policy areas, 218; and the precautionary principle, 214–15; and realism, 18; and reputation of states, 78–79, 101; and scope of agreements, 163; and strategies over time, 58; and uncertainty, 96; and variable payoffs, 56. *See also* specific agreements

escape clauses: and credibility, 134, 138, 141–42, 228n. 13; and customary international law, 187–88, 199; described, 147–52; and form and substance of agreements, 131–32, 133,

escape clauses (*continued*)
155; and membership of agreements, 153, 173; and risk mitigation, 124; and soft law, 160–61; and state credibility, 9; and variety of agreements, 120. *See also* exit clauses

ethnic cleansing, 47
European Commission (EC), 14, 53
European Community, 66
European Convention on Human Rights, 6, 158
European Court of Human Rights (ECHR), 6, 50, 158, 223n. 23
European Court of Justice, 223n. 23
European Parliament, 14
European Union (EU), 14, 209, 223n. 23
evaluating agreements, 155–56. *See also* costs and benefits of agreements
ex post facto laws, 45
executive power, 145–46
exit clauses: and credibility, 134, 138, 141–42, 228n. 13; described, 147–52; and flexibility, 136; and form and substance of agreements, 131; and membership of agreements, 153; and soft law, 160–61. *See also* escape clauses
expropriation of assets, 88, 159–60
externalities, 170, 172, 174–79, 181, 233n. 64. *See also* collective action issues; free-rider problem
extradition treaties, 105, 123

federalism, 4, 170–72
Filartiga v. Pena-Irala, 196, 204
Financial Action Task Force, 231n. 41
flexibility in agreements, 135–36, 136–38, 229n. 15. *See also* reservations
foreign investment, 11, 50, 60, 88–89, 158–60, 184
Foreign Relations Authorization Act, 7
form of agreements: and credibility, 138; described, 130–32; and flexibility, 137; interaction with substantive elements, 154–61; and membership, 172–73; selection of, 140; tradeoffs, 154–56, 157–67; and treaties, 180–81
formal agreements, 28, 134–35, 140. *See also* treaties
France, 98–99, 111–12
Franco-Polish Military Alliance, 98–99
Free Trade Commission, 27–28

free-rider problem: and customary international law, 197; and escape clauses, 153; and membership of agreements, 174–77; and multilateral agreements, 65, 66–67, 212; and retaliation, 71–72. *See also* collective action issues

game theory: "battle of the sexes" game, 28; and commitment levels, 59; and cooperation, 25–29; games states play, 25–33; and payoffs, 55; repeated games, 32, 36, 41, 49, 55–58, 191; "stag hunt" game, 221n. 5. *See also* prisoner's dilemma
General Agreement of Tariffs and Trade (GATT), 7, 50, 61, 150, 164
General Agreement on Trade in Services (GATS), 168–70
general custom principle, 199
genetically modified organisms (GMOs), 151–52
Geneva Convention Relative to the Treatment of Prisoners of War, 67–68, 93, 102, 113
Germany, 60, 80, 111–12, 226–27n. 25
global warming, 64–65, 78, 114, 155–57, 170
good-faith assumption, 94
Gorbachev, Mikhail, 89–90
Great Britain. *See* Britain and the UK
Great Lakes Water Quality Agreement, 175–76
Guantanamo Bay detention camp, 96
Gulf War, 67

habeas corpus, 3–4
hard law: and agreement construction, 120–21; and dispute resolution, 134, 161; and features of agreements, 156; and negotiation, 36; and other agreement types, 9, 134, 136, 142, 144–45, 213, 220n. 27, 229n. 18
Hay-Bunua-Varilla Treaty, 60–61
health and safety issues, 26–27, 97–98. *See also* environmental issues and agreements
Helsinki Final Act, 7, 142, 144–45, 216
heterogeneity of agreements, 167–68
hierarchies in international law, 213–14, *214*

high-stakes policy areas, 112–14, 125–26. *See also* security issues
Hoone, Geoffrey, 6
Hull Rule, 99
Human Rights Committee, 230n. 31
human rights issues: and collective action problems, 64; and customary international law, 184, 186, 196; and escape clauses, 133; and ex post facto laws, 45; and form and substance of agreements, 157–58; and international tribunals, 50; and membership in agreements, 170, 171, 172–73; and multilateral agreements, 66–67, 68; and multiple reputations, 101, 102–3, 104–5, 110–11; and NGOs, 99–100; and rational choice, 20–21; and reservations, 230n. 31; and retaliation, 47; and signaling functions, 95; and soft law, 216; and state behavior, 12; and torture, 7, 104, 125, 186, 190, 196, 203–4; and uncertainty, 96
Human Rights Watch, 209

immunity, 184, 192–93, 196. *See also* sovereignty issues
imperfect information. *See* uncertainty
imports, 151
India-Patents case, 115–16
Indonesia, 148
inferred consent, 188
informal agreements, 19, 28–29, 57–58, 127, 157, 214
information about states: asymmetry of, 41; and Bayesian updating, 225n. 8; and compliance decisions, 16, 33; and coordination problems, 27; and court rulings, 51–54; dissemination of, 51–53, 53–54, 98; and estimating payoffs, 44; and monitoring, 133; and *opinio juris* doctrine, 186; and reputation, 72, 77, 91–100, 101–3, 109–10, 212; and reservations, 154. *See also* uncertainty
inspections, 85, 114. *See also* monitoring and verification
instant custom principle, 199–200
institutionalist approach, 18–19, 21
intellectual property, 115–16, 162, 164, 165–66, 167, 168
inter arma silent leges doctrine, 113
interaction of policy area, 104

Inter-American Commission on Human Rights, 104, 143
Inter-American Convention on Human Rights, 95
Inter-American Court of Human Rights, 143
interest groups, 19
Intermediate Range Nuclear Forces (INF) Treaty, 90
International Atomic Energy Agency, 82, 114
International Civil Aviation Organization (ICAO), 127
International Convention on the Elimination of all Forms of Racial Discrimination, 158
International Convention on the Protection of the Rights of Migrant Workers and Members of Their Families, 172–73
International Court of Justice (ICJ): and advisory opinions, 223n. 26; and customary international law, 184–85, 191, 200, 207–8, 223n. 26; and dispute resolution, 50; and information dissemination, 52, 54; and international tribunals, 50, 52, 54; and the *Medellin* case, 3–6; and soft law, 142, 143–44; and state obligations, 234n. 18; and state practices, 234n. 16; and the U.S., 226–27n. 25
International Covenant on Civil and Political Rights (ICCPR): addressing violations, 231n. 39; and escape clauses, 131–32, 148; and ex post facto laws, 45; expressive function, 20; and form and substance of agreements, 157; and membership in agreements, 170, 173; and multilateral agreements, 66–67; and multiple reputations, 103, 104; Operation Protocol, 95; and reservations, 230n. 31; signing vs. ratification, 177
International Criminal Court, 147–48, 154, 223n. 23
International Joint Commission, 42, 222n. 15
International Labor Organization (ILO), 162
International Load Line Convention, 161

International Monetary Fund (IMF), 20, 103, 108
International Olympic Committee (IOC), 29
International Organization, 120, 122
International Tribunal for the Law of the Seas, 50
international tribunals, 49–54, 143
investment agreements, 11, 50, 60, 88–89, 158–60, 184
Iran, 45, 81–82, 95, 96, 107
Iran-Iraq War, 96
Iraq, 67–68, 96, 103, 113, 126
Islamic law, 148
Israel, 68
issue areas, 100–106, 165, 167

Japan, 67, 109–10
jurisdictional issues, 184, 231n. 39

Kaldor-Hicks efficiency, 171
Kazakhstan, 91
Kosovo, 126
Kyoto Protocol: and externalities, 175; and federalism, 171; and monitoring and verification, 114–15; and multilateral agreements, 64–65; and reputational sanctions, 78–79; and scope of agreements, 162; and the U.S., 177

law and legal issues: contract model of agreements, 128, 135; and customary international law, 195, 228–29n. 14; and extradition treaties, 105, 123; and form and substance of agreements, 134; illegal actions, 96–97; and Islamic law, 148; legal obligations of states, 217; legalizing nonperformance, 149; and multiple reputations, 101–2; quasi-legal agreements, 217; and reputation, 226n. 23; and risk aversion, 123; and treaties, 127, 177; and uncertainty, 93–96, 100; and warfare, 113
Law of the Sea Tribunal, 50
legislatures, 146, 177
legitimacy, 17
liberalism, 18–19, 20–21, 215
Libya, 87
Limited Test Ban Treaty, 30, 45
limits of international law, 125
linking issues, 165, 167

Madrid Protocol, 58
managerial school of international law, 15–16, 98
maritime law, 127, 149–50, 164–65, 189
McKinnon, Gary, 7
Medellin, Jose Ernest, 3, 6
mediation, 52
Mediterranean Action Plan, 10
membership in international agreements, 153, 170–73, 174–77, 181
methodological issues: assumptions, 12–13, 215–16; Bayesian probability, 84, 225n. 8; case studies, 10–11; Coase theorem, 121; empirical testing, 120; measuring state practices, 185–87; modeling international agreements, 121–22, 228n. 9; overview, 15–22; risk aversion assumption, 230n. 28; and social sciences, 13, 211; and state actors, 126–29; and theory, 120–21, 207, 215–16, 218; and transparency, 216
Mexico, 3–4, 6
migrant workers, 172–73
military force: and breaches of agreements, 79; and retaliatory sanctions, 47; and risk diversification, 125; and the stag hunt game, 221n. 5; and the UN, 220–21n. 1, 223n. 25
Mine Ban Treaty, 6
modeling international agreements, 121–22, 228n. 9
monitoring and verification: and arms control, 96; and credibility, 134, 138; and exceptions, 231n. 41; and form and substance of agreements, 131, 133, 155–56; and inspections, 85, 114; and membership in agreements, 173; and multilateral agreements, 64; and negotiation of agreements, 130; and obligations of states, 85; and prisoner treatment, 113; and reporting requirements, 98; and risk aversion, 138; and types of agreements, 119
monopolies, 172
Montreal Protocol on Substances That Deplete the Ozone Layer, 168
Morocco, 202
motivations for international agreements, 120–21. *See also* costs and benefits of agreements

multilateral agreements: and
cooperation, 63–69; and customary
international law, 189; and
externalities, 176; and free-rider
problem, 212; and ratification, 177–78;
and reciprocity, 64–66; and
reputation, 68–69, 71–72; and
retaliation, 66–67, 196; and scope of
agreements, 119, 168; and transfers, 166
Munich Accord, 111–12
mutual defense agreements, 95, 98–99,
220–21n. 1
Mutual Defense Assistance Agreement,
95

Namibia, 6
national crises, 113
nationalization of assets, 88, 103
natural law, 187
Nazi Germany, 111–12
negotiation, 129–30, 138, 166
neoliberal economics, 103
neutrality, 122
New York Times, 5
New Zealand, 45
Non Proliferation Treaty (NPT): and
collective action issues, 68; and legal
obligations, 85; and monitoring, 114;
and new states, 91; and
nonreputational payoffs, 79–80,
80–82, 83–84; and reciprocity, 45
nongovernmental organizations
(NGOs), 29, 99–100, 209
nonnuclear weapon states (NNWS), 45,
79–80, 91
nonreputational payoffs: and
compliance decisions, 44, 73–75, 75–78,
78–80, 81–82, 84–86, 94, 112–13, 217;
defined, 56–57; estimating, 56; and
existing reputation, 83–84; and
incomplete information, 91–93,
225n. 14; and multilateral agreements,
72; and multiple reputations, 105; and
signaling, 41
nonstate actors, 11. *See also*
nongovernmental organizations
(NGOs)
norms: and CEDAW, 141; and
commitment levels, 213–14; and
compliance decisions, 111, 117; and
customary international law,

184, 186–87, 188–89, 190–94, 206,
207–9, 213–14, *214*, 214–15, 234n. 11; and
human rights, 99; importance of, 9;
internalization of, 12; and legitimacy,
17; and liberalism and constructivism,
19–22; and *opinio juris* doctrine, 194,
196, 198, 201; origin of, 94–95; and
politics, 217; and reputation, 80, 87, 89;
and soft law, 142; and state practices,
203–4; treaties contrasted with, 57–58;
types of, 23–24. *See also* customary
international law (CIL)
North American Free Trade Agreement
(NAFTA), 6, 27–28, 50, 67, 108, 158–59
North Atlantic Treaty Organization
(NATO), 126, 212
North Korea, 67, 81, 86–87, 104, 148
nuclear weapons. *See* arms control
agreements
Nuclear Weapons Advisory Opinion,
207–8

objectives of states, 124
obligations of states, 84–86, 142, 157, 179,
230n. 28
Olson, Mancur, 174
Olympic Games, 28–29, 221n. 4
opinio juris doctrine, 185–87, 190,
194–201, 201–2, 203–4, 206, 233n. 67
Optional Protocol on Civilian and
Political Rights, 158, 231n. 39
opt-out provisions, 154
Organization for the Prohibition of
Chemical Weapons, 7
Organization of American States (OAS),
143
Organization of the Petroleum
Exporting Countries (OPEC), 172
organized labor, 106

pacta sunt servanda doctrine, 15, 204–5
Palestinian territories, 223n. 26
Pan Am Flight 103 bombing, 87
Panama Canal Zone, 61
Paraguay, 226–27n. 25
Pareto efficiency, 60, 62, 167, 171, 206–7
Paris Memorandum of Understanding
on Port State Control, 127
payoffs of cooperation: and compliance
decisions, 78, 222nn. 9–11; and
customary international law, 190–91,

payoffs of cooperation (*continued*)
193, 194, 206–7, 209; and facets of
compliance, 33–41; and form and
substance of agreements, 155–56; and
legal obligations, 85–86; and the
prisoner's dilemma, *32, 37, 39*; and
reputation, 74–75, 78–80, 80–82,
83–84, 217; and risk diversification,
124–25; and scope of agreements, 180;
and state responsibility, 55; and
strategies over time, 55–58; and
uncertainty, 72, 92–93, 225–26n. 14.
See also nonreputational payoffs
peace agreements, 60, 103, 104
Permanent Court of International
Justice, 55
persistent objectors doctrine, 188, 197–99
Pinochet, Augusto, 103, 106
Poland, 98–99, 111
policy areas, 107–8, 218
political science, 8, 73, 216
politics, 216–17, 223–24n. 32
precautionary principle, 209
prisoner's dilemma: and coercive
enforcement, 49; and cooperation
efforts, 29–33; and customary
international law, 189; and form and
substance of agreements, 155; and
payoffs, *32, 37, 39*; and rational choice
assumption, 121–22; and reciprocity,
42–45; and reputation, 36–41; and
state actors, 127–28; strategies over
time, 57–58; and types of agreements,
120
prisoners of war, 104, 113–14, 131–32
private rights of actions, 158–60
Proliferation Security Initiative (PSI), 68
protectionism, 6, 151
Protocol on Environmental Protection
(Madrid Protocol), 58
public choice theory, 19, 20–21, 124,
128–29, 150
public goods, 66–67, 68, 124, 175–76

quasi-legal agreements, 217

radio frequencies, 28
ratification of agreements, 145–46,
177–79, 233n. 67
rational choice theory: applicability to
international law, 211; assumptions,
12–14, 121–22, 215–16; and collective
action problems, 174; and
constructivism, 19–22; critics of, 17; and
customary international law, 9–10,
188–90, 194, 201–2, 204, 206, 207; and
focus of book, 24; and form and
substance of agreements, 130; and goals
of states, 132; and multiple reputations,
107–8, 109; scope of, 218; and self-
interest, 224n. 3; and soft law, 160; and
spectrum of commitments, 144; and
state actors, 128; and types of
agreements, 119; and uncertainty, 98;
and value of reputation, 77
"Rational Design of International
Institutions" (Koremenos, Lipson,
and Snidal), 120
realism, 18, 31–32, 122
reciprocity: and compliance decisions, 9,
42–45, 175, 211–12; and customary
international law, 191–92; and
externalities, 175; and the law of
treaties, 233n. 65; and multilateral
agreements, 63, 64–66; and the
prisoner's dilemma, 32–33; reciprocal
noncompliance, 141; and reputation,
71; role in international law, 42–45
regulatory agreements, 157, 162
renegotiating of agreements, 48
repeated games, 32, 36, 41, 49, 55–58, 191
reporting. *See* monitoring and
verification
repression, 103. *See also* human rights
issues
reputation: and agreement dyads, 107–8;
and commitment levels, 59;
compartmentalization of, 100–111; and
compliance decisions, 9, 33–34, 34–41,
78–82; and cooperation, 212–13; and
cost of sanctions, 139–40; and
customary international law, 191, 192,
194–201, 202, 205, 206–7, 208–9; factors
affecting, 77–78; and form and
substance of agreements, 133–35, 180;
and imperfect information, 91–100;
and international tribunals, 52, 54; and
issue areas, 100–106; and legal
literature, 226n. 23; and levels of
obligation, 84–86; limits on, 111–15;
managing, 86–91; and multilateral
agreements, 64, 66–67, 68–69;

multiple reputations, 100–106, 107–8, 108–11, 209, 213; and the prisoner's dilemma, 32–33; and rational choice theory, 211–12; and reciprocity, 42, 141; and retaliation, 46, 48; and signaling functions, 89–90; and treaties, 178, 234n. 12; types of, 115–17; and uncertainty, 96–97, 225–26n. 14; value of, 75–78, 76
research and development, 165–66
reservations: conditions for, 153–54; and credibility of states, 134, 228n. 13; described, 147–52; and form of agreements, 131; and membership of agreements, 153; and state interests, 132; Vienna Convention rules on, 141, 230n. 31
resolve of states, 33, 77, 101, 115
responsibilities of states, 55, 184
retaliation: and arms control agreements, 81–82; and collective action issues, 67–68; and compliance decisions, 9, 33–34, 46–48, 211–12; costs of, 139–40; and customary international law, 192, 209; forms of, 46–48; and international tribunals, 52; and multilateral agreements, 63, 64, 66–67; and the prisoner's dilemma, 32–33; and reputation, 71, 141
risk, 122–26, 136, 138, 230n. 28
rogue states, 102
Rome Statute of the International Criminal Court, 147–48, 154, 223n. 23
Roosevelt, Eleanor, 140
rule of law, 17
Russia: and arms control agreements, 45, 81–82, 83; and multilateral agreements, 66, 67; and reputation, 89–90, 109–10; and signaling, 90–91; strategies over time, 55–56

safety standards, 26–27, 97–98. See also environmental issues and agreements
Sanchez-Llamas case, 4
sanctions: and coercion, 63; costs of, 139–40, 141; and credibility, 138; and customary international law, 192, 193, 194–201, 206–7, 208–9; and design elements of agreements, 160; and escape clauses, 151–52; and expectations, 83–84; and facets of compliance, 33–41; and the free-rider

problem, 174; and international tribunals, 52–53; and legal obligations, 85–86; and multilateral agreements, 67, 68–69; and reputation, 44, 106; and retaliation, 47; and scope of agreements, 167; and types of violations, 78–79
Sanitary and Phytosanitary Agreement, 97–98
satellite communications, 28
scope of agreements: broad scope, 163–65; economies of scale and scope, 64, 163, 168–70, 181; and effectiveness, 163–65; and enforcement, 119–20; and form and substance of agreements, 156; and generalizability, 120–21; and membership, 170–73; narrow scope, 161–63; and payoffs, 180; and transfers, 165–68
security issues: and compliance decisions, 78; and form and substance of agreements, 131–32; and multiple reputations, 103, 104, 107; and nonreputational payoffs, 86; and realism, 18; and reputation, 72, 113; and risk aversion, 125; and self-defense, 125–26; and soft law, 144–45; and territorial waters, 150. See also arms control agreements
self-interest, 224n. 3
service sector, 164, 168–70
signaling: and commitment levels, 58–59; and customary international law, 95; and reputation, 89–90, 108; and sanctions, 48; and signing treaties, 178; and soft law, 146
Slaughter, Anne-Marie, 19
social psychology, 77
social sciences, 8, 13, 211
social security benefits, 173
soft law: and commitment levels, 59, 134, 213–15; and credibility, 134; and customary international law, 204, 207, 208; described, 142–47; and flexibility, 136; and form and substance of agreements, 156, 180; and the Helsinki Final Act, 216; and membership in agreements, 173; and other agreement types, 9, 23–24, 120, 131, 160, 214, 214, 220n. 27; and reputation, 234n. 12; and state actors, 126

World Trade Organization (WTO)
(*continued*)
multiple reputations, 108; and
retaliation, 48; and scope of issues, 6,
163, 164, 167, 168–70; staffing issues, 13;
and transparency requirements, 97–98
World War I, 60, 89

World War II: and failures of
international law, 111–12, 140; and
human rights issues, 20; impact on
Europe, 14; and military alliances,
98–99
written agreements, 126. *See also*
treaties